3000 800011 54866
St. Louis Community College

D1568055

ILLUSTRATING FASHION

E. Sloane

ILLUSTRATING

HARPER & ROW, PUBLISHERS, NEW YORK, HAGERSTOWN,

1817

FASHION

REVISED EDITION

SAN FRANCISCO, LONDON

Drawing by Eula,
courtesy Geoffrey Beene

The illustrations credited to *The New York Times*, on pages 6, 7, 8, 9, 68, 80, 104, 120, 121, 140, 141, 155, 160, 161, 185, 200, 201, 231, 244, 250, 252, 253, 254, 255, and 256, are copyright © by *The New York Times*. The illustrations credited to *Mademoiselle*, on pages 116 and 211, to *Glamour*, on page 69, and to *Vogue*, on pages 84, 85, 143, 145, 154, 194, 261, 262, 263, 264, 265, 266, 267, 268, 269, 270, 271, 272, 273, 274, 275, 277, 278, 279, 280, 281, 282, 283, 289, 290, 292, 293, 294, 295, 296, 298, and 299 are copright © by Condé Nast Publications Inc. The drawings by Leslie Saalberg, on pages 234, 236, 237, and 238, are from "The Traditions of Elegance Abroad," copyright © 1962, by *Esquire*. A drawing on page 27 was reprinted by permission from *The Christian Science Monitor*, copyright © 1968, The Christian Science Publishing Society, all rights reserved. Illustrations from *Women's Wear Daily* are reprinted by permission of the Fairchild Syndication Service. Illustrations that were advertisements for Bonwit Teller are reprinted by permission of Bonwit Teller.

For those
who wish to carve
a career in the fashion world
as illustrators
or designers,
this book has been planned
as a basic guide
to interpreting fashion
and expressing it
in good drawing, with
style and flair.

ACKNOWLEDGMENTS

I would like to thank
the following persons, who generously
lent original artwork,
and their publishers and advertisers for
reproduction permissions granted.

Mrs. René Bouché (private collection).
Miss Anne-Marie Barden, artist.
Mr. Antonio Lopez, artist.
Mr. Lou Beres, artist.
Mr. Kenneth Paul Block, artist.
Mr. Juke Goodman (private collection).
Mr. Tod Draz, artist.
Miss Esther Larson, artist.
Miss Barbara Pearlman, artist.
Mr. Leslie Saalburg, artist, writer.
Mr. Harry Rodman, Advertising Director, Lord & Taylor.
Mr. John Robinson, Assistant Advertising Manager,
   Bergdorf Goodman.
Miss Patricia Peterson, Fashion Editor, *The New York Times.*
Mrs. Jean Chiesa, Executive Editor, *Harper's Bazaar.*
Mr. Harold T. P. Hayes, Editor, *Esquire Magazine.*
Miss Lynn Stevenson, Public Relations Director, Du Pont.
Mr. Rudolph Millendorf, Art Director, *Women's Wear Daily.*
Miss Helen Finch, Associate Editor, *Woman's Journal* (London).
Mr. Silas Rhodes, Director, School of Visual Arts.
Miss Wendy Seabrook, Advertising Manager, Henri Bendel.
Miss Anny Queyroy, Art Director, Bonwit Teller.
Mr. Lawrence Goodman, Sales Promotion Manager, Stern Brothers.
Mr. Carl Ziltz, Assistant Merchandise Manager, Carson Pirie Scott.
Mr. Roger R. Jones, Hallmark Gallery.
Mr. Paul T. Kearney, Vice President, Galey & Lord.
Condé Nast Publications, for *Vogue, Glamour,* and
   Mademoiselle illustrations.
Hearst Publications, for *Harper's Bazaar* illustrations.
The New York Times.
Women's Wear Daily.

CONTENTS

ILLUSTRATING FASHION

1. INTRODUCTION

It is my intent to offer in this book not only a formula for drawing but also a guide for awareness: to sharpen your ability to observe and think is the first step toward expressing your ideas in an individual way. To be correct simply in a mechanical sense without a spirited imagination can be dreadfully dull. A knowledge of anatomy cannot be over-estimated as the basis of good drawing, but rules for measurements and proportions can be learned by anyone. There is much more to being an artist.

Art is an expression of ideas and emotions, a feeling for line and form, color, light and shade, and texture. To portray these elements in an understandable and exciting way is to learn to see as an artist sees. Each one expresses himself in a different way, even though influenced by the work of others. It is sound, therefore, to acquire knowledge of the subjects involved as a basis for working and for developing a perceptive eye and an assured point of view. To listen to everyone's criticism is to allow one's own thinking to waver. A trite remark, sometimes expressed by nonartists, is "Well, from a layman's point of view, it is out of drawing," or, even worse, as commendation, "It looks great—just like a photograph." To the knowing, this is no goal.

A dress, for example, might be drawn exactly as it looks in every detail, yet the drawing would completely lack buyer appeal. In creating a fashion impression, one might ignore realism and produce an idealized version that is sensational. The right effect and the fashion news is there, and accuracy of proportion becomes secondary to the statement made. This is not "bad drawing," but exaggeration to give the picture more impact—the difference between excellence and mediocrity.

In using this book, make a point of reading all of it, perhaps a chapter a day, before starting to draw. It is helpful to get a brief, even shallow, grasp of the whole subject in the beginning. Once you begin on the lessons and exercises, be prepared to turn out quantities of drawings. Avoid being miserly with paper; one learns through mistakes. If you expect miracles overnight it is easy to become discouraged. Do not get overserious and exacting in the beginning. Let yourself go, and try the next chapter. You will want to return and review some lessons again and again to refresh your thinking and improve your drawing, even after years of working.

As in any specialized field, perseverence is a requisite for success. Nothing is accomplished without effort and application. Halfhearted efforts produce dull drawings that have appeal for no one. Along with knowledge and awareness, it is hoped that you will, in the end, have acquired the inspiration to work hard enough to meet your goal and to find joy in the doing. As a career fashion illustration can be fascinating, and the field can widen to the breadth of your vision and capabilities.

2.
AN EXPLANATION OF FASHION ILLUSTRATING

WHAT MAKES A GOOD FASHION DRAWING?

Fashion illustrating is sketching a garment or a plan for one. The ability to portray a fashionable figure, showing the design and detail in an appealing way, is acquired only through knowledge of the subject and practice. It looks so simple to the layman that few realize the knowledge behind a well-drawn illustration. Some artists in other fields think of it merely as exaggerated drawing of exaggerated clothing, requiring little need of good drawing. The fact is that without knowledge of "what makes fashion," good drawing alone is not enough.

Exaggeration *is* part of fashion. Knowing what to exaggerate or emphasize is the story of fashion. Without emphasis on current lines

Courtesy of *Harper's Bazaar*, 1964

THE MANY WAYS TO TELL A FASHION STORY

ANTONIO (Lopez), a very young contemporary, displays great versatility and a spirited imagination with fine drawing and fashion sense. Frequently changing technique and style to suit the subject, he avoids the dullness of repeating a set formula. Reproductions of Antonio's work appear throughout the book to represent the various qualities of good fashion illustrating.

SOPHISTICATES, EXOTIC AND CONSERVATIVE ■ Using the same theme and charcoal technique for the exotic type in palazzo pajamas (1966), Antonio repeats an idea used two years earlier for the editorial pages of *Harper's Bazaar*.

Done with flair and accuracy, the earlier drawing represents a conservative elegance. The fashion story is told with realism. The flowing lines and well-placed black accents form a pleasing design. The later drawing portrays a more exotic fashion on a suitably flamboyant type.

and proportions, there is no news—just a picture of a person wearing clothes without distinction or flair. It does not take a genius to recognize the difference between a dowdy, out-of-date look and a new and exciting look of current chic. It does take a trained eye and knowledge, however, to know what subtleties make the difference in the total look.

There is much to know on the subject, and it can be fascinating. There are constantly new and exciting styles. The changes come faster today than in the past, and it is essential that one keep up to date. There is more to the fashion story than changing waistlines and skirt lengths—differences obvious to anyone.

Antonio, courtesy of *The New York Times*

DYNAMIC ACTION ■ Young pace setters of the speed age are geared for action here in brief dresses and divided skirts. The vibrating patterns of black and white are repeated in the bold stripes of the background, which is done with appliquéd transfer sheets. The illustration successfully tells a fashion story with verve and good drawing in another Antonio style.

Lines and proportions change. Hair styles must conform. Even the "fashion face" has a different aspect—expressions and features alter the look. Periodic changes in clothing construction alter the general outline, sometimes in a very subtle way. The new fabrics with body (double-faced, bonded, etc.) have simplified tailoring. It is no longer necessary to stiffen and pad with various body-giving materials, formerly essential. Linings, too, have been eliminated in some cases. All these add changes of contour and line.

The Courrèges styles of 1964 in these new fabrics set off a completely new concept of tailoring and line. It was the space-age look—uncluttered, short, and suggestive of a uniform. Courrèges' mannequins had to have the right look to wear them—young, tanned, and active, with an alert, neat head, short hair, zingy walk, and expressionless face. The over-all effect created a great impact. Although extreme, the ideas were eventually used in a modified, more feminine way by all the other designers.

There are many facets of quality in a good fashion drawing, and many points to consider. The "look" can be achieved through the pose of the figure, the type of model indicated, the technique of rendering, and emphasis on the important lines of the garment. It can be stated in a crisp, definite, knowing way, or be muddled and wavering, making no statement at all. One must recognize and seek the best for inspiration. To be influenced by the work of an artist whose drawings you admire is perfectly natural. One learns through observation, developing a personal style later on.

The artist with imagination develops more self-expression as he works. If he really loves what he is doing, the results are apt to be better than if he is overly worried about pleasing. This does not mean going to the extreme of producing something unsuitable to the sphere you are trying to reach. The degree of realism varies with the type of fashion depicted. To be 100 percent realistic, however, is not interpreting fashion. One has to glamorize an item to make it appeal to the buyer—to give it a little "pizzaz."

Courtesy of *The New York Times*

THE SWINGER ■ The action skirt of a simply cut black crepe dress incites interest through the pose of the young swinger. The bold, fluid lines and strong blacks show the influence of the Art Nouveau period.

A successful illustration sells fashion. It makes a spontaneous and definite statement that conveys a mood from the brash and bold for action clothes to the romantic looks of evening chiffons. Model and pose should be in tune with the character of the fashion, suggesting the naïve, the exotic or whatever type, convincingly. New lines and proportions are emphasized with a knowing indication of garment to body lines.

To the inventive artist, ideas to animate the story suggest themselves as he works. The whimsical, the humorous or the provocative may provide a fillip if handled in a subtle way. Emphasis on either personality or situation can be distracting, however, defeating the essential purpose of illustrating fashion. The ideal model projects an aura of detached self-assurance, a natural style and ease.

A well-designed composition unifies the whole with movement of line and arresting patterns of dark and light areas. In advertising illustration, much depends on the skilled layout artist who arranges art and copy and open spaces in a planned design that is simple and direct.

FASHION ASSETS

Sensibility, the intuitive capacity to recognize style and quality, is the gift of awareness that grows with exposure to the best. Discerning taste and skill develop with the accumulation of knowledge. It sparks enthusiasm and adds zest to creative effort. To know what you wish to convey establishes a base for interpreting fashion. Bold, sure-handed drawing is acquired through understanding what to emphasize or minimize. Drawing that appears labored reveals muddled thought or timidity. Successful effect appears effortlessly simple. It is the substance of quality in both design and illustration.

SPACE AGE FASHION ■ This sleek action figure is appropriately orbiting in outer space (pasted on a photographed galaxy of stars). The coat dress illustrated is one of the first pared-down, military-cut styles of Paris designer Courrèges. The angular pose, expressionless face, and wrap-around goggles project a consistent image of cool chic. The off-beat approach and mood of fantasy attract attention in an entertaining way.

Antonio, courtesy of
The New York Times

THE LONG TRENCHCOAT
■ This example of the classic style made up in canvas is illustrated in a bold poster style. The 24-inch original in red, white, and blue was done with appliquéd colored papers. The pattern of the stars and stripes scarf adds impact to the planned design.

Courtesy of *Harper's Bazaar*, 1965

CONTEMPORARY ART, FAR-OUT CHIC ▪ The work of artist Katharina Denzinger has the bold painting style and color of a Picasso. The original of this illustration was done in clear bright green, yellow, red, and light blue; the Tiffeau dress in shocking pink. The stride of the figure and the design of the composition are contemporary. The emphasis on the fashion leg was the beginning of a strong trend.

STYLE is the undefinable expression of individuality, separating the distinguished from the ordinary. "Mode passes. Style remains," said Coco Chanel. First to recognize the great style of functional design, she made trench coats, pea jackets and polo coats fashionable for women in the twenties. She was then wearing tailored pants in the country. The soundness of her convictions remains. The Chanel classics have outlasted their creator.

TASTE is controversial, since it is a personal point of view. A current fashion, enthusiastically accepted by some, may be considered atrocious by others. For the illustrator, a light-hearted flexibility adjusts to variety as another mode of expression.

ACQUIRING A KNOWLEDGE OF FASHION

Advanced news of fashion trends can be found in the leading fashion magazines, some newspapers and dailies—for example, *Women's Wear Daily*, which reports news of the top designers and couture houses in New York, London, Paris, and other European cities. Some of these periodicals may be found in public libraries. One must do more than just look at pictures, however. There is much reading to be done to explain a trend or stress a point, to learn the story behind some of the extreme styles and exaggerated photographs. Fashion news must be daring in order to create interest. Conservatism does not make news.

Fashion dictates tend to minimize or exaggerate figure proportions. Not only the pose, but the proportions, too, change in drawings. In an era when attention is drawn to a great exposure of leg, the rest of the figure is minimized by the loosely fitted shift, the "slow fit" in clothing, with little or no indication of a waistline. As in all good design, there should be one dominating center of interest. The artist should be aware of these trends and influences and interpret them knowingly. To be "with it," one must not only sense the new but be up on the news, and being "with it" has nothing to do with personal taste.

Fashion is always a reflection of the times, of a way of life. It is part of history and part of today. In the sixties, as students traveled more, a young, international look developed. Their nonconformist, free-thinking, uninhibited attitude toward dress and behavior set a general pattern of long hair and a very young, Bohemian look. Their "groovy gear" set the pace for even the Paris couture. Included were the influences of thrift-shop Victorian and the western frontier, both leaning to the romantic past. Their "little money" was important because of its volume.

YOUNG MODERN ▪ Anne-Marie Barden's contemporary style appears in many chapters of the book exemplifying the best qualities of design in art and a very young slant on fashion. This fine pencil-line drawing with a clever repetition of black ink dots combines a quality of young chic with interesting rendering. The pose of the figure is pleasingly designed with emphasis on the one boot. The long, straight hair, the pale mouth, and the non-expression of the eyes are an important part of the sixties' young international look.

Bigi ad, courtesy of Bergdorf Goodman

Kenneth Paul Block, courtesy of *Women's Wear Daily*, November, 1966

FASHION NEWS ■ The swagger of casual styles in simple fabrics is the story in this fashion report. A young, fresh, calculated chic, worn without pretense, is typified in these amusing and lively sketches.

Some of the fashions were wild, some practical, some outrageously nutty, but they had a positive quality and a casual look of independence.

There is always more than one influence at a time. The leading designers try different ideas. One general trend finally comes through as dominant, sometimes taking five years or more to be accepted generally. The radical ideas, given much notoriety by the press, are often dropped soon after a mad rush of copies appears in the bargain-basement price range. No matter what the price level, there is an avid interest in fashion change and excitement in everything new. The subject is challenging and fascinating.

EMPHASIS ON CURRENT LINES AND PROPORTIONS ■ Pure line, with nonessentials eliminated, can make a strong statement. The silhouette of the garment is dramatized in these drawings by accentuating contour lines of fit and seaming. To indicate the style of a garment with such assurance requires a knowledge of the subtle changes of each new trend. To know what to leave out and what to emphasize is the basis of illustrating fashion.

Ben Morris, courtesy of Du Pont Company

GALA EVENINGS

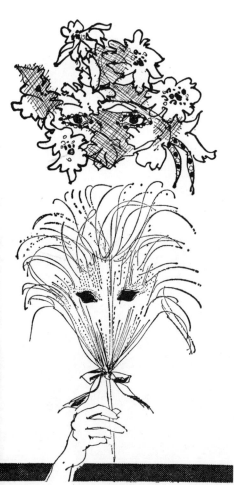

KENNETH PAUL BLOCK, whose sketches and drawings of fashion and fashionable women cover a broad field, manages all with excitement and flair. He maintains flexibility and a professional standard in both the diverse problems of fashion reportage and fashion advertising. His sketching for fashion news covers showings from New York to Paris. In advertising, his well-defined figures and accurately portrayed merchandise appear in magazines and newspaper pages for one of New York's leading fashion stores. Examples of both are reproduced here and throughout the book to illustrate various objectives.

FASHION NEWS, A MASKED BALL ■ Fashion reporting on this ball of the year covered many newspaper and magazine pages before and after the event. Many of the gowns and fanciful masks were designed by famous members of the Paris and New York couture. This decorative pen-and-ink drawing, reflecting an influence of the Aubrey Beardsley style, shows three of the guests as sketched by Kenneth Paul Block. It appeared on the front page of *Women's Wear Daily* (1966).

ADVERTISING ILLUSTRATION ▪ The couture fashions illustrated here for newspaper and magazine ads retain the flair of high fashion with a greater degree of realism in the detailed rendering of the merchandise. Beading and fabric are accurately indicated without being overworked in a mechanical way. The effect is rich. The hair styles and the types portrayed are suitably chic.

Kenneth Paul Block, courtesy of Bonwit Teller

Courtesy of *Woman's Journal,* 1966

THE INTERNATIONAL BOUTIQUE SCENE ▪ Sketched on the scene in
Paris by Tod Draz for the British magazine, *Woman's Journal,* this bustling
shop is one of the Left Bank favorites. Young spenders, looking for amusing
top-to-toe chic, haunt the boutiques for clothes and accessories all over
Europe and America. In tune with the times, these small shops fill the demand
for a young "total look" in new fashions. The clubby atmosphere and way-out
decor have contributed to their phenomenal success.

ADDED ATTRACTIONS ▪ Interesting props and backgrounds have attention value in advertising. Artist Barbara Pearlman injects a whimsical note here by adding the mysterious figure from the Middle East behind a fashion figure. The arrangement of figures within the space makes a pleasing composition.

The well-drawn basset hound, looking relaxed and rather bored beside the swingy fashion figure, relieves an otherwise serious approach to illustrating a dress that is not dramatic. The free-flowing line, achieved by direct sketching from the model, gives the drawing vitality and realism.

Barbara Pearlman for Galey & Lord, courtesy of Johnstone Advertising

PARIS

BALENCIAGA

Courtesy Women's Wear Daily

ADVANCE NEWS OF FASHION TRENDS

PARIS COUTURE, 1967 ■ Fashion reporters covering the collections were occasionally accompanied by artists. On-the-scene sketches and news were rushed via wireless photo to the New York newspapers. Skill and keen observation were needed to record quick impressions from the mannequins on the runway.

PHOTOGRAPHY AND ART IN FASHION

Of the visual arts, photography has probably made the greatest strides in the past decade or two, because of the vast improvements in equipment and techniques of developing. The creative talent and artistic genius of some photographers set an exciting standard for magazine editorials and advertising. Among these men and women are many whose taste and knowledge of composition and other aspects of art give them much more to offer than photography that is simply mechanically good. Such techniques as clever use of photomontage and varied effects in developing have provided endless possibilities.

The artist can learn much from photography and use it to advantage in his drawing. Many artists use the camera as a quick way of recording pictures for future use—action shots, good poses and situations, with background atmosphere included. To resent the inroads made by photography in advertising is futile. Art still has certain advantages, and it is the artist who must prove this by producing something the camera cannot. For many types of advertising, photography often surpasses available art. The camera registers a mechanically exact image and can record instantaneously interrupted action. It also has limitations, which the artist should recognize.

Drawings, first of all, can be imaginative, producing images from the human mind, giving a personal interpretation of what the artist sees or imagines. In fashion illustrating, he can simplify, accentuate, and with the hand put down on paper a line that no camera could imitate. He can flatter not only the clothes but also the model or type to be indicated, whereas the photographer is completely dependent on a model with the right look and flair as well as photogenic features.

It would seem that time is on the side of photography because of its advantage of being immediate and direct in recording a subject, but actually much time may have been spent in

DIOR 1976 ■ The look is long, lean
and supple. The Bohan suits, in wool
gabardine with a slightly military influence, are broadened in the shoulder and narrowed in the skirt. The
dropped draw-string waist and blazer
lapels of both suit and slim coat show
a new trend. The hooded raincoat of
tissue-weight silk taffeta is shown
over dot printed crepe de chine. For
evening a loose tunic of silk chiffon
over a long dress confirmed a new
direction.

Kenneth Paul Block,
courtesy *Women's Wear Daily*

19

setting up the scene for the camera and then in the darkroom, experimenting and developing to achieve the right effect. Often, if the job is sufficiently important, the photographer submits to the agency or editor many shots, from which a single photograph is chosen. Although this practice may give the art buyer a gratifying choice, it does consume considerable time. In some cases, retouching may be necessary to eliminate non-essentials or to correct defects.

The artist, on the other hand, can make a direct statement in his first portrayal, eliminating unnecessary lines and detail immediately. Even interpreted realistically, artwork can pick up and explain with imaginative changes or additions what the camera cannot. The right model, the right hair style, accessories, or even the garment itself may be developed out of thin air if necessary, adding glamour where it does not exist. The camera cannot fake a face or figure or the right accessory.

In newspaper work especially, the time element favors the artist, who may be asked to get out a drawing in short order. The illustration might be for a rush ad or for part of a reporting job that must meet a close deadline. For newspaper reproduction, artwork is more clean-cut and quicker than photography. It also makes the necessary simplifications of line and tone for the kind of paper used.

Photography has set a pace that the artist should strive to meet. The registering of motion in a picture has created a taste for dynamic action in art and advertising artwork. The staid poses of the past look static and dull, and the challenge to produce figures that are "with it" in action gives the artist today's point of view.

THE ISADORA DUNCAN LOOK ▪ St. Laurent's new dress shape for spring of 1976 is gathered with elastic at the shoulders, waist and hips.

Robert Young,
courtesy *Women's Wear Daily*

PARIS 1976 ■ The tunic was in almost every collection, St. Laurent's in rich Oriental colors. Marc Bohan continued with new versions of the classics in the Chanel tradition.

PARIS 1974 ■ The Givenchy halter-neck sheath and cape, accordion-pleated on the bias, holds to the timeless qualities of couture. The black velvet jacket and skirt, rib-quilted in gold, is from the era of evening theater suits.

ST. LAURENT
(1976)

(1976)
CHANEL

(1974)
GIVENCHY

Kenneth Paul Block,
courtesy *Women's Wear Daily*

Courtesy of *Women's Wear Daily*

FASHION NEWS, THE MINI-SKIRT ▪ The controversial short skirt that became almost no skirt inspired the decorated leg. High boots and textured stockings became an important part of the total look of fashion.

FASHION NEWS, THE PRETTY GIRL ▪ A new, softer look was bound to follow the 1965-66 "tough chic." The young had been haunting thrift shops for some time seeking old finery to express their individuality with a more romantic flair. Designers on the same wave length followed through.

Courtesy of *Women's Wear Daily*

Jack Geisinger, courtesy of *Women's Wear Daily*

LONDON COUTURE, 1966 ■ The constructed shape of tailoring represents the period of mid-thigh skirts and bouffant hairstyles. The evening dress with ruffled lace top and sashed moire skirt suggests a costume influence from Nell Gwyn's London, significant of a trend for timeless design from other eras.

London Mods 1966

Carnaby Street

Kings' Road

THE MOD MODE ■ The other side of London, at its most extreme, is caricatured here by Charlene Glascock for *Women's Wear Daily*. The London Mods rocked the world with their fashion revolution. An instantaneous success everywhere with nonconformist teen-agers, who made it young and gay in some quarters, kooky in others.

Courtesy of *Women's Wear Daily*

Givenchy, 1976

Dior, 1970

Givenchy, 1976

PARIS NEWS ■ Similarities of shape exist between the 1970 Dior and the 1976 Givenchy dresses. The later model expresses the trend toward more casual dressing with the looser fit above the waist. The long, bare-backed, deeply-slit dress for the terrace was Moroccan-inspired. The varied ways of summer bareness were fashion's news.

Kenneth Paul Block,
courtesy *Women's Wear Daily*

FASHION TRENDS AND INFLUENCES

Fashion takes on a new image in predictable 10-year cycles, according to James Laver, once curator of engravings and design at London's Victoria and Albert Museum. A prolific writer in many fields, he left a heritage of books analyzing fashion throughout history as a reflection of social change. As today's designers well know, nothing happens overnight. There is constant change, but general acceptance of change is slow. The strict silhouette of the sixties, the era of Courrèges and the space-age image, was replaced by a relaxed, easy look that followed body lines. Shape became a matter of individual choice, lengths a matter of esthetic proportion.

Lancetti, 1972

Galitzine, 1972

THE PARIS COUTURE, more than a hundred years old as the last quarter of the twentieth century began, retained its following of private customers who can still afford the price of quality and expertise. The major couturiers remain the most influential fashion authorities as the gap between ready-to-wear and couture narrows. The collections are well-covered by the press, but fewer American stores are represented. Many buyers now look for trend-setting clothes in the Right Bank and Left Bank boutiques of Paris. The names of Dior, Givenchy, St. Laurent and others, label scents and cosmetics and a growing list of other products which earn fine profits through licensing. Major pattern companies now carry some of the same names on couture designs for home-sewing enthusiasts.

Kenneth Paul Block,
courtesy *Women's Wear Daily*

PARIS *New Exposures*

Cardin

the Bare Back

the Bare Midriff

Givenchy

Grès

Cut-outs

FASHION NEWS, 1976: Relaxed, easy shapes were in. Conformity was out. The line between country and city clothes blurred. Evening looks were more casual but soft and feminine in crepe de chine and floating chiffon. Many were two-piece and ankle-length at Dior. Fashion, always focusing attention on one exposure at a time, returned to legs as skirts were slit at various levels. Halter necks revealed bare backs and plunging necklines were provocative.

The new chic reflected the "boutique" influence, effectively using lengths or squares of fabric with little or no seaming. Drawstrings and ties supplanted buttons and zippers. Stoles, shawls and ponchos topped everything. The more flamboyant Paris collections appealed to the camp sensibility with parodies of the ethnic idea amid the fun and fantasy.

The new classics showed an influence of the nineteen-twenties and thirties but were far from nostalgic. Unlined and softly tailored, they packed easily for travel. Man-tailored blazers were interchangeable with skirts or pants for day or evening. Timeless styles proved their worth in good fabrics and distinctive cut.

Steven Stipelman, courtesy of *Women's Wear Daily*

Young Paris

Stephen Meisel,
courtesy *Women's Wear Daily*

Far-out London

Kay Gallway Courtesy of *The Christian Science Monitor* © TCPS

Youth continued to influence new trends. Action sportswear was high on the list. T-shirts and tank tops reached classic status as summer tops. Lengthened, they set a trend in knit dresses. Off-beat shops in Paris stocked work clothes, not copies but originals, once indicative of various trades. They were soon a new favorite of the mood for dressing down.

Young London designers, an international group, concentrated on one-of-a-kind originals for a mainly non-English clientele of buyers and private customers. Romantic fantasy designs lead the way as timeless investments having nothing to do with fashion trends.

London - 1975

3. DEVELOPING YOUR

ART-TRAINING POSSIBILITIES

There are no set rules for art training or for the number of years to be spent in learning. The true artist continues to learn all his life. The desire to learn is of primary importance, but talent is the first requisite. Some competent and successful artists have, through their own efforts, managed without formal schooling. If you happen to be able to produce something that sells without having had art training, you are unusual—or lucky. However, to the trained eye, your work may lack the quality of guided taste and assured drawing.

To work as an apprentice with little or no pay was, in the old days, a valuable way of learning. In this age even a beginner must be paid, so

TALENT

it is necessary to have a portfolio of reasonably good samples of your work to show when applying for an art job. You must have a groundwork of training and knowledge in order to compete, though it is still possible to learn and improve through working with artists in the field. Nothing quite takes the place of the practical knowledge acquired this way.

Art schools, either accredited or recognized as top rank, offer the desirable advantages of individual criticism from a qualified instructor, the opportunity to work from live models, and the personal contacts and stimulus of working with other students. For the student who can afford the time and expense, college can be an asset, but the art school concentrates on developing a skill that you can use in much less time.

Self-teaching is still possible if the best schools are beyond your scope financially or geographically. This book can give you the basics of good drawing and a groundwork for thinking, observing, and developing your ability. Improvement comes only through constant drawing and study, which means reviewing the lessons and practicing the exercises. There is no magic in a few lessons nor achievement overnight. Even experienced artists do drawings many times over to obtain desired results. The techniques involved in finished artwork also require considerable practice to develop ease and a professional standard of quality.

To broaden taste and appreciation of art and fashion, learning from many sources is available to everyone. Even in small towns, many popular magazines are sold that carry good articles on art, often with color reproductions. By subscription, art magazines (such as *American Artist*), which are full of news of contemporary artists and carry advertising of art supplies and suppliers, are available. Whatever your goal, there are many roads leading to it.

HOW TO JUDGE AND IMPROVE YOUR WORK

Enthusiasm without well-considered thought is not enough for true accomplishment. With learning, one should acquire a basis for criticism, the ability to judge the good from the bad. Personal taste is of questionable value as a means of discernment. As you learn more, your tastes will grow and alter in proportion. You will learn not only what you like, but why. This is the foundation for intelligent criticism of your own work as well as that of others. A knowledge of the principles of good drawing, design, and techniques of working are therefore invaluable guides to keen observation.

As a check list, you might consider the following questions for analyzing your drawings:

1. Does the drawing stimulate your interest in the clothes illustrated?
2. Does the figure have animation, look alive, or is it dull, stilted, and wooden?
3. Are there good strong contrasts of dark and light areas in a variety of proportions, or is the whole drawing an even, monotonous tone?
4. Are the lines crisp and clear with a definite contour?
5. Is the figure correct in proportions?
6. Does the pose have swing and a direction of line that express movement?
7. Are the head and neck constructed to join the shoulder line convincingly? Is the neck long and graceful?
8. Is the hair style right for the type of fashion? Is it a definite style or a nothing type?
9. Check the hands. Are they drawn carefully or haphazardly?
10. Do the feet really support the figure and look well shod?
11. Have you overworked the face with too much detail, or is it suggested with a minimum of lines that are clean and definite?

12. Is the garment detail accurately indicated without complicated and confusing lines?

RANDOM RULES

1. LEARN TO OBSERVE: This is the first step. It cannot be repeated too often. Think out what you see.

2. DRAW WITH CONVICTION: Make a clear, bold statement on paper. Be definite; better a mistake than timidity. Be convincing. Use a heavy line at times and a delicate one for contrast when it suits the purpose.

3. SIMPLIFY: Omit meaningless, unnecessary lines. Create definite shapes.

4. CREATE AN EFFECT: Learn to attract the viewer's attention to a single impression or point of interest. Tell a story.

5. CLEAR UP YOUR THINKING: Muddled thinking produces dull drawings. Have a single thought in mind and state it simply.

6. LEARN THE BASIC RULES: Rules can be broken, but first of all learn them. They are a guide and plan for working, like a map for direction in thinking or a recipe for procedure.

7. REVIEW WHAT YOU HAVE LEARNED: Having studied each chapter carefully and practiced the exercises many times, go back and review them again occasionally. This gives you a more solid base for improvement and renews your thinking.

8. DEVELOP YOUR IMAGINATION: Avoid the heaviness of being overly serious about realism. To be exact can be dull. Expression and imagination are the lively ingredients of all visual art forms.

9. TRY A FRESH APPROACH: Vary your working methods and techniques now and then. Use a new kind of pen or pencil, a different kind of paper, or work entirely in wash. Uninterrupted routine can produce visual dullness.

4. MATERIALS AND

Before starting any worth-while project it is important to buy the right materials and equipment. There is nothing more discouraging than foundering with inadequate or unsuitable tools. The materials listed herein are separated into absolute necessities and supplies for subsequent projects. The second list covers materials needed for doing finished artwork, as well as unusual items for experimenting and producing new effects. Although new artists' materials constantly appear on the market, the following are the most practical and proven ones to date. It is up to the individual to experiment if he chooses.

On some items it is possible to cut costs; for others it is important to buy only the best. Good brushes, for instance, are worth the investment. It is also important that they be kept in good condition. Good papers are

QUIPMENT

also requisite for some media. A pen line, for example, may be beautifully clear on one paper and simply blot and blur on another. The best art materials are usually stocked by regular art-supply dealers. A few items on this list may even be found in a neighborhood stationer's or five-and-ten.

SUPPLIES FOR THE BEGINNER

1. A DRAWING BOARD: 20″ x 26″ or larger. Eventually you may wish to purchase a regular artist's drawing table, but the portable board will always be useful. As a substitute for a regular art board, an ordinary new bread board could be used.

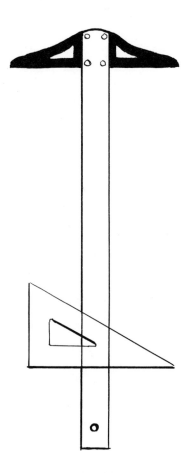

2. RULERS: 1 inexpensive plastic one, 1 metal or metal-edged ruler 18 inches or longer.

3. T SQUARE AND TRIANGLE: A metal T square is the most durable and worth the extra expense. The wooden ones loosen at the joints and are impractical for use in cutting papers with a razor knife. The triangle is usually of a transparent type of heavy plastic. (These to be used in combination for getting parallel lines and right angles.)

4. PENCILS AND SANDPAPER PAD: Buy regulation drawing pencils, which come in varying degrees of hardness. As a start, get a few 2H (hard lead), HB (medium), and B (soft, for sketching) weights. Art-supply stores also have mechanical pencils with replaceable leads in all weights, which are worth the price in the long run. They last indefinitely and eliminate pencil sharpening except for getting a fine point, which may be obtained by using a sandpaper pad.

5. ERASERS: 1 art gum, 1 ink eraser, several kneaded erasers. An art-gum eraser is best for cleaning up a finished drawing since it is soft and will not harm the surface of the paper. An ink eraser may be a necessity at times, but since it is sanded, it cannot be used on a soft paper, only on hard-surfaced ink papers or boards. The kneaded eraser can be broken into small pieces and kneaded into any shape or size. It does the best job of removing pencil lines. After lengthy use it becomes gummy and must be discarded.

6. RAZOR BLADES: Single-edged blades are useful for sharpening pencils and cutting papers. There is also a mechanical knife that holds replaceable blades, which is better for cutting jobs.

7. INDIA INK: Be sure it is black waterproof India ink. Soluble inks come in all colors but are used mainly for washes.

8. PENS: A good selection of pen points for use with India ink should include a couple each of "crowquills," Gillotts #303 and #290, Mitchell's "pen painters," #0708, and bowl-point pens for heavier lines. These are all drawing pens and must have the holders into which they fit. An ordinary penholder is too large. In addition to these, you might get some felt-tip pens for sketching. There are all types, sizes, and prices in this category. The cheaper ones smudge and do not last long. The fountain-pen type is refillable and the ink more dependable.

T Square and Triangle

Method of using T square and triangle to get accuracy of lines and measurements.

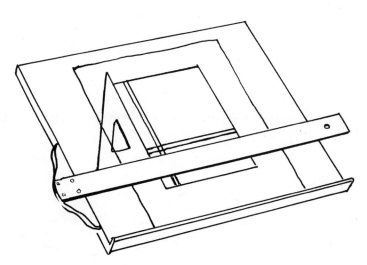

9. COLORED PENS AND PENCILS: In making copies of the exercises on drawing the figure, it is easier to follow the diagram drawings using a colored pencil to indicate guidelines. A colored felt-tip pen would do as well. A strong, bright color such as blue or red makes a more interesting chart and distinguishes the guidelines from the figure drawn in black pencil.

10. PAPERS: 1 pad of tracing paper 9" x 12" or 14" x 17", 1 drawing-paper pad 14" x 17"; 1 pad of Bristol paper 14" x 17"; several sheets of inexpensive illustration board.

11. THUMBTACKS: To attach papers to your drawing board, you need thumbtacks, push pins, or a couple of large paper clamps. Scotch tape or masking tape will also do for some types of jobs.

SUPPLIES FOR MORE ADVANCED WORK

1. BRUSHES: Best red-sable water-color brushes, one each, sizes #1, #3, #4, and #7. (Cheap or inferior brushes are useless for any artwork aside from varnishing or gluing. They are limp, shapeless, and cannot be controlled.) Buy just a few as a start, but be sure the hairs have a lot of spring and that they will "point" when wet, not fan out into a fuzzy mop. There are also special brushes for fashion artists, which have extra-long and tapered brush ends (optional). These are lovely for a delicate or tapered line but unsuitable for wash areas. They are also rather difficult to master. It takes a very delicate touch.

2. PAINTS: Matte-black water color of a good quality—like Winsor & Newton—is best. 1 tube of opaque white or a jar of Johnston's Snow White. Buy all paints in tubes, not cakes. If you eventually decide to purchase colors, you do better to buy them separately rather than in sets. However, you may find the others boxed to your liking. Opaque colors (designer's or poster colors) are optional.

3. PALETTE: There are so many sizes and types of palettes for mixing water colors that this, too, is an individual choice. There are enameled metal ones, plastic ones, and chinalike ones. It is important to have one with fairly deep wells for mixing ample amounts of a color or a tone of wash.

4. PAINT JAR: Any good-sized jar will do to hold clean water for mixing color and washing out brushes. A decorative or interesting one adds to the appearance of your studio.

5. BOARD FOR CUTTING SURFACE: It is wise to have a separate board on which to cut papers with a razor knife. A good, hard-surfaced board is Masonite. Some art stores carry it in limited sizes. Masonite can also be ordered from your local carpenter or lumber-supply house cut to any size (the same size as your drawing board or table top might be useful). It is possible to use the reverse side of your drawing board for cutting, but it ruins the surface.

6. PAPERS: Strathmore paper (heavyweight), sheets or large pad. Illustration board for water color (good quality). Large pad of tracing paper or vellum. Drawing-paper pad for sketching (inexpensive). Newsprint pad for sketching; charcoal paper, sheets or pad; and water-color paper, cold press, heavyweight, are optional.

7. SKETCHING MATERIALS: Charcoal or charcoal pencils. Optional: Conte crayons or pencils, colored pencils, felt-tip pens or markers, and Japanese bamboo or reed pens.

8. FIXATIVE: This may now be had in spray cans rather than bottles (Sprayfix is the name of one brand.) It is a must for all charcoal or soft-pencil drawings, which smudge without a protective coat of diluted varnish.

9. RUBBER CEMENT: For all paste-up jobs, this is the most practical. Once it is dry, surplus cement can be easily rubbed off or picked up with a rubber made of the cement and dried. It is the only adhesive so easily removed. Papers attached by rubber cement can also be pulled off, providing only one surface was coated, and it never causes buckling.

10. PORTFOLIOS: These may be bought in many sizes and types, from the black flap with ties to the zippered ones with carrying handles. The size of your finished, mounted work will determine the size you should purchase.

WORKING METHODS AND PROPER USE OF MATERIALS

First of all, assemble your materials in some kind of order and establish a good working arrangement. Your drawing board and table should be placed in a good light by a window or have adequate artificial light.

Balance your drawing board on your lap, resting it against the table at an angle. Always work on a slanted surface, never a flat one. A flat surface distorts the length of the picture you see, because the top part is further from your range of vision than the bottom. This is called a foreshortened view.

Have pencils, pens, brushes, ink, water, and palette within easy reach (at your right, if you are right-handed) and on a flat surface, for obvious reasons. Have a few blotters handy and a clean cotton rag to use as a paint cloth. Brushes and pencils can be placed in a tall jar or arranged in the type of drawer-organizing tray designed to hold kitchen cutlery. This is also handy for storing them in a drawer. Art-supply stores have a "lazy Susan" type of rotating brush holder with partitions for small articles as well.

For getting straight lines and right angles and accuracy of measurements, get used to working with a T square and right-angle triangle placed together on your drawing board. (See illustration on page 34.) It can save endless time in measuring and checking.

Proper care of your supplies is not only economical but essential in producing a neat, professional job. Listed here are a few hints for getting the best out of your brushes and other equipment.

Brushes should never be left standing in water. Always rinse them quickly in clean water before paint dries in them. If they have become clogged with paint and will not rinse out, use a little soap and lukewarm water and wash out thoroughly. Dry with a clean paint cloth and shape hairs to a point while brush is damp. A good brush is expensive but lasts a long time with care. If abused it is worthless. Be sure to put them away so that the brush end does not get bent out of shape. Either stand them on end in a jar or place them in a long-enough box. If the hairs persist in separating, try moistening the brush and stroking it over the glue side of a piece of gummed tape, then put it away to dry. This will give it a little sizing to hold the shape until you wish to use it. It can then be easily rinsed off.

Pens used with India ink should be wiped off frequently with a cloth. Dried ink cakes on and clogs the pen after a while. Some of it can be scraped off with a razor blade.

Metal paint tubes should be squeezed from the bottom once the cap has been replaced. This forces the paint up to the top and eliminates the air, which causes the paint to dry out.

5.
DRAWING
THE
FASHION
FIGURE

Never was the natural-body look so important. Designers threw out the pinched waist along with the cluttered, restricting styles of past eras and produced a new picture of vitality and freedom of movement. The beauty of today is young, healthy, and on the go. Body proportions are no longer overtly feminine with accentuated curves and tiny hands and feet. Today's ideal is the bikini figure with long, sculptured torso, normal waistline, small bosom, and long legs. Feet stand firmly on the ground and support a strong, active body. A long, slim neck completes the lithe and graceful mien. The pose is uninhibited and completely natural.

The following lessons give you the basics for drawing the fashion figure, starting with measurements for proportion. Construction of the figure is expressed first in block form. Anatomy lessons are here condensed to absolute essentials. The average fashion artist has little need for years of studying anatomy and learning names of muscles and bones, unless he plans to branch out into a field of art that demands more realism.

The opportunity to sketch from living models cannot be overestimated. Life class gives the artist a chance to observe and use his knowledge of constructive anatomy. Sketching from life around you is also invaluable.

With a good drawing pencil (HB or B) and a pad of erasable drawing paper, follow the exercises in this chapter, copying the diagrams and illustrations carefully. Establish exact measurements first, as described, for guidelines (preferably in colored pencil so as to separate guidelines from those of the figure). Written notes on your drawings are also helpful while learning, particularly numbers for checking your measurements. Do not expect to achieve perfection on the first few attempts. Throw out and redo when necessary. Sometimes it is better to start over than to work over a bad beginning.

BASIC PROPORTIONS OF THE FIGURE

The ideal figure is 8 heads tall, slightly taller than the average 7½.

Measure off 8 spaces of equal size with horizontal lines about 1¼" apart. (Your transparent ruler is handy for this.) This gives you the over-all height of the figure. The width of the figure at the shoulderline should be approximately 1½ times the length of the head or 1¾" if the above measurements are used.

Draw a vertical line through the measured spaces to establish the center line of the figure.

Use a colored pencil or pen (red, green, or blue perhaps) for all these guidelines so as to separate them from the black lines of the figure. (See diagram on page 40.)

1. The head should be indicated in the top space, in pencil. Draw the head as an egg-shaped oval, a half circle at the top narrowing to a slightly pointed oval for the chin.

2. Divide space 2 in half to establish the shoulderline and pit of the neck, which is in the middle. Line 2 indicates placing of the armpit.

3. Divide space 3 into 4 parts. The first of these establishes the bustline, the third quarter, the bottom of the rib cage. Draw in the rib cage (chest) as a box, wider at the shoulderline and tapering in at the waistline (line 3).

4. Line 4 places the hipbone (trochanter is its anatomical name), an important part of the bone structure. It is exactly halfway between the top of the head and the heel bone or sole of the foot. Draw in the pelvis as another box below the waistline, about ⅓ down, widening slightly at the hipline. Indicate the hipbone at the extreme width of the hip.

small head

elongated proportions

The fashion figure

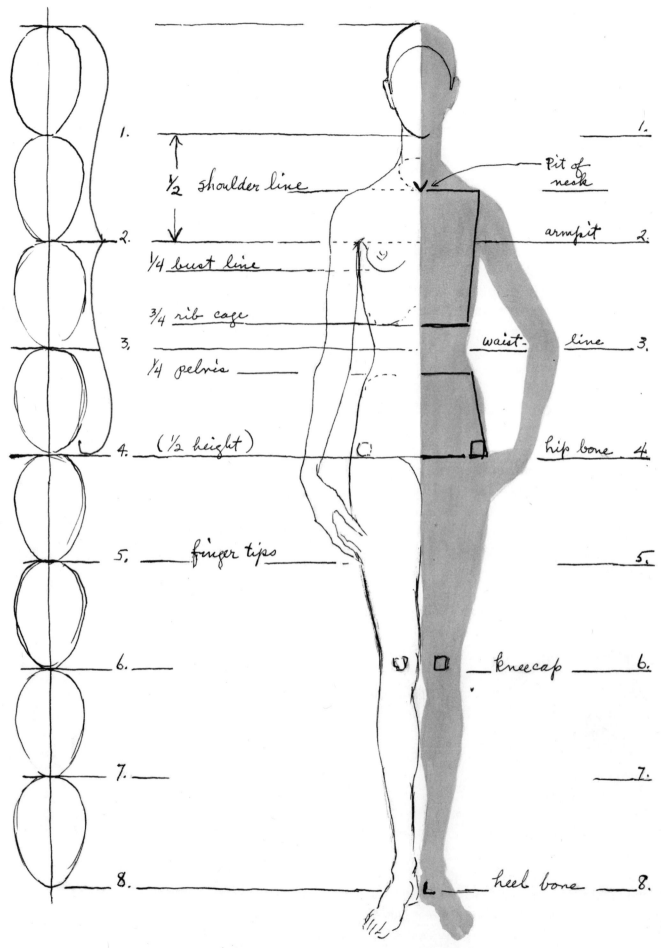

1.

½ shoulder line

Pit of neck

¼ bust line

armpit 2.

¾ rib cage

waist line 3.

¼ pelvis

4. (½ height)

hip bone 4.

5. finger tips

5.

6.

kneecap 6.

7.

7.

8.

heel bone 8.

PROPORTIONS OF THE IDEAL FIGURE ■ Eight heads tall. Study and use these measurements for drawing and checking the figure until your eye is trained to see without measuring.

5. Line 5 gives you the length of the arm and hand to the fingertips. The elbow is in line with the top of the pelvis box, the inside bend at the waistline.

6. The kneecap rests on line 6, halfway between the hipline and the sole of the foot. Indicate with a small square.

7. This marks nothing.

8. Line 8 gives you the heel or the placing of the foot which carries the weight of the body. If the figure is wearing shoes, the heel of the shoe is below this line, of course.

SIMPLIFIED CONSTRUCTION OF THE FIGURE
Using Block Forms

Once you have acquired a knowledge of figure proportions, continue to measure and mark them off as the first step in all drawings while you are still learning. The next step is to work for form, to think of the figure as having three dimensions, not as a flat paper doll. To learn the general construction of the figure, start by drawing it in block forms (blocks, cylinders, and wedges). Small knobs connect these movable parts like a jointed wooden doll. (See diagram on page 42.)

Practice drawing just blocks and cylinders at first, doing them separately until they look right. Be sure they have a third dimension and feeling of perspective (the appearance of some being above the eye level and some below). See Chapter 6, "Basic Steps Toward Improvement in Drawing." This not only develops draftsmanship but teaches you an appreciation of pure form in art.

Draw cylinder shapes for the legs, the arms, and the neck. The torso is made up of two boxes, independent of each other and separated by the waistline. Do not think of the torso as one inflexible form. The upper section, which is the chest area or rib cage, and the lower section, which is the pelvis, move in opposite directions when the body bends or twists.

Above the rib cage a pyramid shape acts as a base for the neck (see diagram on page 42.) This gives the shoulderline a natural and graceful-looking slope. Somewhat similar is the wedge shape that forms the general outline of the foot, with an arch on the inside between the heel and the base of the foot.

EXERCISES

1. Make a careful copy of the figure in the diagram on page 40, working in pencil. If the first try is messy, trace onto a fresh sheet of paper and start over, making necessary corrections. Next, go over your lines with pen and India ink. Erase the pencil lines when the ink is dry, using a kneaded eraser.

2. Find a photograph of a fashion figure in a magazine (in a simple pose) and see if you can use it to analyze construction and proportions.

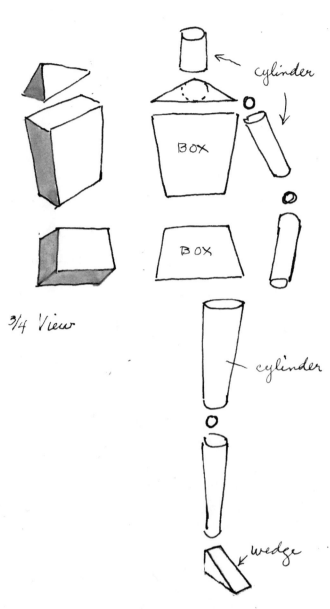

3/4 View

cylinder

cylinder

wedge

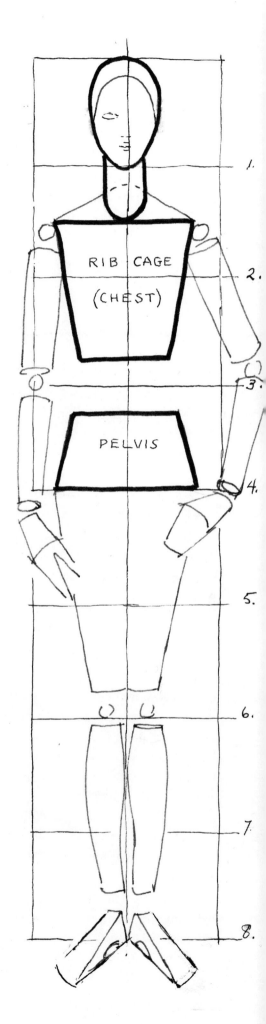

1.

RIB CAGE

(CHEST)

2.

PELVIS

3.

4.

5.

6.

7.

8.

CONSTRUCTION IN SIMPLIFIED BLOCK FORM ■ To learn the main masses of the body, sketch the figure in these three-dimensional shapes. First indicate the head, chest, and pelvis, then add the cylindrical forms of the neck, arms, and legs.

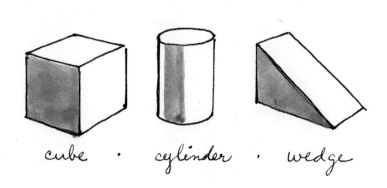

cube · cylinder · wedge

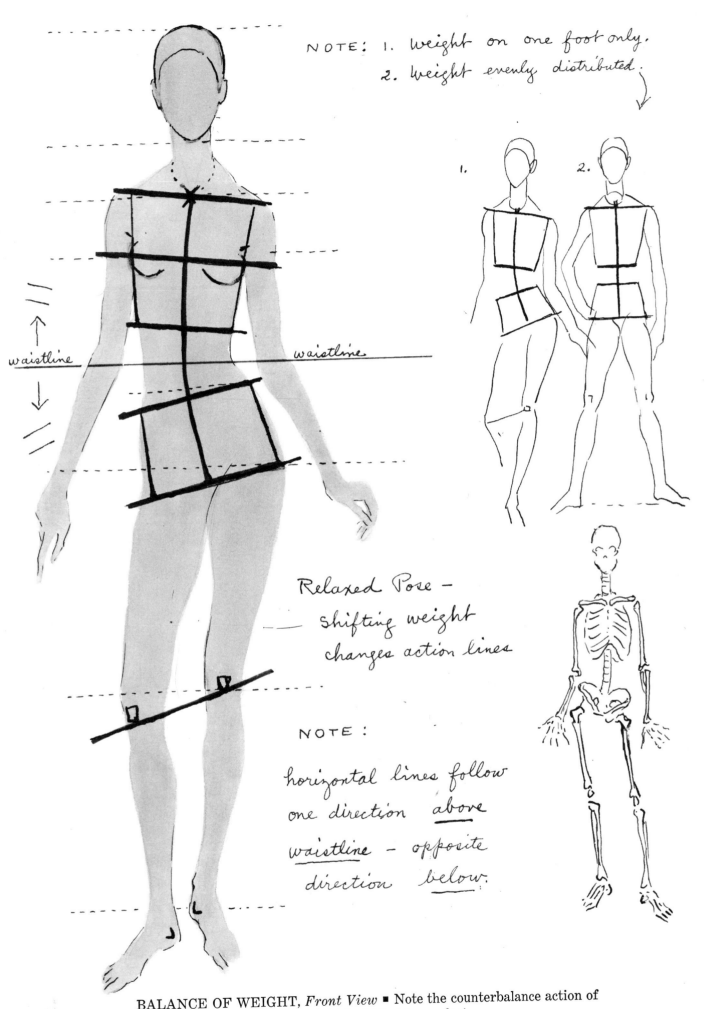

NOTE: 1. Weight on one foot only.
2. Weight evenly distributed.

waistline

waistline

Relaxed Pose –
shifting weight
changes action lines

NOTE :

horizontal lines follow
one direction *above*
waistline – opposite
direction *below.*

BALANCE OF WEIGHT, *Front View* ▪ Note the counterbalance action of
the chest and pelvis as the weight is shifted to one foot.

Place tracing paper over it and sketch in the rib cage, pelvis, cylinder of the neck, arms, and legs. *Do not trace the outline of the figure.* This teaches you nothing of form or drawing and the result is always an obvious, thickened outline of a photograph. Analyzing the construction develops your powers of observation and knowledge of the figure so that later on you will be able to sketch from memory and imagination.

Your tracing-paper sketch should be an interesting arrangement of block forms that portray a figure without outlines and detail. It should have qualities of form and dimension as simplified as those of a wooden doll. Try as many examples as possible, checking with the figure in the diagram for accuracy.

BALANCE OF THE FIGURE AND ACTION LINE

As long as the figure is erect and the weight equally distributed on both feet, all action lines are straight (horizontal and vertical). The relaxed pose shifts the balance of weight to one foot and the lines immediately change direction. Automatically the center line of the figure changes to a curve stretching from the pit of the neck downward. This line, *always from the pit of the neck*, is the center line of action for every pose. It is called the axial line.

Always establish the pit of the neck as the pivotal point of action. Directly under, in a straight line, is the foot maintaining the weight, and the hip swings out on that side. The only time these rules do not apply is when the figure is leaning on or against something for partial support.

As the hip swings out over the foot supporting the weight, the pelvis drops at an angle along with the knee, which is bent. To balance this action, the shoulderline drops at an angle in the opposite direction.

All lines above the waistline follow one direction, all below the waist the opposite direction.

EXERCISES

Sketch with pencil on a pad of regular drawing paper. Practice copying diagram on page 43, for front view. Concentrate on action lines. Do not worry too much about outlines of the figure; these are of secondary importance for this problem.

1. Mark off figure proportions with horizontal lines as before (8 heads).

2. Establish pit of neck and axial line (curved).

3. Put in rib cage as a box with the shoulderline at a slight angle.

4. Next draw pelvis box, dipping at an angle in the opposite direction.

5. Place weight-carrying foot and leg directly under the pit of the neck.

6. Sketch free leg with the knee bent, as illustrated on page 43.

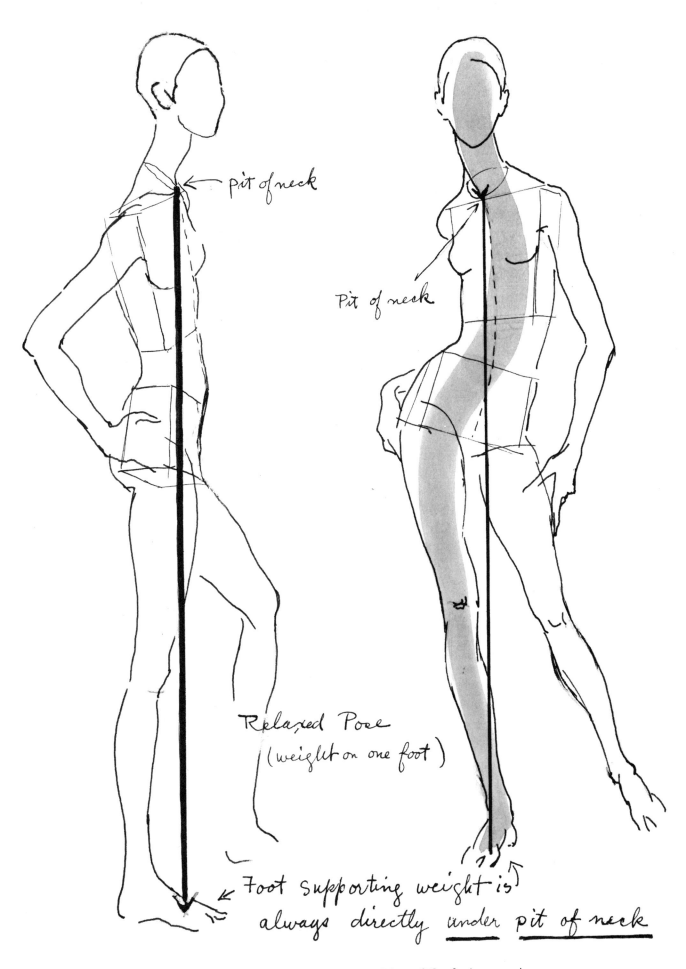

pit of neck

Pit of neck

Relaxed Pose
(weight on one foot)

Foot supporting weight is
always directly under pit of neck

BALANCE OF WEIGHT, *Side View* ■ Note the position of the foot support-ing the weight in relation to the rest of the figure. The same rule applies to the twisted, partly three-quarter view.

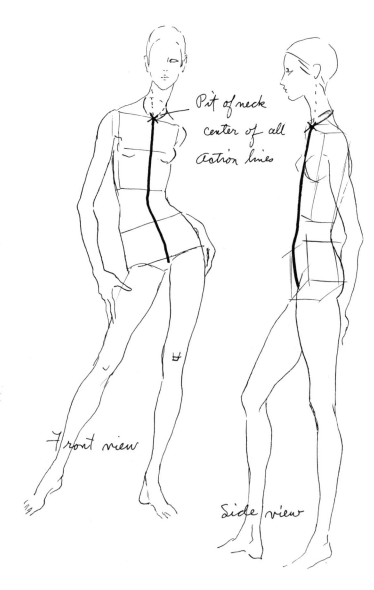

Pit of neck
center of all
action lines

front view

Side view

ACTION LINES, *Front and Side Views* ■ The axial line starts at the pit of the neck. Indicating the center line of the body, it directs the main action line of the pose.

After trying several versions of this exercise, do some small, quick sketches of action lines to get the feeling of different poses. Leave out the outline and details of the figure, using as few lines as possible. If you prefer, work with a fine-pointed felt-tip pen rather than a pencil. These are not meant to be done in careful detail or corrected. They are purely practice drawings, to be done as follows:

1. Draw the axial line in a curve and indicate the pit of the neck.
2. Add oval for the head, with neck indicated by a single line.
3. Indicate arms and legs with single lines, adding simplified hands and feet as well.
4. Try many poses and see how animated these jottings can become.

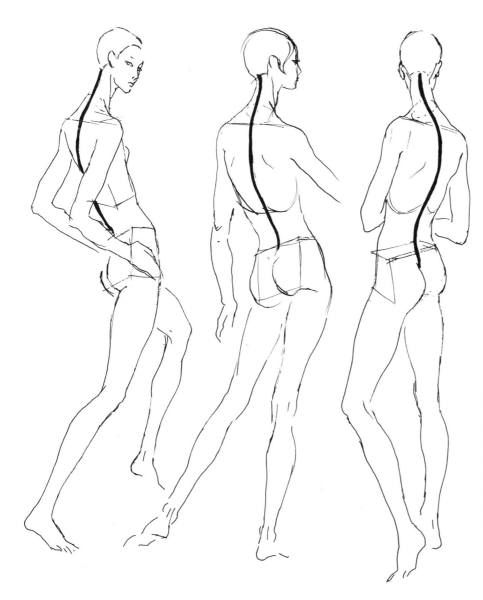

ACTION LINES, *Back View* ■ The spinal column is the obvious center line of action, starting at the base of the skull in all back views, and it must be indicated in order to achieve the character of the pose and to draw it with conviction.

5. Try a line like the letter S. Make it large and work out a pose within that shape. The S line always makes a beautiful and graceful pose.

Next, try analyzing a photograph again as in the previous lesson, using tracing paper to indicate the action lines. As before, be sure that you *do not trace outlines of the photograph*. (This mechanical procedure, to avoid thinking, accomplishes nothing—it is an uninspired, mechanical rendition, obviously traced from a photograph. Exact tracings do not have the proportions of a fashion figure when transposed to a flat line drawing.) Get only the pose from a photograph, not the outline. If you find tracing paper too much of a temptation, simply pin the photograph up nearby or on your drawing board and use it as you would a model, drawing larger or smaller than the picture.

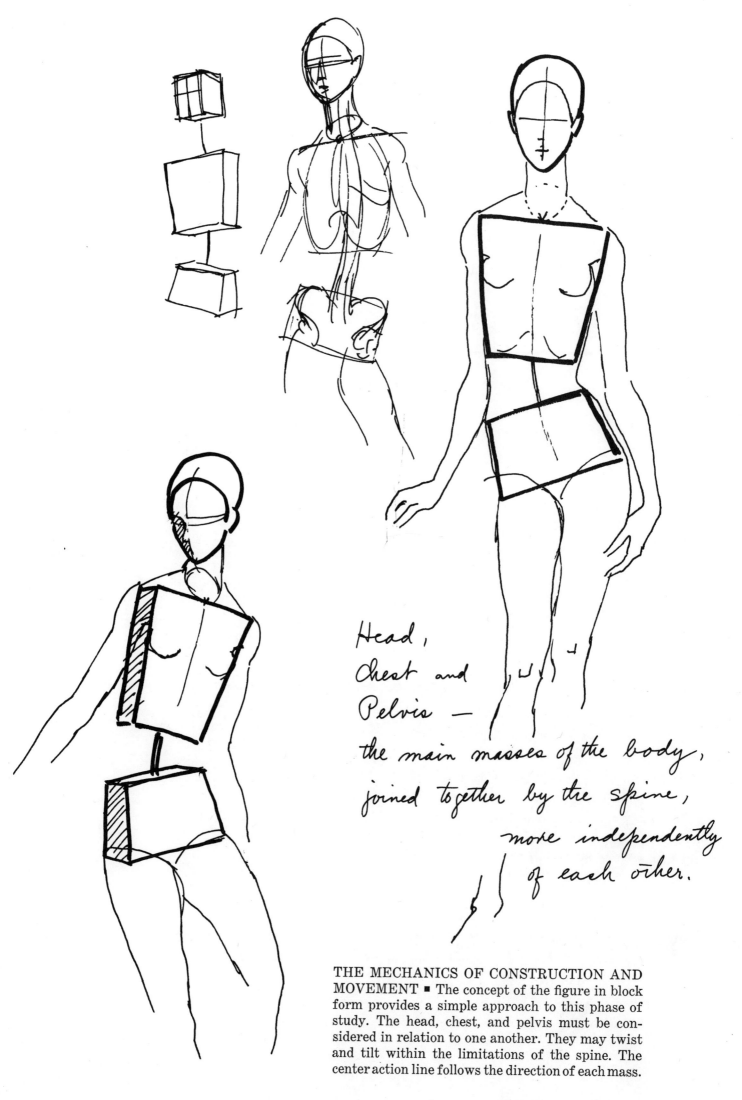

Head,
Chest and
Pelvis —
the main masses of the body,
joined together by the spine,
more independently
of each other.

THE MECHANICS OF CONSTRUCTION AND
MOVEMENT ■ The concept of the figure in block
form provides a simple approach to this phase of
study. The head, chest, and pelvis must be considered in relation to one another. They may twist
and tilt within the limitations of the spine. The
center action line follows the direction of each mass.

THE MECHANICS OF CONSTRUCTION
AND MOVEMENT

Although there is a tendency away from realism in all art, not only fashion art, there are advantages in knowing the basic rules of figure construction. Without knowledge of bone structure and the more important muscles, you will produce a figure that looks like an air-filled rubber toy, and with about as much charm. Ignorance is displayed by a pitiful lack of assurance in drawing.

Realism need not be forced to the point where the drawing is dull and heavy. A knowledge of good drawing need not prevent an artist from making use of distortion or exaggeration for a desired effect. Where there is a desire for an unrealistic or stylized figure, a deliberate fake can have a reason for being. It is usually done better and in a more sophisticated way by the artist who discards the rules than the one who is ignorant of them. For the average fashion artist, however, years of working in life class, studying anatomy, and learning the names of bones and muscles is a needless waste of time.

The drawings of skeletons on page 50 show the underlying bone structure and what happens to it as the body moves. They also show the balance of the figure, the strong spinal column, and the body's curve when viewed from the side. Note the bones descending from the pit of the neck, forming the shoulderline, and meeting the shoulder blades in the back. Note, too, the bones of the leg, joining the pelvis at its extreme width in the front view. All these shapes can influence the way you express a line or draw a well-balanced figure, regardless of the pose. Study them carefully and make copies. Refer to them frequently.

THE NECK

How elegant and expressive the neck can be! The long, graceful lines and well-set head are so important to the fashion figure, so easily

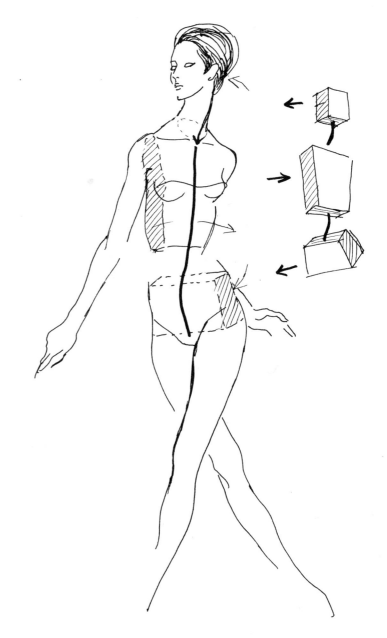

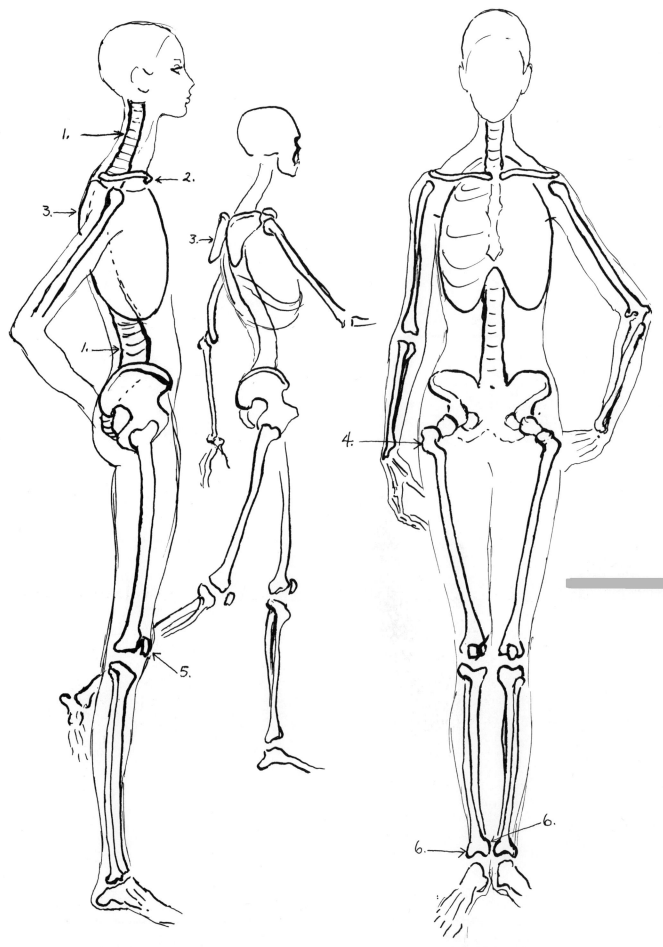

BONE STRUCTURE ■ Indicated in relation to the outline of the figure, the bony masses not only suggest the mechanics of action but directly affect the surface form. Note how near the surface are (1) the spinal column (side view), (2) the collar bone, or clavicle, (3) the shoulder blades, (4) the hip-bone (front view), (5) the kneecap, and (6) the anklebones. The pelvis is the mechanical axis of the body, supporting the muscles of the trunk and legs.

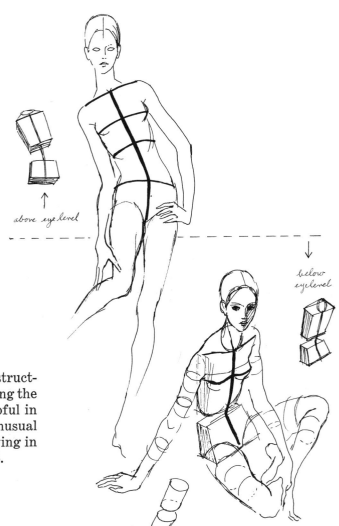

THE FIGURE IN PERSPECTIVE ■ Constructing the body in block form is an aid in sketching the model from various eye levels. It is also helpful in working from imagination to develop an unusual angle for dramatic effect. The rules for drawing in perspective apply, as described in Chapter 6.

THE FORESHORTENED VIEW ■ A basic knowledge of perspective allows the artist to convey foreshortening with conviction. Most seated poses require drawing of arms and legs that appear to be receding at near-eye-level. Practice drawing these as cylindrical shapes in perspective to acquire a subconscious feeling of foreshortened form. As your point of view is sharpened, expressive outlines develop naturally. Sketch anyone available as a subject. Put in as many guidelines as you need to delineate form. Make many rough sketches.

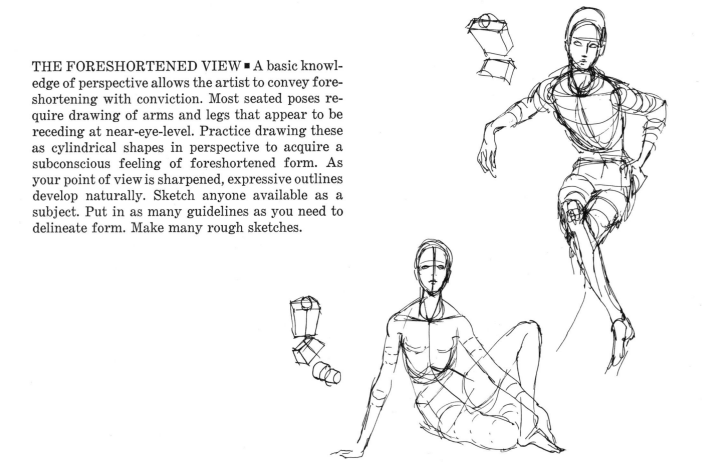

THE FORESHORTENED BODY ■ Tilted forward, as in this pose, the masses of the chest and pelvis are foreshortened without losing proportion. From rough drawings with guidelines a clean outline may be worked out later by tracing the sculptural form. Draw from your imagination or use poses from photographs as inspiration. Do not trace outlines from photographs; try to analyze the construction underneath.

ruined by careless drawing. To draw the neck well one must give a feeling of its underlying construction.

The basic form of the neck is a cylinder, shorter in back than in the front, where it joins the shoulderline. The center of the shoulderline is the pit of the neck. Avoid drawing the neck and shoulderline at right angles or with a continuous curve. The shoulderline slopes from the neck at the back into the straight line in front that reaches from the pit of the neck out to the shoulder proper where the arm is joined to the collarbone.

The important muscles of the neck (see illustration on page 54) give it flexibility and form. They are so apparent from every angle that to ignore their existence is to draw the neck without grace or movement. Viewed from the front, the neck gets its main line from the dominant muscle, which starts at the pit of the neck and rises to the ear, joining the head in back of the ear. No matter what position the head takes, this muscle is always in evidence. A mere suggestion of line will show this knowledge. Note, too, the strong muscle in back, joining the head, shoulders, and spinal column.

Practice copying all drawings and diagrams accurately. Draw in the construction on all figure drawings until you have it firmly in mind. Sketch from a model whenever possible. Once these muscles are well imprinted on your mind, your lines will fall into place as they should.

THE HEAD

FRONT VIEW

1. Draw a rectangle 2″ wide and 3″ high (or twice that size is better).
    a. Divide in half horizontally and vertically.
    b. Draw a half circle at top, taper to an oval in bottom half to create an egg shape.
    c. Take off crescent shape for hairline.

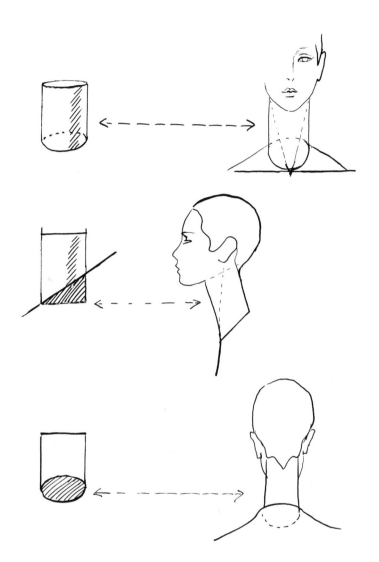

THE NECK, *A Cylinder* ▪ In simplified form the neck is a cylinder and should be indicated as such. Note that the neckline is high in the back but meets the shoulderline in front (the pit of the neck). This gives a natural slope to the shoulderline and a lengthening effect to the front of the neck. Avoid vagueness in drawing the neck. It must look strong and definite. Practice copying this diagram as often as necessary.

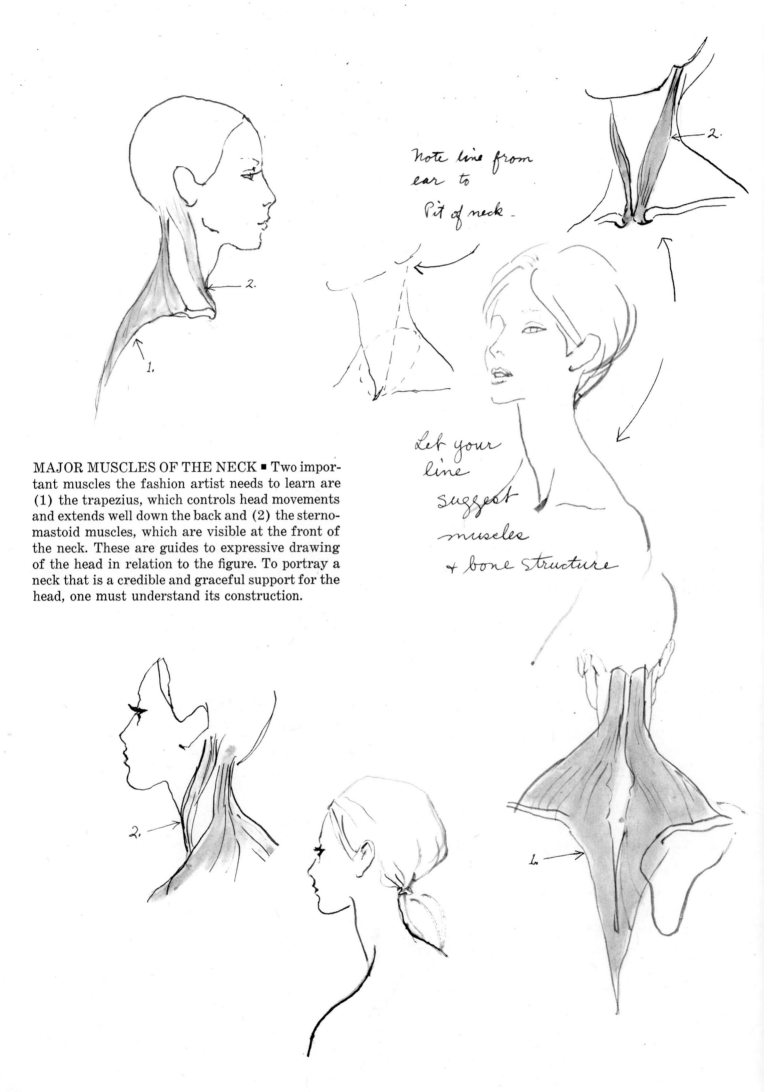

Note line from ear to Pit of neck.

MAJOR MUSCLES OF THE NECK ∎ Two important muscles the fashion artist needs to learn are (1) the trapezius, which controls head movements and extends well down the back and (2) the sterno-mastoid muscles, which are visible at the front of the neck. These are guides to expressive drawing of the head in relation to the figure. To portray a neck that is a credible and graceful support for the head, one must understand its construction.

Let your line suggest muscles + bone structure

d. Divide face into three equal parts from hairline down for line of eyebrows and nose.

e. The eyeline is halfway between the top of the head and the chin.

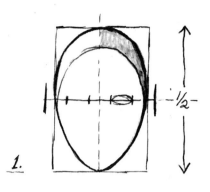

1.

2.

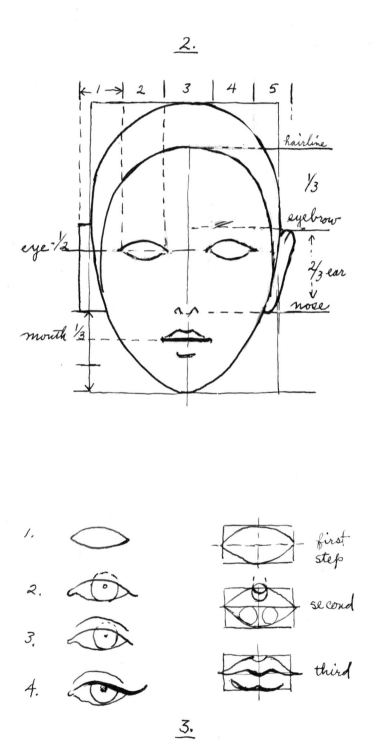

hairline

⅓

eyebrow

eye ½

↑
⅔ ear
↓

nose

mouth ⅓

1.

2.

3.

4.

first step

second

third

3.

curve of cheek bone

4.

THE HEAD, *Front View* ▪ (1) The egg shape within the rectangle. (2) Measurements for placing the features. (3) Guides for drawing the eyes and mouth. (4) The stylized head with undulating curves outlining the cheekbones and rounded chin.

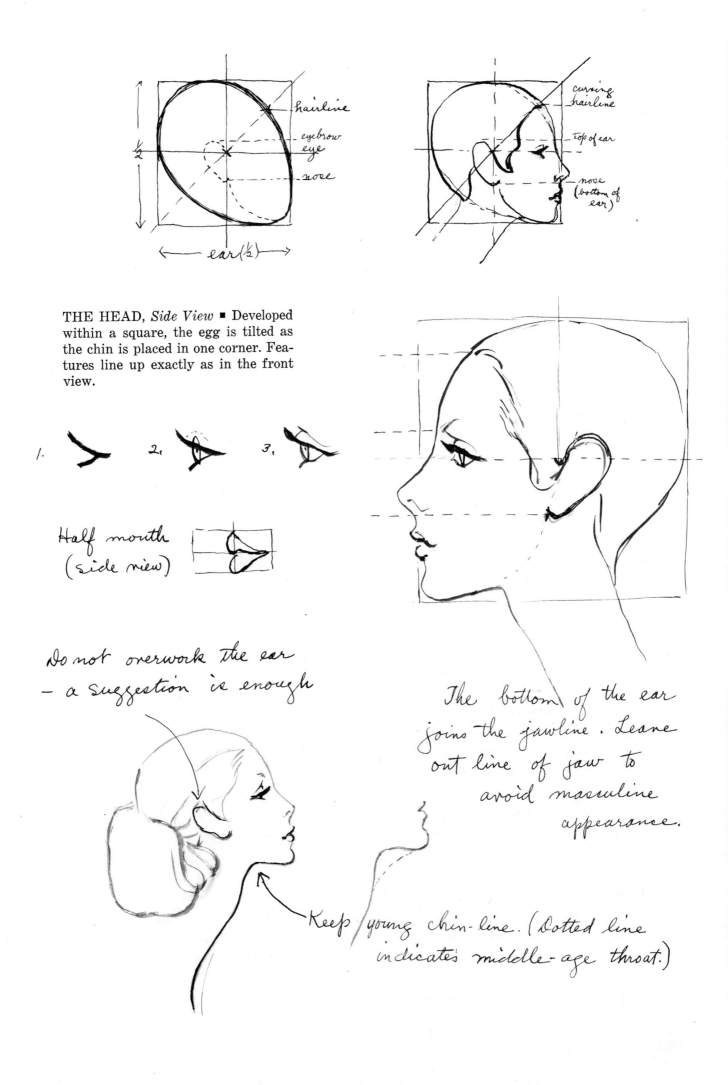

hairline
eyebrow
eye
nose

½

ear (½)

curving hairline

Top of ear

nose (bottom of ear)

THE HEAD, *Side View* ■ Developed within a square, the egg is tilted as the chin is placed in one corner. Features line up exactly as in the front view.

1.   2.   3.

Half mouth (side view)

Do not overwork the ear — a suggestion is enough

The bottom of the ear joins the jawline. Leave out line of jaw to avoid masculine appearance.

Keep young chin-line. (Dotted line indicates middle-age throat.)

2. Draw a line slightly outside rectangle for ears.
   a. The ear is in direct line between eyebrow and nose.
   b. Measure off 5 equal spaces, horizontally, from earline outside rectangle.
   c. This gives exact width of eyes and space between.
3. Divide the distance between nose and chin in thirds. The top line indicates the placing of the center line of the mouth. It should be slightly wider than the width of the eye.
4. The eye.
   a. Draw an almond shape. Next suggest the tear duct at corner of eye nearest nose. Lengthen line on other side to suggest eyelashes.
   b. Draw the iris (a perfect circle resting on the lower lid and partly covered by the upper lid).
      Draw it as if you could see through the lid. Put in a curve for upper lid.
5. Lightly suggest the eyebrows and nose.
6. The mouth.
   a. Draw rectangle; divide in half horizontally and vertically.
   b. Draw almond shape with ball in upper half. Take off curve as illustrated to give shape of upper lip.
   c. Draw curving line between lips, following around ball shape, up and down and curving up at corners.

EXERCISE

Practice drawing, using a colored pencil for measurements, a black one for drawing. If you use a lead pencil, indicate guidelines lightly.

SIDE VIEW

1. Draw a square with lines dividing it in half horizontally and vertically.
   a. Draw egg shape with point in lower corner.
   b. Draw line at angle from opposite lower corner to upper corner, through middle, establishing hairline and ear at point of attachment. Note that the ear is at an angle.
   c. The measurements for placement of eyes, nose, and mouth are the same as front view.
   d. Draw curves of profile, with only nose extending beyond square.
2. The eye.
   a. Draw a curved line, following the cheekline, for lower lid.
   b. Draw a longer line, making a V, for upper lid (eyelashes).
   c. For the iris, an elliptical oval with shallow pupil (very thin).
   d. Place line over it for upper lid.
3. The mouth is equal to half of front view (shaped like a heart on its side).
4. Draw curves from nose to mouth, from mouth to chin.

5. Indicate hairline with curves toward the eyebrow at the temple, in again, then out again in front of the ear, like a short sideburn. Behind the ear (if an upswept hairdo), there is a lovely, curved space following the hairline down to a point at the neck.

EXERCISE

Practice drawing, putting in all measurements carefully. Experiment. Do it over and over. You may get many different faces. Compare yours with the diagram; check for errors. Practice drawing eyes separately, and large.

THREE-QUARTER VIEW

The three-quarter view is more complicated than the front or side views, since this puts the head in perspective. Placement of the features follows the same rules, but the center line becomes curved.

1. Again draw a rectangle and place the egg shape (tilted as in diagram) with chin in corner.
   a. Draw curved center line to one side, following imaginary line of the egg.
   b. Mark off horizontal lines for eyes, nose, and mouth as in front view, the ear within outline of head.
   c. Establish the hairline, partly hidden on far side.
   d. Place nose on center line with tip beyond and the mouth centered underneath.
   e. Indicate eyes at halfway line (the far eye near the nose).
   f. The curved outline of the face should be indented slightly beside the eye, out again over the cheekbone, in again, then out by the mouth, and in once more before rounding the chin.
2. The features.
   a. The eyes. Draw the same as in front view but make rounder (foreshortened).
   b. The nose. Draw a triangle (the same as in side view). The line of the nose and eyebrow join, hiding part of the far eye.
   c. The mouth is divided in half vertically, the near side indicated exactly the same as front view, the far side as a half-ball shape.

Changing the Angle of the Head. If the head is tilted up or down, the horizontal lines become curved, downward in a down view and up when the head is viewed from below. (See illustration on page 59.) These curved guidelines automatically place the ear above or below the lines of the other features as shown.

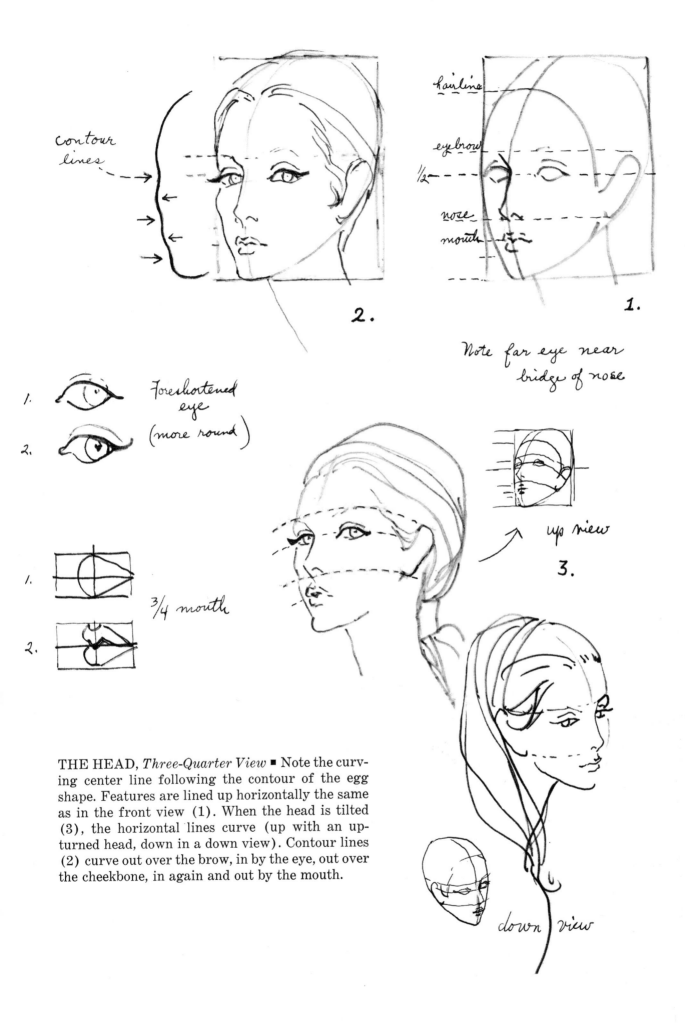

contour lines

2.

hairline

eyebrow

1/2

nose
mouth

1.

Note far eye near bridge of nose

1. Foreshortened eye (more round)
2.

1.
2. 3/4 mouth

up view

3.

down view

THE HEAD, *Three-Quarter View* ■ Note the curving center line following the contour of the egg shape. Features are lined up horizontally the same as in the front view (1). When the head is tilted (3), the horizontal lines curve (up with an up-turned head, down in a down view). Contour lines (2) curve out over the brow, in by the eye, out over the cheekbone, in again and out by the mouth.

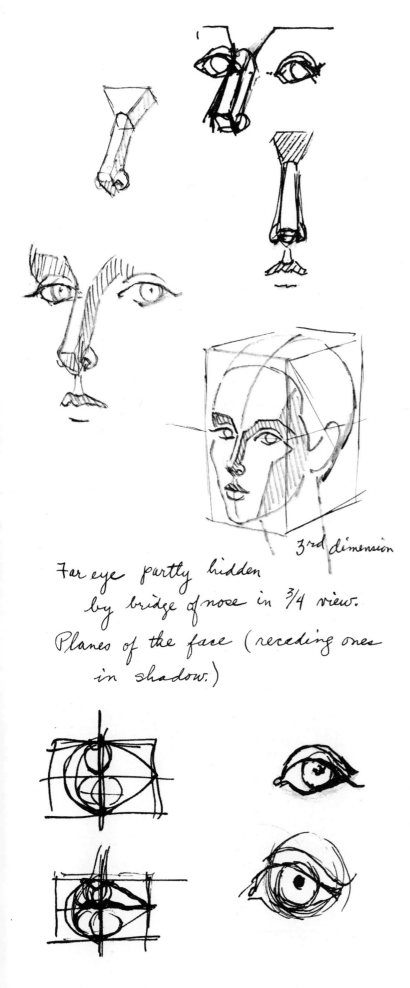

3rd dimension

Far eye partly hidden by bridge of nose in 3/4 view. Planes of the face (receding ones in shadow.)

THE HEAD IN THIRD DIMENSION ▪ Copy these diagrams to learn the sculptural planes of the head and features as explained in the lesson.

EXERCISE

Practice drawing the head from all angles. Check carefully for placement of features.

THE THIRD DIMENSION

Modeling of the head and figure may be expressed either through light and shadow for emphasis of depth or through a simple outline that defines form through contour. In either technique it is essential to have a knowledge of the surface planes and the block construction of both techniques. The basis of good drawing is to understand exactly what your line should reveal before you put it down.

The head fits into a general block form. In the three-quarter view illustrated, three sides (side, top, and front) are revealed. Draw it as you would an oblong box in perspective. The head is chiseled into a rounded skull and blocklike planes of the face. Projecting planes catch the light; receding planes are in shadow. Projecting planes are the forehead, nose, cheekbones, upper eyelid, and lower lip. The nose, in simplified form, is a triangle or wedge with a narrow, flat surface over the bridge that widens into a triangle between the eyebrows.

Lines curve out over the projecting planes and in at the receding ones. Your knowledge of form thus gives your contour line authority and meaningful expression. *Lack of that knowledge* may produce a grotesque or distorted face with misplaced features. It is worth the hours of practice and study necessary to acquire this ease of drawing. The head can make or break an otherwise passable drawing.

In shading a drawing or water color do not copy shadows in great detail as they may appear on the live model or in a photograph. They may be confusingly complicated or too sharp or too indefinite. Light and shaded areas should be simplified and indicated through knowlege of the planes rather than copied literally. This also allows the artist to work from imagination and portray realism without a model. All planes on one side (whichever side is lighted) reflect a light surface. All planes away from the light are in shadow.

Another way to express the third dimension in drawing the figure is to work for roundness through direction of lines. Try drawing lines *around* the figure, around the arms, around the legs in a continuous spiral. Think of the figure as made of glass. You can see through to the back surface, and the lines drawn on the surface show through as they circle the body.

EXERCISE

Practice drawing the figure from life as directed in this chapter. If this is difficult at first, try using tracing paper over one of your drawings and draw only circular lines to define the figure. Leave out the original outlines. Remove the tracing and study the results.

Try this same method for drawing the garment. Correctly indicated, circles should give you guidelines for the placing of neckline, armholes, beltline, and even some seaming. They should all go around the body in graceful curves.

HAIR AND HAIR STYLES

HOW TO DRAW HAIR

Natural-looking hair must have the appearance of growing from the scalp. The first step is to establish the hairline correctly. Look around at people, or take a mirror and study your own hairline. Obviously the hairline is hidden on someone wearing bangs or hair down on the neck; study from an off-the-face or upswept hair style.

Although hairlines vary slightly, there is usually a definite, curved line arched across the forehead. The so-called widow's peak gives this line a heart shape. From the brow, this line curves in at the temple and out again over the cheekbone in front of the ear. The line then swings up over the ear and down in a wide curve, leaving a good space behind the ear, and then downward to a W shape at the nape of the neck. It is the series of lovely, flowing curves that gives length and grace to the neck itself. Mistakes made through lack of observation can result in a grotesque and false look.

The hairline never has a hard line, or edge, against the face. The fine hairs at the hairline

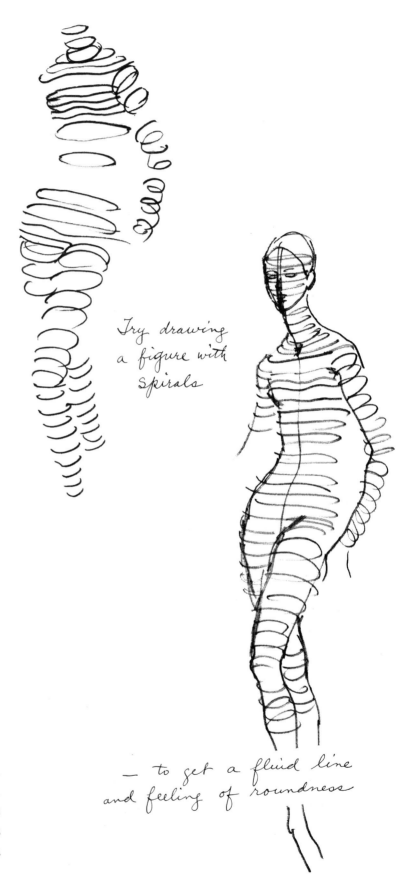

Try drawing a figure with spirals

— to get a fluid line and feeling of roundness

THE ART OF SUGGESTION ▪ A few deft brush-and-ink strokes by artist Antonio stimulate the imagination. This provocative sketch of the eyes creates the idea of an alluring female at a masquerade ball. Glitter is conveyed with a sprinkling of dots. A knowledge of good drawing is evident in the simply stated and sure strokes.

EYE CLOSE-UPS ▪ Illustrations from a full-page newspaper ad for eye cosmetics. A realistic wash drawing by Dorothy Hood for Lord & Taylor. Done actual size on a handmade water-color board with a medium surface, the washes are clear with sharp contrasts of dark and light. Lines are handled with pen and brush and highlights are added with opaque white.

blend gradually into the skin tones of the face. For this reason use only a delicate pencil line as a guideline. Once the hairline is established, begin to think of the hair as lines starting from the scalp and flowing out in a definite direction.

All hair styles should have direction. Start drawing these lines out from the face, beginning at the center of the forehead and working downward. Try pen lines or soft brush lines directed from the face. Use delicate, tapering lines.

Avoid even spacing of lines, since this looks too mechanical and gives the hair a dull, lack-luster appearance. Rather place the lines in varied spacing, some close together, some widely spaced. Flowing lines of hair might be likened to the stylized interpretation of ocean waves found in a Japanese print. Working in pen line will give you a feeling of hair as a series of lines. It will also force you to be definite in your drawing and get shading without gray tones.

Once you feel that you have achieved the look of hair in your drawing, try doing some finished heads. Indicate the head and features according to the instructions given earlier in this chapter. Draw lightly in pencil, including the guideline for the hairline, then outline a simple hair style brushed back from the face. Draw in the hair with strong, definite lines. Try finishing the sketch in pen and ink or brush and ink. The hair can be rendered with an almost dry brush (dry with a blotter). With practice, this method can give a soft, silky look to the hair. Experiment until you have control of your brush line, working on a separate scrap of paper or on tracing paper.

draw lines out from scalp

HAIRLINES ■ Definite directional lines suggest texture and styling. Note the curves of the hairline outlining the face. The undulating line arches over the forehead, in at the temples and out over the cheekbone. Behind the ear, the line curves out again before dropping low on the neck. Fine hairs soften the outline blending into the greater mass of hair.

As you learn various methods of rendering (wash, charcoal, and so on), these techniques will give you ways to indicate hair as a mass. The main objective, in the beginning, is to interpret hair and hair styles with good drawing. Do not be discouraged by your first attempts. Quality develops with practice.

HAIR STYLES

Hair styles change as fashion changes. The outline of the head and hair is part of the fashion silhouette, part of the total look. The hair, as a mass, should become integral in proportion and balance of line to the whole aspect of the figure.

Suitability of style should also be considered. For example, the elaborate type of upswept coif with added hair piled high on the head is suitable only for evening wear. The daytime look should be simple and well-groomed. The active type should have hair that looks free and easily brushed, not arranged with pins or sprayed with lacquer. It could be one of the short-cropped styles or, for the very young and slim, long and swingy. To look chic, hair must be controlled, brushed in a definite direction. Even the loose, careless-appearing hair styles worn by Brigitte Bardot in her early films were actually carefully arranged by her hairdresser. It was a studied carelessness, which set a definite style trend in the sixties.

This history of hair styling can be a fascinating subject. From ancient times, man has been intrigued by the endless possibilities of hair arrangement. Today's hair stylists may be influenced by the ideas of any era—from classic Greek sculpture to the sleek, short hair of the nineteen-twenties, which no doubt suggested the geometric cut of 1965. It was inevitable that it reappear with the short skirts and leggy, boyish look. It looked bizarre or chic, depending on the wearer.

Head proportions and outline are completely changed by hair styles. In the nineteen-thirties, hair was brushed in a smooth line over the crown of the head and out around the head in various ways. The nineteen-sixties brought the height-

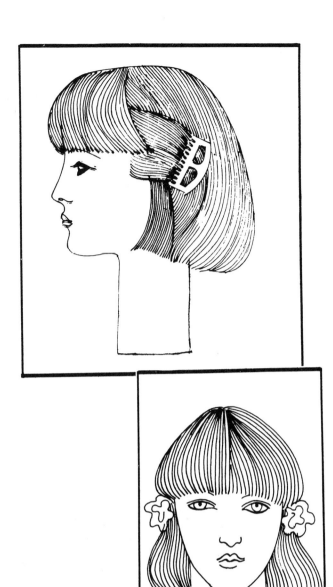

Pedro Barrios,
courtesy *Women's Wear Daily*

Courtesy of Bonwit Teller

THE FASHION HEAD BY KENNETH PAUL
BLOCK ■ Hair-styling illustrations executed in
Conte crayon on charcoal paper. Fine lines of the
hair follow a pattern of controlled design. Dark accents of shading are added with the dull side of the
crayon, giving a polished, well-brushed look to the
hair. The accurately defined features are delicately
suggested with pale lines and shading, the eyes accented with a minimum of black. The total look is
the conservative one of natural beauty. The expression is self-assured without affectation. Good drawing and control of the medium are outstanding factors contributing to the fine result.

ened crown, achieved by back-combing and spraying with lacquer or by special cutting and setting on mammoth curlers. Textures of hair were also altered by the development of the permanent wave, then by hair-straightening methods (from the too curly to the unnaturally straight).

In finding the right hair style for an illustration, it is helpful to get ideas from the leading fashion magazines. If you are lucky enough to find a model whose hair style is right, there is no problem. To avoid monotonous repetition, one should vary styles and learn to improvise.

Remember, whatever the style, hair should have direction of line and a pleasing silhouette. Even if the desired effect is careless abandon, it should be a planned arrangement, a definite style. There is nothing duller than a no-type, characterless hair arrangement without plan or design.

SWEEPING LINES ■ Sketched with obvious abandon, this head by Barbara Pearlman achieves a breezy quality with a minimum of line and a few smudges of gray shading. The lyric flow of lines and the effect of space add to the charm.

PENCIL SKETCH ▪ Indicated with a few light pencil lines, the hands help to frame the face of this dreamy-eyed beauty sketched by Antonio. The hair, too, serves as a frame and is merely suggested.

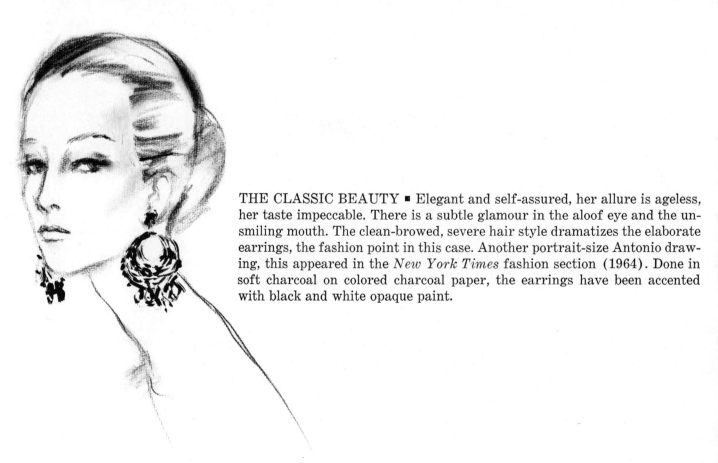

THE CLASSIC BEAUTY ▪ Elegant and self-assured, her allure is ageless, her taste impeccable. There is a subtle glamour in the aloof eye and the un-smiling mouth. The clean-browed, severe hair style dramatizes the elaborate earrings, the fashion point in this case. Another portrait-size Antonio draw-ing, this appeared in the *New York Times* fashion section (1964). Done in soft charcoal on colored charcoal paper, the earrings have been accented with black and white opaque paint.

Courtesy of *The New York Times*

Antonio, courtesy of *Glamour*

THE YOUNG CONTEMPORARY ■ The casual, sultry look, childish but worldly, is interpreted by Antonio in this illustration for *Glamour* magazine. The long, carefree, straight hair with bangs low over the eyes, the pale, sulky mouth, and the small, childlike proportions of the face compose the look of an era. Part of the bohemian image adopted by the international student groups, it gained momentum in the mid-sixties. The original art was done life-size in felt-tip pen line.

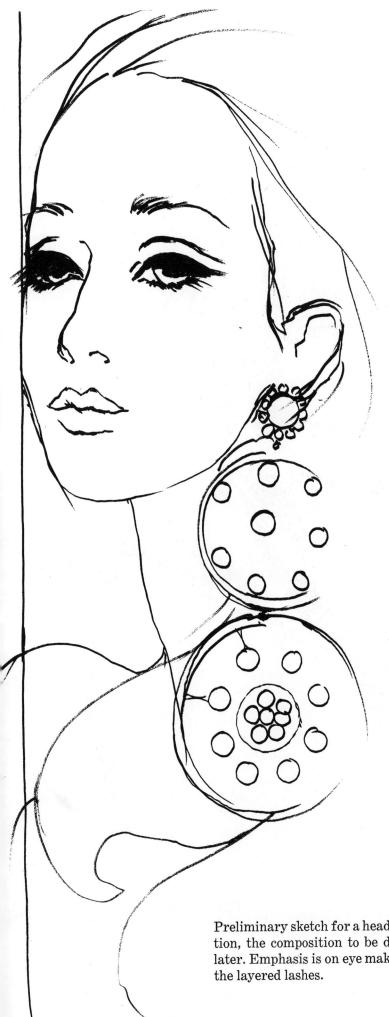

THE HAND

CONSTRUCTION

The hand has two distinct masses: the hand proper and the thumb. The knuckles of the hand form an arc, and the fingertips follow the same arc. (See illustration on page 71.) The mass of the thumb dominates the hand. The first segment of the thumb joins the hand at a slight angle and moves in a more independent way than the fingers. The thumb may be at almost a right angle to the hand or completely hidden except for the large joint.

The bones of the hand radiate from a common center at the wrist, and the fingers open like a fan from the first knuckle, forming a wide arc at the tips. The joints of the fingers, as seen on the back of the hand, are like steps or wedges tapering down to the fingertips. There are three steps, including the first knuckle, which is the largest. The bones of the hand are fine and delicate and, like all bones, larger at the joints and thinner in the middle. Thus the knuckles are evident in a good drawing of the hand.

The hand and wrist move as one part. Muscles of the wrist move the hand in all ways except twisting, which is accomplished by the forearm. The two bones of the forearm cross each other when the hand is turned in toward the body. When the hand is turned palm outward they are parallel. These bones are noticeable where they join the wrist, especially the one on the outside which appears as a small knob. The back of the hand is lower than the arm at the wrist. The wrist itself appears rounded and high only when the hand is bent in or down.

THE FASHION HAND

The muscles and tendons are more obvious in the male hand, but the feminine hand should

Preliminary sketch for a head illustration, the composition to be developed later. Emphasis is on eye make-up and the layered lashes.

Antonio

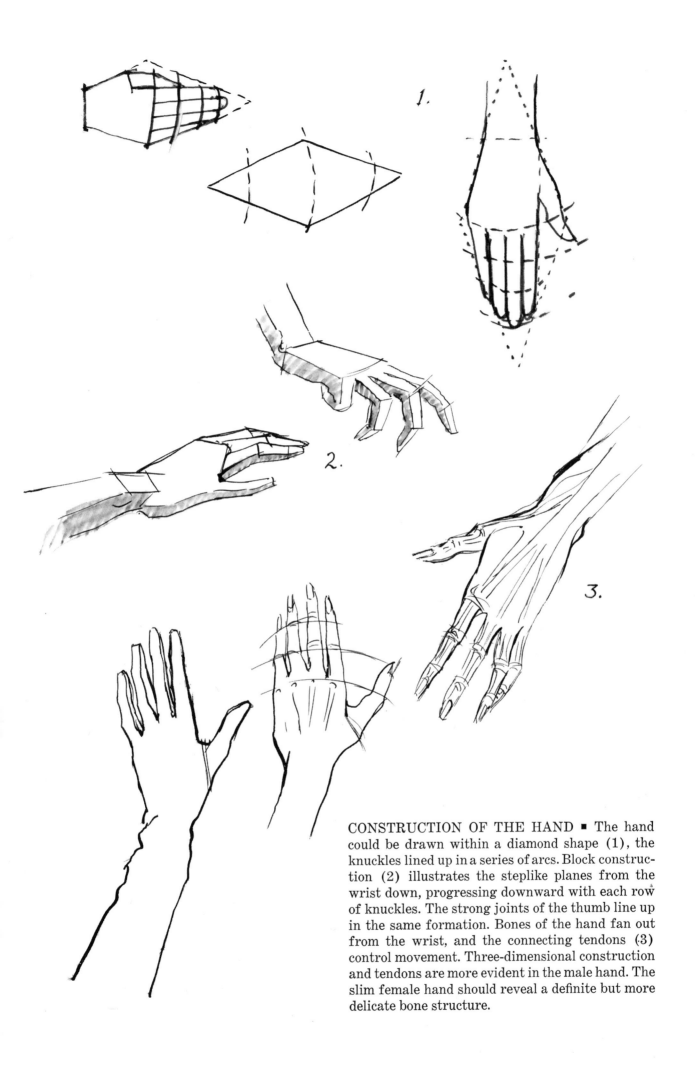

CONSTRUCTION OF THE HAND ■ The hand could be drawn within a diamond shape (1), the knuckles lined up in a series of arcs. Block construction (2) illustrates the steplike planes from the wrist down, progressing downward with each row of knuckles. The strong joints of the thumb line up in the same formation. Bones of the hand fan out from the wrist, and the connecting tendons (3) control movement. Three-dimensional construction and tendons are more evident in the male hand. The slim female hand should reveal a definite but more delicate bone structure.

THE FASHION HAND ■ Relaxed but not limp, the hand should have definite character. It should look slim and delicate, but capable. Avoid self-conscious prettiness and coy attitudes. The pose of the hand should be completely natural, either relaxed or in action. Think form and construction as you sketch the hand from a model. Work for smooth, flowing lines. Be slow and deliberate in drawing. Repeated efforts are the only formula for successful results. Make sketches of any hands available, even your own.

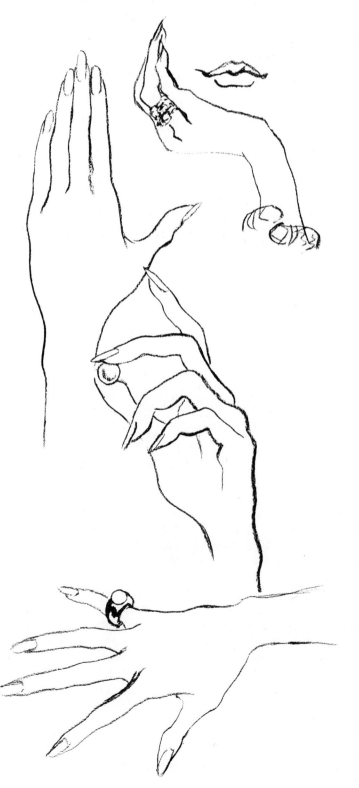

also have strength and character. It should be long and slim, relaxed and delicately boned, not soft and fleshy. Suggestion of the bone structure avoids a shapeless, rubber-hand look. Poses of the hand should be natural and unaffected. Avoid too-small hands. They were fashionable in the Victorian era but look insipid today. The too-thin hand can look clawlike or spidery. The average hand is about the length of the distance from the chin to the eyebrows. A slightly exaggerated length, however, is more graceful.

EXERCISE

Study diagrams and copy carefully. Try sketching all the hands you see—even your own. Draw large, even life size. Try different angles and poses. Make use of your knowledge of construction, putting in planes and bones at first; then draw in simple outline. If you have a willing model, sketch her hands doing or holding something, or relaxed and down at her sides if the figure is standing. The more you sketch, the more you learn and improve. Strive for a natural look. The elegant hand should be relaxed, the pose assured, never self-conscious or coy.

THE FOOT

The general form of the foot is a wedge. The outer side is flat on the ground, the inner side arches gradually into a bridge between the ball of the foot and the heel. The ankle interlocks the two sides, and the heel bone juts out slightly in the back as a separate wedge.

When the foot is viewed from the front, the interlocking anklebones fit into a curve and jut out, higher on the inner side of the foot. The inner bone is part of the heavier bone of the lower leg, the tibia. The smaller bone on the outer side of the leg joins the foot farther down, so the anklebone is lower on the outer side of the foot.

The large, or greater, toe is the equivalent of the thumb. It is the strongest of the toes and not only carries the heaviest load in action but is separated from the other toes. There is a large pad of muscle which curves from the small toe back to where the heel begins.

When the foot is flat on the ground, the foot and leg are at right angles. This applies to the foot in flat shoes as well. When the weight is thrown onto the ball of the foot, the angle is obviously changed.

In the back view of the foot, the heel narrows up into and is controlled by a long tendon of the leg. This tendon is very apparent and gives the narrow look behind the jutting-out anklebones.

Practice drawing the foot in all views as shown in the diagrams.

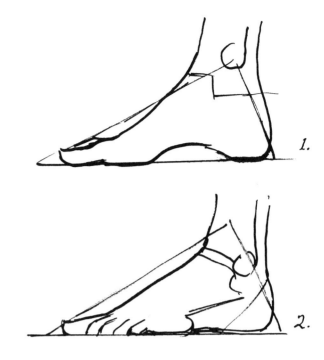

1.

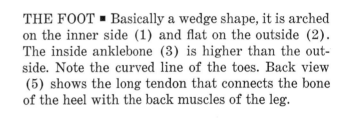

2.

THE FOOT ■ Basically a wedge shape, it is arched on the inner side (1) and flat on the outside (2). The inside anklebone (3) is higher than the outside. Note the curved line of the toes. Back view (5) shows the long tendon that connects the bone of the heel with the back muscles of the leg.

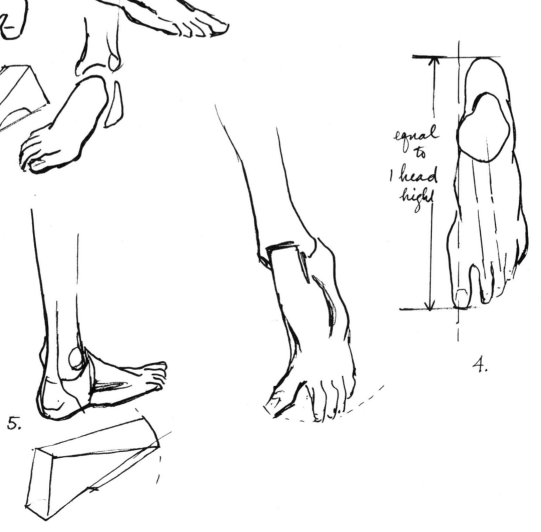

3.

equal to 1 head high

4.

5.

6. BASIC STEPS TOWARI

DRAWING OBJECTS FOR FORM

To acquire facility in drawing, there is no better way to learn form than by sketching simple objects and basic shapes. It is the artist with experience and advanced taste who discovers the beauty of pure form. The beginner, unfortunately, has a tendency to ignore simple forms in his desire to produce flashy, seemingly complicated drawings in a hurry. The results can be sadly amateurish.

A famous portrait painter and instructor at the Art Students League in New York used to enjoy telling about a woman who brought her eleven-year-old daughter to him to learn portrait painting. He suggested that the child start with something simpler, like learning to draw first.

MPROVEMENT IN DRAWING

The mother replied, "Oh, she doesn't want to waste time on all that." The artist, whose efforts covered a span of many years, smiled and said, "Madame, I'm glad your daughter didn't decide to take up brain surgery." Many persons realize that they cannot become concert pianists just by wishing, but somehow they imagine good drawing to be an effortless accomplishment. To make use of a talent takes consistent effort and organized thinking.

To lay the groundwork for good drawing, guided thinking is as important as endless sketching. For this reason, learning to see more in everyday objects helps one's drawing. Sketch what you see in terms of line and form. Try boxes and cylinders from imagination, or sketch an apple or other simple shapes. It may sound dull, but an imaginative artist can make it interesting or decorative. Stop worrying, relax, and enjoy each line you put down. Follow the outline or form of whatever you are sketching, using one continuous line. Avoid a lot of unsure, short lines. Exactness of line is not as important as sureness. Acquire ease in your drawing. Remember that you may not seem to be improving at all sometimes, but suddenly there is a noticeable difference between your early attempts and the later product—the result of time and effort. Save some of your early sketches to check your progress.

DRAWING IN PERSPECTIVE *(The Third Dimension)*

In the Middle Ages pictorial art was usually rendered in two dimensions, all the objects appearing flat. Artists were unable to convey an impression of depth, the third dimension. Little was known of perspective until an Italian of the Renaissance period, Piero della Francesca (1420-1492), wrote a book on the science of perspective which gave artists an exact method for delineating form and portraying distance.

During the fifteenth and sixteenth centuries painters also developed the use of light and shade to project the feeling of a third dimension. The Italian school of the sixteenth century exerted much influence and referred to the method as *chiaroscuro*. In depicting light and shadow, a knowledge of form and surface planes guides the artist in placement of light and dark areas.

Today, a realistic or academic approach to drawing may seem of little concern to the fashion artist. In some cases flat, two-dimensional, stylized drawing is used deliberately in fashion art to produce a decorative effect. Good drawing, indicating depth and form, however, requires a general idea of the principles of perspective.

To simplify the theory of perspective: Look straight ahead of you at an imaginary line on the wall. This line should be at the same height as your eyes, lower if you are sitting, higher if standing. A horizontal line drawn on paper establishes the line of eye level. Your eye level also establishes the horizon line out-of-doors. Place this line on paper at the level you have decided to use as the horizon line or eye level. All objects at this level appear flat. Everything above or below shows a third dimension.

METHOD OF DRAWING PERSPECTIVE LINES ■ For mechanically accurate perspective, draw converging lines with a paper ruler anchored by thumbtacks pinned to the vanishing points at eye level. Vanishing points may be established at whatever distance you choose on the drawing board. A T square and triangle provide a simple means of drawing all vertical lines.

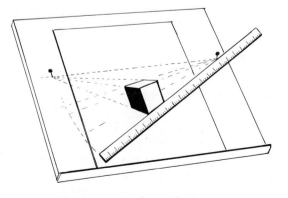

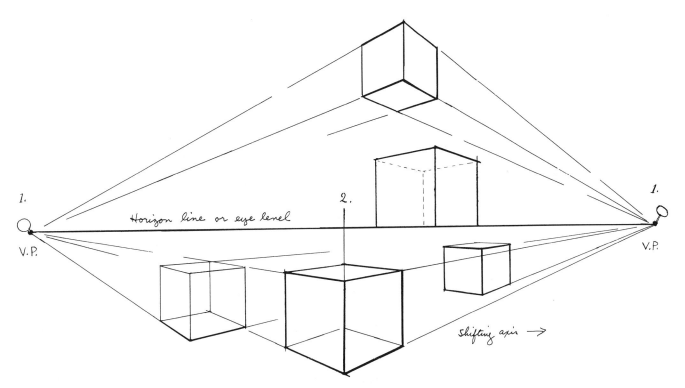

OBLIQUE PERSPECTIVE ■ To draw a perfect cube from the diagonal view, (1) establish a right-hand vanishing point and a left-hand vanishing point on the horizon line (eye level). The sides of the cube are thus diminished according to the distance from the vanishing point. (2) Draw a vertical line (the perpendicular axis) to establish the angle nearest you. (3) Draw converging lines from this point to the vanishing points and establish the remaining perpendicular lines and third surface of the cube (the top, if the cube is below the eye level, the bottom if it is above eye level). Experiment with all views and angles.

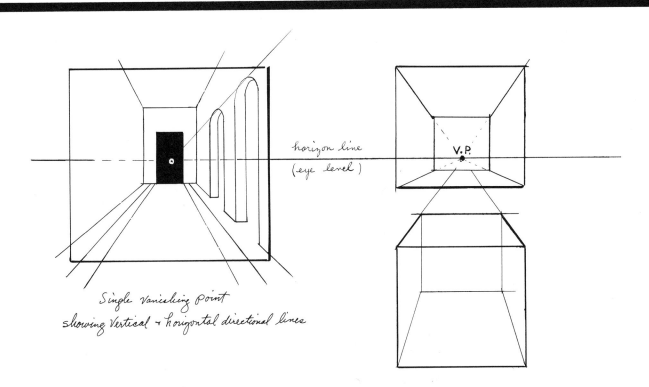

PARALLEL PERSPECTIVE ■ In drawing from a flat plane (one side directly front view), there is only one vanishing point. This is centered at eye level. All perspective lines converge at this one point, and all horizontal lines are parallel to the horizon line. Experiment with this problem. It offers endless possibilities, producing architectural as well as purely decorative compositions.

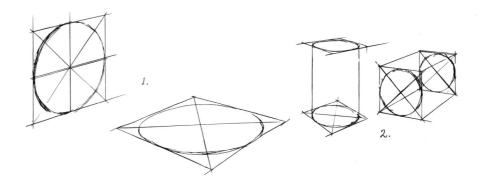

THE ELLIPSE, *A Circle in Perspective* ■ To achieve visual accuracy, draw the circle within a square. The square, drawn in perspective, will dictate the shape of the ellipse. (1) The cylinder is merely a series of elliptical circles, as illustrated. (2) If you have difficulty drawing either, use this method for checking and correcting inaccuracies.

If you place a box-shaped object parallel to your line of vision so that only one flat side is toward you, the lines of depth converge to a center vanishing point. If the object is turned at an angle so that you see two sides of the box, there are two vanishing points, one at either side. There are then two sets of lines, one converging to the right-hand vanishing point and another to the left-hand one. (See illustrations on page 77.)

It is seldom necessary to indicate perspective lines unless you are drawing furniture or an architectural exterior or interior. These principles, however, teach you to observe and to get depth or roundness into your figure drawing, and give you the feeling of receding and projecting forms.

The cylinder shape follows the same principles of perspective, except that the top and bottom, being circular, become elliptical. The ellipse, which is always oval, narrows near the eye level and becomes rounder as it moves higher or lower than eye level. See illustrations on this page. Note how this affects the drawing of the arm and sleeve. The arms are like a series of cylinder shapes above and below the elbow.

EXERCISE

Practice drawing boxes and cylinders as if they were made of glass. Draw perspective lines with a ruler, starting with the horizontal line to indicate the eye level. Establish your vanishing points as far out on the drawing board as possible. Mark them with a thumbtack. This will guide and hold the ruler at the vanishing point so that all converging lines can be drawn easily. All vertical lines in this exercise may be drawn with a triangle and T square for exactness. You might get some rather interesting drawings from these exercises by using a little imagination and adding color to some of the planes, showing light and shadow.

unlike all Gaul

our French coat's graceful line
flows undivided—thanks to
the smooth touch of concealed
buttons. Dazzling diamond
design in black and white or
brown and white; yoke
detail front and back. 100%
lightweight wool; from Paris,
naturellement. 8 to 14. **90.**
Foreign Exchange, Dept. 126,
Fashion Third.
And at Bergen Mall.

THERE'S A GROWING EXCITEMENT AT STERN BROTHERS

**check Her Majesty's
border...** the check of the
double-breasted jacket bounces—down
...to make a matching border on
the solid color knife pleated skirt. From
Britain, luv. 100% wool; gold and
blue or lavender and blue. 7 to 13. **65.**
Foreign Exchange, Dept. 126,
Fashion Third. And at Bergen Mall.

DRAMATIC EFFECT ■ Visual impact is achieved here through the use of perspective to develop an impression of heroic scale. The relative placing, in perspective, of the two boxes and the exaggerated size of the forward leg of the main figure take on the avant-garde approach to art in newspaper advertising. The over-all plan of the composition is successfully carried out through the use of transfer sheets in varied patterns.

Russian dressing...

sleek, dyed black rabbit
cuffs wrap up the "Zhivago
look". Wrist-snuggling slip-on
length kidskins lined with dyed
white rabbit. From Italy,
warm enough for Siberia—
without a samovar. Black or
mocha brown. **9.** Gloves,
Dept. 230, Street Floor.
And at all branches.
All furs labeled to show country
of origin of imported furs.

compute square root

Angelyn calculates a most
uncommon denominator for fall
fashion with the squared-off
toe of this suede from the French
Collection. Wide, opulently
pleated bow; petite flat heel.
Tivoli green, Granada taupe, Paris
red. **25.** Shoe Salon, Dept. 211,
Fashion Third. New York
store only.

in Spain, the plain

envelope bag is transformed
—with pure Castilian
elegance—into a rich fitted
calfskin with two compart-
ments and a graceful little
handle. Black, burgundy,
brown, green or navy. **23.**
Handbags, Dept. 250,
Street Floor.
And at all branches.

STERN ❦ BROTHERS

41 WEST 42nd STREET, N. Y. · PARAMUS, PATERSON, PREAKNESS, N. J.

A PROVOCATIVE ANGLE ■ The point of vision in this amusing illustration might well be from a manhole in the street. The effect of height is given the foreshortened figures through an above-eye-level perspective. Originally done in color, this space-age composition appeared in the fashion section of *The New York Times*

Gerhardt Leibman

Antonio, courtesy of *The New York Times*

INTERIOR IN PARALLEL PERSPECTIVE ■ Accuracy of perspective is
retained throughout the patterns of floor tiling, ceiling décor, and plaid walls
in this charming sketch of the Bigi shop at Bergdorf Goodman. Although
carefully planned with ruler and pencil, all ink lines have been rendered
free-hand with a very fine crow-quill pen on vellum paper.

Draw a single box first, then try lining up several in formation so that they recede and grow smaller as they approach the vanishing point. There are endless possibilities, as you may discover while experimenting. It is not necessary to be overly exact about ruled lines as long as you are developing a structural approach to drawing. If you happen to be gifted with a natural eye for perspective, it is possible to sketch accurately what you see without establishing vanishing points and horizon lines. Lacking that ability, these rules are an infallible means of checking your drawing and acquiring an image from which to work. Eventually, the artist must decide his own personal approach to drawing. Precise lines and fine detail may be his natural bent, or free-hand drawing may be the only way to express his talent, tossing out T square and triangle except for accuracy in sizing a drawing.

ELLIPTICAL LINES ▪ Correctly indicated in perspective, the elliptical circles and fanning spokes of this Japanese parasol are beautifully executed in wash and ink line. It is one of many fine accessory drawings from the Henri Bendel direct-by-mail Christmas pages.

7.
DRAWING
THE
GARMENT

CORRECT FIT

The beginner should concentrate on the figure first, drawing it carefully and in proportion, then indicate the outline of the garment so that it follows the body lines. As proportions become automatic in drawing, one starts to see the body and garment as one silhouette, the fashion story dominating the illustration. Fit and contour are of first importance.

It is impossible to cling to set rules about fit, since fashion dictates constant changes. The only basic rule is that fit does not mean the glued-on, body-revealing characteristics of comic-strip-siren dress. The truly chic fashion figure is never voluptuous; it must never put bulges into a costume.

PARIS COUTURE, 1962 ■ Fro[m]
the Givenchy fall collection, the[se]
fashions were sketched on the sce[ne]
by René Bouché. They are not t[o-]
day's fashions, but the mood of t[he]
haute couture during an openin[g]
has been revealed through the pe[r-]
ceptive eye of the artist. The dra[w-]
ings are fine examples of magazi[ne]
illustrating for international fas[h]-
ion reportage. Working quickly wi[th]
a felt-tip pen and a minimum [of]
charcoal shading, Bouché has subt[ly]
expressed the spirit of the fashion[.]
He has keenly observed and recor[d-]
ed the attitudes of the figures [as]
they move along the runway at [a]
fast pace and the importance [of]
garment shape in relation to th[e]
figure in motion. A few brisk lin[es]
in the background suggest the usu[al]
exclusive gathering of buyers an[d]
members of the press.

Courtesy of *Vogue*

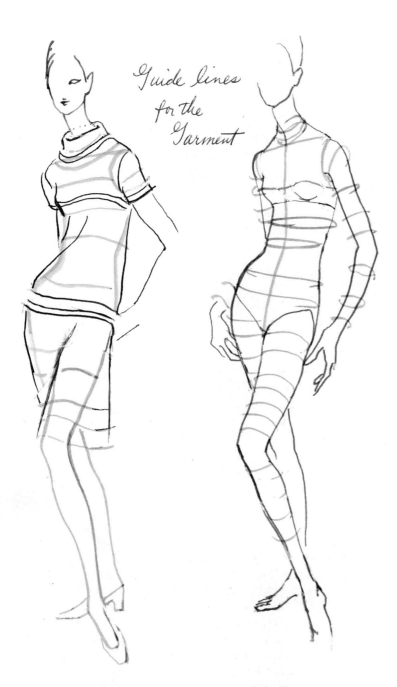

Guide lines for the Garment

GUIDELINES FOR THE GARMENT ■ If your figure drawing follows the methods described in Chapter 6, garment lines automatically fall where they should. All necklines curve around the neck, seam lines follow body lines, and the center action line of the figure indicates the center line of the garment (front closings, etc.).

To reveal all is too obvious. Fashion designers take a more subtle approach to allure, that of focusing on one part of the female anatomy at a time. In eras of the long skirt, the accent may be on plunging necklines or tiny waistlines. When much leg is revealed by very short skirts, interest in the rest of the body is minimized by a loose fit with little indication of waistline or bosom. The artist learns to accentuate fashion news and subtleties of fit as well as changing proportions. This knowledge can be acquired in various ways from available sources. The few suggestions listed here are for the artist aiming at the top bracket, which is always ahead of the trends. Others, more conservative, are always a few steps behind.

To see the new lines there is nothing quite as enlightening as a good fashion showing with top-ranking models gliding along the runway with their special walk and insouciant flair. Occasionally, an important showing is filmed for television and is well worth viewing for fashion news and general flavor. Seeing the clothes in action, with the right accessories and hair styles, is a rare treat not often available to the average artist. The opportunity to see a fashion showing should not be passed up.

Fashion publications are the most important and easily available source of news. The fashion designer relies on them implicitly, and the fashion illustrator should keep equally well informed. One outstanding publication is *Women's Wear Daily*, a newspaper published in New York and devoted entirely to news of fashion and the fashion business both here and abroad. Since it has more drawings than photographs, it is especially helpful to the artist. The sketches are not to be followed as examples of accurate or detailed representation of actual merchandise, but they give one an over-all expression of the new fashions. A mere glance at sketches and photographs is not enough to get a real understanding of new lines, however. It is important to read a good report that analyzes and explains the highlights and subtleties of new fashions. In this way you learn the character of new trends, such as emphasis of

Action lines : body + garment

fit, flare of skirt, shape of neckline, and so on. Such subtleties are constantly changing, especially in the more expensive fashions. Sometimes a buyer or fashion director will explain the effect he wants achieved for a specific job, but most of the time it is up to the artist to know the current look of fashion.

One can also learn from top magazines such as *Vogue*—which also publishes English, French, and Italian editions — and *Harper's Bazaar*. *Glamour* magazine emphasizes the younger American approach. There are numerous others which could be added to the list, but these are outstanding. French magazines worth mention are *Elle*, which has the young international approach, and the more expensive *L'Officiel* and

BODY–DEFINING GATHERS ▪ Elongated proportions of the figure accentuate the flowing, easy lines of the body and garment. Soft, thin fabrics gathered in at the waist create directional lines that change with each movement. A new ease is suggested by the relaxed, unposed action of the figures.

FABRIC AND CUT ▪ Both influence the character of fit and contour in relation to body lines. Bulky woolens skim the body without cling or folds and are indicated with a heavy outline as shown in Halston's boxy white steamer coat above. The silk chemise dress, gathered at the neckline, is cut on the bias. Off the figure, the dress falls in a straight line, but the bias cut shapes it gently over body lines in a subtle way.

Kenneth Paul Block,
courtesy *Women's Wear Daily*

L'Art et la mode. Although the foreign magazines are rather costly, it is interesting to see one occasionally for a fresh point of view.

The Paris openings and fashion news from London and Italy are reported and illustrated in most of the publications mentioned as well as in some newspapers. Paris has been the important fashion center of the world for many generations and is still the location of the top couture houses. Famous couturiers such as Dior, Balenciaga, and St. Laurent, leaders of the nineteen-fifties and sixties, are familiar to everyone interested in the world of fashion. Their stories make fascinating reading and their openings are eagerly awaited by buyers, the press, and other designers. The press is given a preview before the formal openings. Buyers and manufacturers pay large sums in advance for an invitation to the opening of a collection, but these fees are later applied to the purchase price of the very expensive original models. Designs and ideas used to be closely guarded secrets, and the people who wanted to attend were carefully screened. Today there is less concern about being exclusive. Originals purchased are brought to New York and copied by manufacturers. Copies are sold to department stores all over the country, and popular styles end up in all price ranges. Your bargain-basement dress may be a copy of one originally designed in Paris or London.

Sketching new trends is the next step. Once you have grasped the general aspects of the current styles, try making sketches that give expression to them. Make quick notes of important directional lines that indicate the character and contour of the garment. It is better to jot down what you know quickly, for practice, than to labor over notes. Take time on finished drawings but not on sketching ideas.

Fabric and cut strongly influence the character of fit. Silk crepes cling slightly to the body, especially when cut on the bias. Chiffons have a tendency to cling where fitted and, in movement, to float out where full or circular in cut. (See illustrations on pages 88 and 89.) Thick woolens and tweeds should have an accentuated bulki-

Romantic notions

Kenneth Paul Block,
courtesy *Women's Wear Daily*

THIN FABRICS, THIN LINES ▪ Delicate pen
lines here suggest an airiness characteristic of
sheer, thin fabrics. The circular flare of skirts and
cape sleeves is done with many fine lines indicating
folds that drop into place without gathers. The
composition and sweeping gesture of the figures
and the exaggerated length of skirt add dramatic
effect to a romantic mood.

ness. Heavy brocades and hard-surfaced woolens, especially the bonded and double-faced types, do not cling at all. They have the crisp, exact tailoring of a well-cut uniform, without folds or gathers.

Remember that fabric can be indicated by the way you draw the outline. A fuzzy line suggests a thick, soft wool; a thick black line, a heavy fabric; and so on. A thin or transparent fabric should be shown with a delicate line. Vary your lines for expression of surface texture as well as weight, stiffness, and other characteristics.

If you have the actual garment from which to draw, seeing it on the right model is a great advantage. (See Chapter 8, "Working With or Without a Model.") If it fits your model, proportions of the garment, such as length of skirt or jacket, and fit of sleeve, are established without guesswork. You also have the opportunity to try various poses to find the one that best shows the

NEW TRENDS ■ Forecasts of changes, like radar warnings, appear regularly in the top fashion publications. At times they are several years ahead of current fashion dictates. It is fascinating to follow the acceptance of a new look after you have been alerted to it.

garment. Without a model you must gauge these details from seeing the garment on the hanger and making notes, planning a pose from sketches or photographs.

GARMENT DETAIL

Construction and fit of any garment are its most important details. They give the over-all look and immediately suggest the era of a fashion. A bias cut or a new type of seaming can change the silhouette in subtle ways. A simple shift dress may have flowing, body-skimming lines if well-designed; badly designed, it may look like a sack, having no relation to body lines. To see well-cut fashions on a model is most important to the artist. It is also useful to study the lines of garments in the better fashion publications. In pattern drawing all construction seaming must be indicated. In other types of fashion illustra-

1963
1965
1965
1966
1966

ourtesy of *Women's Wear Daily*, 1966-67

CASUAL WRAP-UPS ■ Easy clothes that travel well is the story here. An assortment of interchangeable knits, the pullover jacket, the poncho and the Noh coat all pack flat. The multiple accessories provide extra warmth for cold climates. Adding pants and a long cashmere sweater-dress for evening completes a versatile wardrobe.

The trend away from fitted clothes reached the ultimate with the blanket as over-sized shawl. (See opposite page.) To be used indoors or out, the "body-blanket" ranged in price from a $25 plaid blanket to a custom-made luxury version of Russian sable.

The illustrations are handled with authority. The sketchy technique and action of the figures above add an imaginative sense of easy exuberance. The blanketed figures, sketched from the model, depend on assured rendition of folds and materials along with the easygoing style of the figures.

Kenneth Paul Block,
courtesy *Women's Wear Daily*

tion, only seaming that is of fashion importance should be indicated. Eliminating all unnecessary lines puts emphasis on more significant details and produces a more striking, clean-cut picture.

Other details, such as necklines, sleeves, beltlines, and skirtlines, require careful attention and definite interpretation. To place these lines correctly, be sure they line up with body-construction lines. (See illustrations on page 86.) Basic garment lines are obvious on the dressmaker's dummy: The neckline, armhole, waistline, and seaming construction are all guides for drawing.

Necklines and collars change with fashion and must be observed carefully. A well-tailored collar curves with the neckline and dips slightly at the back, avoiding the appearance of reaching the hairline of the neck. The Japanese kimono, as worn by the geisha, is a charming example of the back-dipped neckline, considered by the Japanese to be a seductive and graceful line. The long, oval line, deep in back and high in front, elongates the neck in a charming way. Various necklines, from high turtle necks to all types of open and low-cut styles, should be indicated by lines that follow the construction lines of the neck.

Kenneth Paul Block,
courtesy *Women's Wear Daily*

High armhole

Summer Suit:
(Classic blazer)

Jersey tunic

Knife-pleated
silk skirt

Gathered

+ wrapped

Man-tailored classics change only in subtle detail and proportion. Linings have been eliminated in most lightweight blazer-styles but the basics of distinctive cut and hand-finishing remain the mark of quality. Fit at its best is never tight, shape never exaggerated. The well-cut sleeve is eased into an armhole cut right for freedom of movement (not too low). The raglan sleeve has a looser fit but should also allow easy action. In sketching from the model, limit wrinkles and folds to action lines defined at meaningful points such as those at the bend of the elbow.

Pleats, used in a great variety of ways, require assured drawing and keen observation. Inverted pleats of the classic kilt should be of uniform width and fall in a crisp line, flaring slightly in action. Sunburst pleats have an entirely different character, flaring from narrow to wide in flowing lines that must be seen on a model. The Fortuny style of superfine accordion pleating adds a textural quality to gauzy silks and subtly-clinging lines to the slim evening silhouette. The original Fortuny dress compressed like an accordion into rope thickness which could be coiled and stashed away in a very small box.

Folds and gathers form interesting lines that vary with the fabric used. From draped squares of thin silk to bulky stoles of mohair or wool, the character of style is dependent on well-defined folds sketched directly from the model. As seamed shaping was overtaken by styles that wrap and tie, gathers became an integral part of design. Draw-strings and elastic shirring altered the general outline with emphasis on easy shapes. In sketching, many short lines should be used at the gathering point, fading off into a few long lines (or none), according to degrees of fullness. Among the draped folds, a few cowl necklines have reappeared in the softer evening looks, as well as draped interest at low-cut armholes.

Knits, the most packable, easiest look around, have also become the most versatile. They can be found in every type of apparel from sportswear to evening dress. Fibers include cotton, linen, silks and woolens and a variety of synthetics

Soft Fabrics, Soft Tailoring

The easy-sleeved Blouson

1.

2.

3.

4.

Slim lines / classic proportions

Emphasis on Shape

INDEPENDENT STYLE ▪ Soft and easy shapes vary from slim to full. For spring 1976, a two-piece, pleated silk dress (1) is topped with a slim, knit cardigan. In the timeless Chanel mood (2), a knit coat and skirt with bowed silk blouse. On the young side (3), a pale knit dress has borders of bright red. Layered dressing (4), a matching skirt of fake suede wraps over a shirtdress of crepe de chine.

Kenneth Paul Block,
courtesy *Women's Wear Daily*

Sunburst-pleated chiffon dress

Crepe evening pajama

Even spacing ↓ at top

knife pleats

flaring open at hemline

zig zag line at bottom

Inverted box pleat

Figure drawing courtesy *Women's Wear Daily*

PLEATS ▪ For desired effect in each type of pleating, it is important to note its construction. For the simpler, straight types, folding a piece of paper into pleats may serve as a guide. The sunburst pleats shown above were sketched from the model in order to get the direction of draped and flowing lines on the figure.

GATHERS, FLOUNCES, AND RUFFLES ■ Many short lines at the gathering point and few, if any, as the material flairs out are characteristic. A minimum of lines with pleasing dark accents in these pen-and-ink sketches tells the story with simplicity and style.

Ben Morris, courtesy of Du Pont

SOFT FABRICS, LOOSE CUT ■ New versions of the Greek influence are noticeable in the classic lines of the 1976 embroidered jersey and the spiral dress from London. The evening looks from New York, at left, are a shirred bias top in floral print georgette, floating over a matching flounced skirt and a shirred matt jersey jumpsuit which can be worn off the shoulder. Worn with it is a top of pale gray chiffon gathered at the low waistline. The effect of sheerness is achieved by outlining the figure underneath and adding tone with a charcoal pencil. Well-placed accents of strong blacks add character to the fine pen line drawings.

Steven Meisel and Robert Young,
courtesy *Women's Wear Daily*

sometimes mixed with the naturals. Outlines are as varied. From sweater looks to clingy silks, texture and thickness are indicated by the character of pen or brush line defining shape in relation to body lines.

EXOTIC SHAPES: Caftans, djellabas and tunics reflect Mid-Eastern and Moroccan influences, a popular trend for evening wear in luxury fabrics and for resort wear in cool cottons. Loose shapes with no fit challenge the artist's imagination. Having the right model is a distinct advantage since attitude and pose create the mood which should be sublimely relaxed. Lines should be simplified, only decoration detailed.

PANTS REVIEWED, 1976:

A fresh spirit in pants-dressing brought infinite variety, although many women were relieved to have the alternative of new dresses and skirts in flattering lengths again. Evening pants in silk crepes and sheers had graceful, flowing lines, many topped with tunics. Man-tailored suits with nineteen-thirties pants were shown by the Paris couture. More casual styles included the work clothes or army-inspired jumpsuit and the safari-jacketed. Summer collections offered all lengths and versions for resort or city wear, including Bermuda shorts, culottes and a variety of longer pants to or above the ankle. Stereotypes were out, so were set rules for sketching. Illustration concentrated on mood, the essence of the "new." Although styles differed wildly, most had the timeless qualities of proven design from other eras, other cultures.

THE EQUESTRIAN CLASSICS:

The best-cut pants have always been found in riding clothes. Since they had to sit a horse with ease as well as look trim standing, equestrian standards of tailoring and fit were all-important. Design is essentially functional, line and proportion the ingredients of style. The original English riding pants ended below the knee to fit properly into the classic riding boot which was made to order or adjusted for exact fit at the top. Pants curved out slightly to create continuity of line harmonious with the flare of the hacking

Figurines of the third century B.C., Metropolitan Museum of Art

DRAPERY ■ Although drapery is in and out of fashion periodically, the cowl neckline and the semiclassic draped chiffons and crepes are always somewhat in evidence. Tied, pinned, and gathered, cloth falling in fluid lines over the body has never been done with more grace than in ancient sculpture. The curving folds are best sketched from the model with pencil, pen, or brush line. Practice develops a relaxed and flowing stroke.

Kenneth Paul Block,
courtesy *Women's Wear Daily*

FROM THE NEW YORK COLLECTIONS ▪ For spring 1976, the soft, flowing lines of the crepe de chine tunic over soft pants for evening and the toga top over an asymmetric, handkerchief-hemmed skirt reflect an ultra-feminine mood. Both shapes by de la Renta are uncontrived, uncomplicated. Enhanced by the right pose, the hang and drape of garment on the figure is all-important. The long, narrow dress of satin by Halston (at the left) has a bias cut and serpentine seaming for body-conscious lines. The gathered, off-the-shoulder neckline with large, flowing bow are subtle parts of the whole. The drawings express the mood and emphasize shape with economy of line, handled with conviction.

Kenneth Paul Block,
courtesy *Women's Wear Daily*

INFINITE VARIETY ▪ More news from the New York Collections include the Turkish-inspired skirt in white chiffon by Mary McFadden (left). The jacket is quilted white silk with tied closings.

The casual figure (center) in suede-like culottes and bright jersey shawl over a cashmere sweater has an air of luxurious ease. The narrow dinner suit with self-belted top is of silk jacquard print. Both are Halston designs in timeless styling. Flowing lines and softened shapes are the message, here. Bold outlines and accents are done with felt pens. Details of quilting and design of print could be more explicit for advertising purposes.

THE COTTON KNIT TOP ▪ The summer T-shirt becomes an all-occasion basic design with unlimited interpretations for any season.

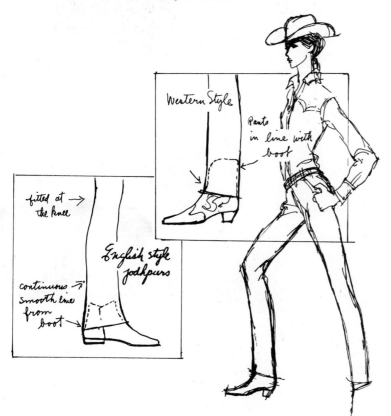

Western Style

Pants in line with boot

fitted at the knee

English style jodhpurs

continuous smooth line from boot

PANTS, *Equestrian Style* ▪ Correctly cut, they fit over the right boot in a clean, continuous line, never jut out beyond the heel in back. This is also true of well-tailored pants in all styles for men.

jacket. Jodhpurs also fit at the knee but taper out over the ankle-high boot in a smooth line with the boot itself, never jutting out beyond the heel. (See illustration on page 102.) The correct boot is an important part of the look. The flat-heeled jodhpur boot, the western boot, and the thin-soled boot with elastic sides of the Civil War period were all originally designed for men who spent time in the saddle.

Simplified versions of the hacking jacket (with modified flare) team successfully with some skirts and tailored pants. Line-for-line copies of the traditional classics, however, become straight camp when worn in the city where the functional details become extraneous.

The "western look" of denim Levis, the hip-riding cowboy pants which evolved as youth's international uniform in the sixties, continued. As faded denim jeans, topped with the cotton knit T-shirt, it became a way of life. It is not fashion news. Variations on the theme offer a wider choice of colors and styles. Holding to the same concept of carefree fabric and design, the T-shirt has become the casual, all-occasion dress.

THE CROQUIS

As a working fashion artist, you may frequently be called upon to make a quick sketch of an item to be drawn carefully later. Since the garment cannot be left for you to work from, it is necessary to observe and draw with accuracy, making written notes that can be followed later. This type of rough sketch is referred to as a *croquis* (pronounced "croakee"), a French word used generally by artists, especially in the fashion field.

Sometimes you have the opportunity to sketch a garment on a model. In this case you can use the exact pose later for your finished drawing, so it pays to draw carefully. To sketch hurriedly is not to sketch carelessly. Careful thought put into a sketch always pays off.

These sketches may be done on any kind of paper or in a notebook, provided it is not too small. A 9″ x 12″ tracing pad is probably best, since sheets can be torn off and filed for future use.

To test your ability to observe detail, try sketching a garment on a hanger. Do not draw it literally, showing the hanger, etc. Simply get the general outline first, indicating skirt length and sleeve length. Add details of unusual seaming, the right number of buttons, if any, type of buttonhole (bound or stitched, vertical or horizontal). Note exact type and size of collar or other neckline detail, sleeve width and style, and any other particular features. Add brief written notes about the colors used, description of fabric, and details of trim (such as metal buttons, leather belt, or anything that seems important). If the fabric is a print or a plaid, make an enlarged sketch of a portion in detail.

If you need examples of new and exciting fashions to sketch, why not try some window shopping? Dress shops and department stores often show their newest acquisitions in window displays. This can give you an opportunity to see details of fabric and styling. If the clothes are displayed on a mannequin (dummy), you can also see the exact fit and contour of the garment. Study what you see carefully, look for details such as decisive shaping (straight lines, shaped contour, flared skirt, general style of cut) as well as placing of waistline, and so on. Without being obvious, make a few notes in a small notebook or sketchbook—preferably away from the scene or you may appear to be stealing designs. After you have made a quick sketch, go back for another look to check for accuracy of detail. Did you get the neckline right? The exact width of the collar? The position of patch pockets or indication of concealed pockets? The sleeve and shoulder detail? The belt in its proper place? You will soon learn to develop your memory and keenness of observation by checking such details and recognizing important differences.

Use these sketches and notes for working up finished drawings later. They may prove to be very good samples of your work. All these seem-

Kenneth Paul Block,
courtesy *Women's Wear Daily*

SUMMER PANTS ■ From a two-part swimsuit to the complete cover-up of a bright red butcher's apron over white pants and T-shirt, pants come in a variety of lengths and shapes. The bold black and white areas of this illustration emphasize the message of summer white with bright, strong contrasts in a well-planned composition.

Courtesy of *The New York Times*

PANTS SUITS ON THE GO ▪ An editorial illustration by Antonio *(The New York Times, 1966)*. Stylized action figures with Pop Art influence provide an eye-catching picture in this composition. The somewhat complicated arrangement was carefully worked out from preliminary sketches. The original measures 22½″ x 24″.

EVENING LOOKS ▪ Dress or pants of soft, clinging satin; topping the pants, a cashmere poncho or
a sable-cuffed tunic. The look is luxurious and
casual.

Kenneth Paul Block,
courtesy *Women's Wear Daily*, 1976

THE CAFTAN ▪ A good pose gives the roomy garment style. It also achieves an interesting design of background (as shape) as well as subject within the space.

Dorothy Loverro,
courtesy *Women's Wear Daily*

ingly minor details are important to the designer or buyer of the garment illustrated. If you do not furnish an accurate picture, your drawing will no doubt be rejected in favor of a more carefully done drawing that is faithful to detail.

LEARN TO OBSERVE. This cannot be repeated too often. To prove your capability as an artist you must learn to observe. It is the first step to learning and the key to improving your skills.

OBJECTIVES

In illustrating fashion for advertising, the chief objective is to attract the prospective buyer. To put it plainly, "You've got to flatter the merchandise." Whatever special qualities the item may have should be accentuated in the drawing. Does it suggest luxury, glamour, youthful zest, the casual life, or is it simply attractive and practical? Each quality appeals to a different type of customer. If the garment happens to be uninspiring, the artist must use his imagination to give it a tantalizing quality, adding flair and his own fashion knowledge.

The artist should have an objective in mind. His point of view may be his own, or may be guided by the effect the employer wishes conveyed. In working from actual merchandise, details are obvious, but the style as a whole must be interpreted.

To achieve your objectives, the following are major points to consider. The pose of the figure is probably of first importance. If the pose is dull and tired-looking, throw it out and try another. Is the pose of today? Poses change with the times. The coy prettiness of a past era is not part of the current scene. Today's model has an easy, bold stance. Good poses can be used again and again with enough changes to avoid monotony. What angle or pose shows off the lines and detail of the garment? Is the pose suitable? (One can hardly use the same pose for a long chiffon dress as for western-style jeans.)

Man-tailored Classics

TIMELESS SEPARATES ■ For clothes that span the seasons and last from year to year, the staying qualities of traditional style and classic tailoring win renewed appraisal. The man-tailored suits (his and hers) or odd jacket that can be teamed with skirts or pants extend a limited wardrobe with changes of shirts or blouses and sweaters to suit the weather. These casual interchangeables, shown in classic tweeds, gray flannel or gabardine, are designs for home-sewing by three major pattern companies. The figures in the drawing have a youthful ambiance, and the easy style and fit of softened tailoring are well defined.

Steven Meisel,
courtesy *Women's Wear Daily*

Steven Meisel,
courtesy *Women's Wear Daily*

STYLE ▪ The mood here is self-assured, luxurious ease. The all-black evening separates are interchangeables with a classic simplicity of line. The pants, of black georgette, are topped with a quilted satin jacket (fur lined), a chiffon jacket over a georgette bandeau and (right) a poncho that is a huge triangle of georgette. The airiness of the sheer fabrics contrasting with the thickness of quilted satin is suggested by the character of the outlines. Wash tones, varied in density, add to the effect of sheerness and indicate the body lines. The relaxed attitudes of the figures, the close-to-the-head, uncontrived hairstyling complete a well-polished, consistent style.

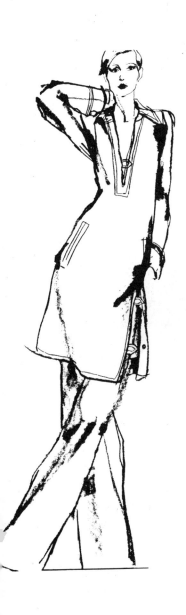

Robert Young,
courtesy *Women's Wear Daily*

ANIMATION ■ The lively, natural action here achieves a spirited image that invites attention. More than an accurate rendition, the leisurely look of tunic-over-pants comes off with charming abandon. Narrow shape and easy fit are fashion points stated gently but with conviction. The soft, carbon pencil rendering is controlled and expressive in flowing lines and good drawing. A minimum of lightly-shaded areas is punctuated with dark accents for effective contrast.

Action poses are great for the right garment and mood, but relaxed poses create interest in a different way—perhaps by being intriguingly sultry or glamorous.

Using a suitable type of model is another important point. Should you suggest active youth or the glamorous sophisticate? Does the hair style suggest the type you are trying to illustrate? Long, swingy hair styles are right only on the very young. The action girl wears the bikini, slick rainwear, practical but gay footwear, and suitable gear for whatever she undertakes. The look is young and uninhibited—fun clothes with an easy fit.

Couture fashions with the expensive, elegant kind of glamour demand a more sophisticated type of model, more assured, perhaps a bit more dignified. The hair must be well-groomed and chic, never carelessly arranged or overlong. There are two main types in this group—the exotic, who can wear extreme styles and flamboyant jewelry, or the more classic beauty whose tastes lean toward understated chic. The latter are women

YOUNG MODERNS, JUNIOR GRADE ■ Interpreted here in decorative, stylized drawings, the junior types emerge as fashion independents. The mod influence is here, the far-out fads such as the beauty patch under each eye, the long hair and bangs, and the no-expression with pale, pouting mouth. The artwork is in tune. Both fashions and illustrations show the influence of the mod revival of Art Nouveau. The new emancipated fashions not only shortened skirts but took on a completely new shape first developed by Paris designer Courrèges and a few young English forerunners like Mary Quant. Previous concepts of fashion for the young suddenly looked outmoded and dull.

Illustrated are some junior clothes in the 3-to-13 size range, which are cut to fit the immature figure. The young look of long, straight hair with a well-brushed sheen and the clean-cut, pared-down clothes are true to trend. Avoiding the kooky, the look is fresh and succeeds as youthful chic.

whose wardrobes might include floating chiffons and rich brocades for evening and beautifully cut tweeds or linen for daytime. Their poses are easy and casual, but restrained.

Some artists concentrate on one particular type. Their thinking may be more in accord with the young, and therefore they portray that type more convincingly. Whatever you decide to do, be definite. A "no type" is always dull and uninteresting, as is a person with no character or personality.

Mood can also be suggested, sometimes, through the right accessories, background, or even the pose. A muffled, cozy look for casual winter furs, for example, can be achieved through the right headgear and boots, or the way the coat is worn. For a summery effect, hair blowing in the breeze gives a cool look and dark glasses suggest sun.

Finally, a clean-cut drawing in a pleasing technique is needed to present all the other qualities to advantage. (See Chapter 10, "Finished Art.")

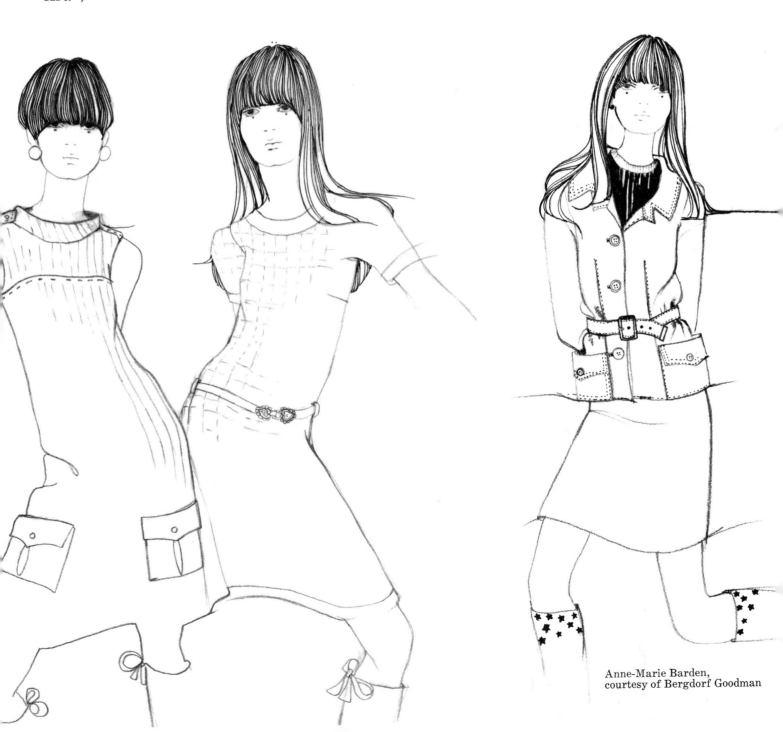

Anne-Marie Barden,
courtesy of Bergdorf Goodman

easy-off

Robert Passantino,
courtesy *Women's Wear Daily*

CASUAL SUMMER GEAR ■ Drawstring pants and a T-shirt that ties with a bright floral print are designed from a young viewpoint. The interesting face and artful eye makeup are beautifully handled, the expression is young, aloof and self assured. The delicate pencil outlines, geometric forms and even washes are in the 1920s tradition.

1. Choose a simple dress with new lines, one of the current, basic styles. If you do not have an actual garment at hand, find a photograph of one in a recent fashion magazine or in a window display. Make quick sketches and notes from the garment so that you have something from which to work. Next, try sketching it on a figure. If possible, work from a live model. Otherwise, use poses from photographs or draw from your imagination and knowledge of the figure. Try several poses to find which one shows off the dress in the most pleasing way, front, side, or three-quarter view. In the side view keep the pelvis forward. This minimizes the bust and makes the garment hang gracefully in back, avoiding bulges. (See illustration on page 125.)

2. Once you decide on the best pose, sketch the figure carefully on tracing paper. Draw figures at least 11 inches tall. Indicate the general outline of the dress first, then sleeve length, armhole, neckline detail, and belt and buttoning, if any. If the dress buttons up the front, be sure buttons are evenly spaced and in line with the center line of the body. Check neckline, armholes, and sleeves for direction of line (the feeling of lines going around the arms and neck in a continuous line from the visible front to the invisible back).

3. Stress the important lines and eliminate the unimportant ones. To simplify your lines, try placing an overlay of tracing paper on your pencil sketch and trace with bold, definite lines only the main lines of direction and detail. See how few lines you need to have a good, clean drawing, and how many fussy ones can be eliminated. Some of the wrinkles or folds can probably be simplified. Remove the tracing paper and compare it with the original sketch. It should be an improvement. Use it as a guide for finishing your sketch.

4. Next, trace your corrected figure onto a clean sheet of kid-finish Strathmore or similar hard-surface paper that will take pen-and-ink lines and light erasing. A good illustration board is also dependable, especially if you plan to use

wash tones or water color. To transfer your drawing onto the final working paper, simply pencil over the lines on the reverse side of the tracing paper, using a 2H or HB pencil. Never use standard carbon paper. To keep your paper clean, wipe lightly over pencil lines on back of paper with cotton or cleansing tissue; this removes surplus lead and avoids smudging. Before tracing the figure onto the board, be sure you have placed it so that there is a good margin at the bottom of the drawing and the figure is more or less centered on the paper. Trace over your lines with a sharpened 2H pencil. When you are finished, you should have a good, clean, pencil-outline drawing.

OBJECTIVE: FASHION NEWS ▪
Demand for tennis wear increases as the game's popularity broadened beyond a once exclusive group of players and spectators. The classic white tennis dress is here color-highlighted with geometric stripes and panels in an interesting choice of styles for the active player.

The artist emphasized the mood with freshness and verve in the abstract style of the Art Deco period. Realism would not have been as effective as the clean-cut line and strong patterns of color for this imaginative drawing.

Pedro Barrios,
courtesy *Women's Wear Daily*, 1975

Kenneth Paul Block,
courtesy Bonwit Teller

OBJECTIVE: ADVERTISING ■ A greater degree of realism is essential for illustrating a specific item through magazine or newspaper advertising. From the pages of *Vogue*, 1974 the ankle-length evening dress from Bonwit Teller is simply stated with meticulous accuracy of detail. The flat wash over Conte crayon line was done on a full sheet of charcoal paper. The character of matte jersey in medium-pale color is clearly defined. The illustration, with brief copy, could sell the dress unseen to an out-of-town customer.

Kenneth Paul Block,
courtesy *Women's Wear Daily*

FASHION NEWS ▪ The diaphanous, color-splashed silk tunic over a slim, ankle-length skirt was one of the evening looks by Mary McFadden from her spring collection, 1976. The illustration, done as fashion reporting, has great freedom of expression. The easy pose of the seated figure artfully suggests the mood. Exact details are unimportant. Lucid effect derives from sensitive and accomplished draughtmanship.

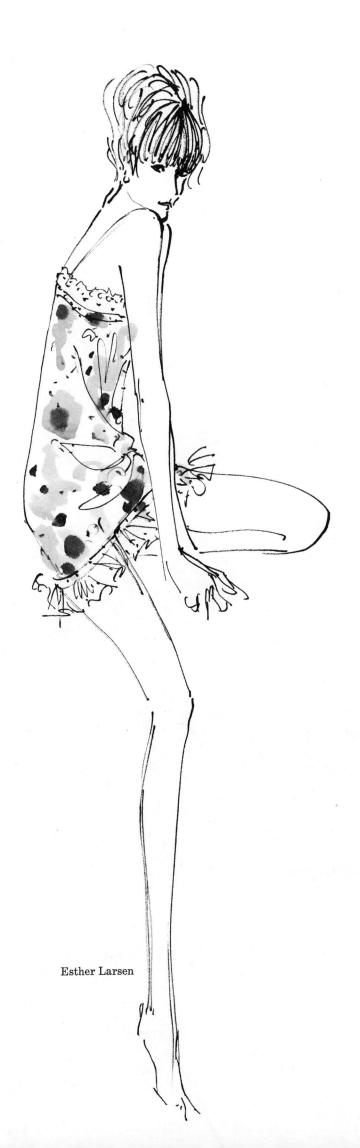

Esther Larsen

TINY PETTIS

Anne-Marie Barden, courtesy of *Mademoiselle*

UNDERCOVER FASHIONS ■ The light touch helps here. Heaviness of technique or an overserious attitude toward the subject does not convey the qualities of lingerie and sleepwear. Delicate pen lines suggest delicate fabrics, filmy laces, and lightweight nylons. Suitable pose should be considered; figures in gay or amusing attitudes incite interest and lure the buyer.

5. You are now ready to finish your drawing in pen and ink. Practice your pen line on a separate piece of paper or on tracing paper again. When you feel confident in your approach, go over the pencil lines with definite pen lines but a delicate hand. Do not use pressure or scratchy lines. When the ink is thoroughly dry, any visible pencil lines may be gently erased with a kneaded eraser. This method of working first in pencil is used exclusively by some artists. It is also good for the beginner who does not have a model available. In sketching from a model, however, the artist is apt to work more freely and quickly with pen, brush, or soft carbon pencil, and the effect is more spontaneous. A pen-and-ink, or brush-and-ink, sketch done directly from a model may also be traced and corrected later. It is possible to sketch more quickly this way and to achieve greater freedom of expression. Each person needs to experiment and decide on the methods that produce the best results for him. Time is also a factor once you are on a real job and short cuts become a necessity. While you are learning, however, it is better to be extravagant with both time and paper. If you make a mistake, start over again. It is better to make several drawings than to work one to death correcting and erasing. Learn from your mistakes and keep your thinking fresh.

6. If your sketches seem to lack good drawing, go back to the figure lessons and check for possible errors in proportion and construction. It is important to be aware of what mistakes are spoiling your drawings. Perhaps the construction of the neck is wrong, or the pose of the figure is out of balance. Learn the rules as a guide to criticizing your own drawing. Continue to draw more and more, redoing a figure until it is right, practicing as a musician must practice for perfection. Keep some of your first sketches in a file. Put them away and do not look at them for a few months. When you feel discouraged with your progress, take them out. You may be astounded at your improvement if you have been truly concentrating on your lessons and working.

PRELIMINARY SKETCH ▪ Quickly sketched from the model, this outline drawing by Antonio was used as the pattern for a finished illustration. The final drawing was more stylized. Areas of gray and black were added with cut-out transfer sheets, and fine detail was done with pen and ink.

8. WORKING WITH O

WORKING FROM THE MODEL

Finding the right model may or may not be easy, but there are certain qualifications that make a model right for the fashion artist. If you are working from nonprofessional models, look for one who is tall and slim enough to wear clothes well (sizes 8 to 10, preferably). Height without shoes should be 5'6" to 5'9". Her hair should be well-groomed and adaptable to varied styles, better short than overabundant and uncontrolled. Extra hair can always be added or faked in drawing.

Prettiness is not essential. Some models who lack ideal proportions may put so much character into a pose that the artist is inspired to do his best. Unlike in photography, shortcomings can be overcome in drawing

WITHOUT A MODEL

with a little imagination. Character and style are most important. To model clothes well, the right stance or posture is essential. The pose must suit the fashion and must look contemporary, since poses change with fashions. Above all a model should be relaxed and at ease. It is impossible to be both tense and graceful. If a model is nervous or uncertain, do your best to put her at ease.

In posing the model, let her move about naturally and try a few ideas. Stop her in the middle of an action if you think it would make a good sketch. Avoid stiff, self-conscious poses. You might suggest an action or mood you wish to convey. If the model has no ideas, do a little stage directing or show her some poses from good fashion clippings. Let her try some walking or sitting poses as well as standing ones—anything that

THE NATURAL POSE
■ Preliminary drawings for a *New York Times* fashion story. Antonio sketched the model absorbed in a television program. The same background theme was carried through a series of drawings later developed into full-color illustrations. The dreamy-eyed model appears convincingly enraptured. Her clothes are shown with style and perfection of detail. The situation adds human interest and creates a mood, enhancing rather than detracting from the fashions. Figures and backgrounds are arranged to form pleasing compositions.

ONE DRESS, FIVE VIEWS ■ A series of quick brush-and-ink sketches was done from the model by Bouché. Experimenting with many poses developed the best interpretation. In this case the choice was made by the fashion editor.

gives expression or character to the clothes being illustrated. Use your imagination.

Poses can be timed from five minutes to twenty or, at most, twenty-five, depending on whether you are doing a quick action pose or a more detailed drawing. Five-minute rests should be taken every twenty-five minutes. If the pose is difficult (a straining, action position), five or ten minutes should be enough time for the artist to put down a quick outline of the pose. If a model absent-mindedly turns her head or shifts weight halfway through the allotted time, the pose may be lost. If you find that your model cannot hold a pose at all, try someone else or, if you have no choice, shorten the poses and mark off the position on the floor by tracing around her feet with a piece of chalk. If she forgets the pose on second try, you really have a poor model. Solving this problem is up to you.

Apart from general appearance, such as good proportions, the right style, chic hair, choosing the right model also depends on compatibility. If there is no rapport between you and your model, work may become frustrating. There is no way of finding out except by trying different

ones. A model perfect for one artist may not be right for another. Once you find a good one, make it worth her while to come back. Either give her a guarantee of a certain amount of work or a generous hourly fee that shows your appreciation. The fees of top fashion models, especially photographers' models, are much too high for an artist. However, some very good fashion models (not so photogenic) are happy to put in otherwise unprofitable time working for artists at a minimum fee. Be sure to settle the matter of price before starting to work.

Finding a good model sometimes takes a little ingenuity. Apart from model agencies, which charge a fee (usually paid by the model), there are other possible sources from which the artist can obtain models. Some unemployed actresses or dancers are excellent models and may be found through their schools or clubs. Art students are another source. Sometimes a telephone call to one of these schools or clubs will bring results, or you might write a letter, enclosing a notice to be posted on the school bulletin board. Some artists, I am told, have had satisfactory results from a newspaper ad in the help-wanted section.

EDITORIAL ILLUSTRATION ■ Sketched directly from the model, these drawings express the substance of style with a sure hand. Subtleties of shape, keenly observed, underlie the casual simplicity of these notable drawings from the pages of *Vogue*.

Drawings by Joe Eula, Copyright © 1975 by The Conde Nast Publications, Inc.

WORKING WITHOUT A MODEL

Working without a model is sometimes difficult, especially if the clothes present a problem of fit or swing. However, it can develop imagination and ingenuity. It is even possible to become too dependent on a model and unthinkingly to copy too literally what one sees. Unwavering routine eventually produces monotony and dulls the imagination. To change methods of working stimulates one's thinking.

There are numerous other sources of inspiration to give you ideas for poses, hair styles, fit. (See mention of fashion publications, Chapter 7, "Drawing the Garment.") Photographs are, of course, next best to having a model. You may want to take your own—even quick ones with a Polaroid camera. It is also wise to start a scrap file of good clippings from magazines. Included in your collection might be pictures filed under such headings as "Figures in Action," "Ideas for Backgrounds," "Winter Sports," "Hair Styles," and so on. Once you have learned to draw the figure, you should have a file of your own quick sketches to use and adapt with a little imagination.

Some large public libraries and museums have collections of pictorial material for the use of artists. The average fashion artist, unfortunately, is usually expected to meet very close deadlines. Time spent in widening one's knowledge and developing taste is never wasted, however. Art exhibits, museums, and the like enrich one's background and add to the joys of aesthetic discovery.

FASHION-MODEL TYPES

A suitable type of model, as discussed in Chapter 7, "Drawing the Garment," is an important factor in creating the right look for a fashion to

THE FORWARD-THRUST PELVIS ■ Professional show models learn to walk with the pelvis forward and knees slightly bent. This posture gives a concave curve to the front of the body and an easy "hang" to the garment.

be illustrated. Practically speaking, it is impossible to have exactly the right model for everything. The artist must decide on a definite type and improvise when necessary. If possible, find a model who is adaptable to the type or types you wish to illustrate. Proper measurements and proportions are necessary. The lithe or supple figure is always more graceful. The curved line of the pose, not the curves of the flesh, does most to make a beautiful fashion sketch.

Do *not* copy literally from the model. Use her as a subject to be interpreted in an imaginative illustration. Pick up her interesting characteristics and overlook any quality that detracts from the right effect. With luck, you may find a model with a long, graceful neck; if not, elongate it in your sketching. To draw literally indicates a meager imagination or lack of concentration on your objective, which is to stimulate interest and attract the prospective customer. Do not be afraid to exaggerate a pose or emphasize action lines for desired effects.

The model with assurance and flair is invaluable to an artist. Let her swing into a pose naturally. One who is self-conscious or wooden is of little help except to show the fit of the garment.

Popular fashion types change with fashion's swing to a new look. In the size range termed "misses" (mainly 8 to 16), there are during each period separate groups, which can be roughly classified into three fashion types.

The first is the young, active (more recently, international) group whose enthusiasm for the new and sometimes for radical change is stimulating. These are the "swingers" of the sixties. To interpret their fashions with zest is to see the light side of fashion and to delight in the whimsy of some of the more bizarre styles. With a tongue-in-cheek approach, illustrating this fashion group can be exciting fun.

A second group might be termed exotic. It includes the more flamboyant type of sophisticate who can wear striking styles, daring colors, and boldly designed jewelry with dramatic effect. These styles, when worn with authority and instinctive flair, achieve a look of great chic; with-

THE BOLD STANCE ▪ A suitably exuberant young model type swings naturally into the right pose for the breezy, active fashions of an era. These quick outline sketches are to be used and adapted to more finished drawings.

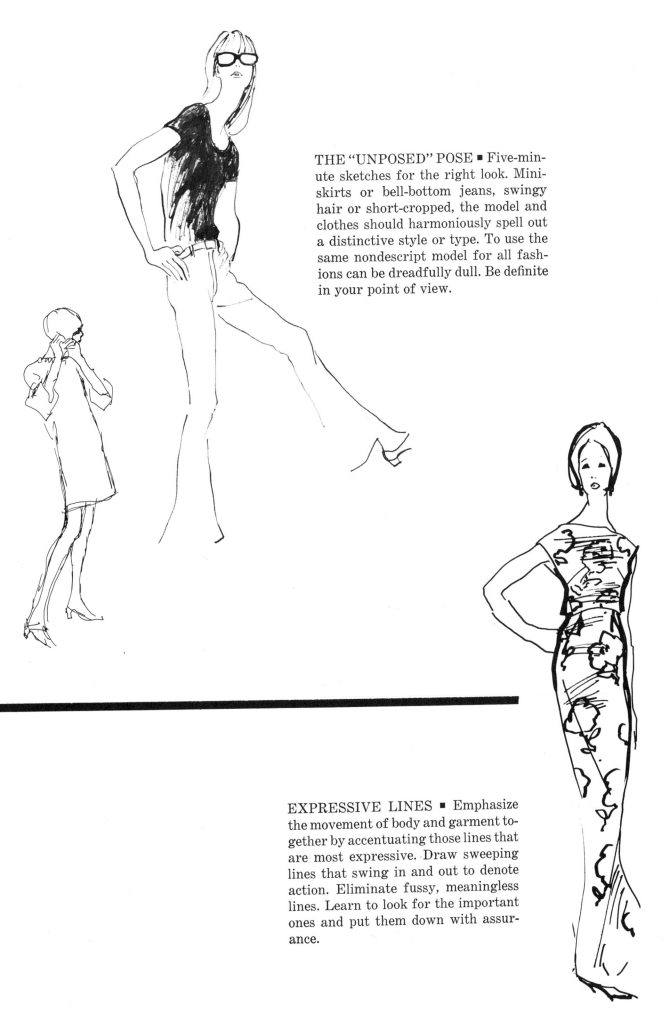

THE "UNPOSED" POSE ■ Five-minute sketches for the right look. Miniskirts or bell-bottom jeans, swingy hair or short-cropped, the model and clothes should harmoniously spell out a distinctive style or type. To use the same nondescript model for all fashions can be dreadfully dull. Be definite in your point of view.

EXPRESSIVE LINES ■ Emphasize the movement of body and garment together by accentuating those lines that are most expressive. Draw sweeping lines that swing in and out to denote action. Eliminate fussy, meaningless lines. Learn to look for the important ones and put them down with assurance.

Ben Morris, courtesy of Du Pont

out taste and assurance the merely daring can be ludicrous or garish. Hair styles for this type are often severely simple, with perhaps an oriental influence. Whatever the style, brushed back and down on the neck or swept up, the hair has a smooth, definite line. This type does not need the softening effect of loose or fluffy hair.

The third important group wears more conservative fashions. Included here are the young, classic beauty, the pretty type, and the dignified sophisticate whose tastes run to understated elegance. Their wardrobes may contain expensive clothes bearing the labels of famous designers here and abroad. They may also contain those simpler, less expensive clothes of flattering cut and good material in classic styles acknowledged to be in good taste. Hair styles, although following current trends, are never extreme. Flattering style and good grooming rather than dramatic effect should be emphasized. Money has little to do with conservative taste, and this group includes women from all income brackets and with varied interests, from career girl to homemaker.

"Juniors," a term used to describe sizes for the teen-ager, is a line designed for a different figure type. Sizes run from approximately 5 to 15, and the cut is for the shorter, not-quite-mature figure, proportionately high-waisted, with minimal bustline. As these fashions are designed chiefly for the teen-ager, who likes lots of changes, they are usually found in a lower price range. Although some of the styles are much the same as misses' models, many are younger and gayer than the more expensive lines. The junior model should be a college or precollege type who loves all the favorite fads current on campus. Magazines featuring this group include *Glamour*, *Mademoiselle*, and *Seventeen*.

Most department stores have their junior departments arranged and decorated as a "College Shop" or "Junior Boutique." The young customers' point of view and tastes are their own. They know exactly the way they want to look. Long hair and affectations of dress are becoming only to their age group and should be illustrated accordingly.

S CURVES ■ The curved lines (direction lines) do more than the curves of the figure to make a graceful and interesting fashion figure. Stiff, wooden poses produce static lines. A pose may be strong but never tense, relaxed but never tired-looking. An inspiring model has spirit and imagination, which the artist should encourage and appreciate.

ACTION POSES ▪ Clippings of photographs can suggest lively poses provided the idea of tracing outlines is eliminated in the beginning. The results of tracing are pathetic. The artist can, however, interpret the spirit of the pose by drawing the action lines and using imagination to create his own style. Pin up a photograph within easy viewing range and use it as you would a live model for inspiration. Apply your knowledge of form to make an original interpretation of the pose.

INTERPRETING ACTION POSES ■ Analyze and indicate body construction to get three-dimensional form from a photograph. Avoid copying outlines. Concentrate on form and action. Use various ways of building up the figure—block forms, spirals, etc. Put tracing paper over these rough sketches and redraw them in simplified outline. In this way you achieve freedom of drawing, substituting a photograph for a live model and applying the same approach. Exaggerate and emphasize curves, which indicate roundness and form, such as the in-and-out curves of the leg muscles, as illustrated.

9.
GETTING ACTION AND SWING INTO YOUR DRAWING

LOOSEN UP THAT DRAWING!

Although you have absorbed the basics of drawing and figure proportions, your figures may still look wooden and lifeless. So let's get some swing into those sketches! To work for animation and action in your drawing and at the same time develop an assured line, it is helpful to work large and follow the suggestions below. If possible, work from a live model. (See Chapter 8, "Working With or Without a Model.") If art classes or art groups are not available, perhaps you can find a model who is not a professional to pose for you, or get together a group of interested artists to sketch from one model or each other. Sketch anyone—young, old, male, female, characters.

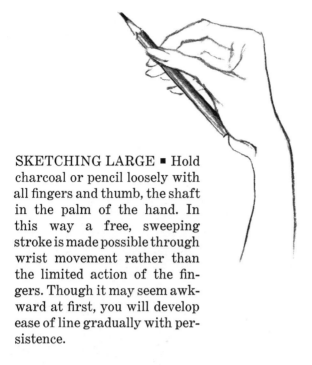

SKETCHING LARGE ▪ Hold charcoal or pencil loosely with all fingers and thumb, the shaft in the palm of the hand. In this way a free, sweeping stroke is made possible through wrist movement rather than the limited action of the fingers. Though it may seem awkward at first, you will develop ease of line gradually with persistence.

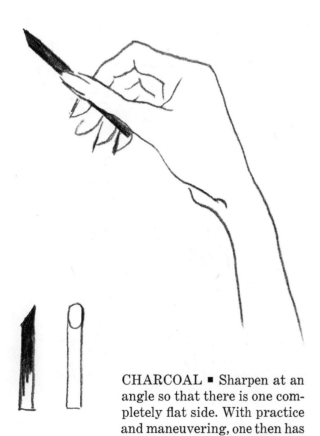

CHARCOAL ▪ Sharpen at an angle so that there is one completely flat side. With practice and maneuvering, one then has the means of producing all types of lines from very thin to very heavy. To retain this flexibility, sharpen charcoal frequently with a sandpaper pad as you work. Small pads of fine sandpaper, especially made for this purpose, are stocked in all art supply stores.

1. Get a pad of newsprint (18″ x 24″). This is the cheapest paper carried by art-supply stores. *Do not save paper.* Feel free to experiment and throw away. Do not expect everything you do to be worthy. Drop your inhibitions. This is purely an exercise for control in drawing and to rid your lines of tension. Your first attempts may be disappointing but this is unimportant. Forget your mistakes. One learns by trial and error, so have fun and let yourself go.

2. Start with a stick of charcoal (or, if you prefer, a black crayon, heavy felt-tip pen, brush and ink). Sharpen the charcoal on your sandpaper pad, holding it at an angle so that it has a flat, oblique point. (Charcoal should never have a round point as is made with a pencil sharpener.) Hold it lightly with the thumb and all four fingers, the end actually in the palm of your hand. (See illustrations on page 00.) This gives you a large scope and sweeping lines that can be controlled in width and weight from a thin, delicate line to a wide stroke and from light to dark. Manipulate the charcoal for varied lines, using the tapered side for thin lines, the flat side for thick.

3. Practice just drawing lines for a while. Work for controlled strokes and lines, trying to achieve contrasts of light and heavy. Next, put down one big, flowing line to suggest the pose of the figure. Be bold and free, but deliberate. Does your one line express action or give an interesting shape? Good. Then build up with a few meaningful secondary lines, some dark and heavy, some light and delicate. Shaded tones of gray may be added or softened by light smudging with the thumb. Do not be tempted to do a lot of smudging to cover up inept drawing of lines. This is the most obvious resort of an untrained amateur. Do have contrasts of definite dark and light areas and precise, controlled lines.

4. If working with brush, use India ink and at least two brushes, one large and a small one for delicate lines and contrast. India ink is hard on brushes, so be sure to rinse them out frequently and to dry them on a clean cloth. Never leave them to dry full of ink.

SOFT CHARCOAL TECHNIQUE ■ Sketched on charcoal paper, this 40-inch figure by Antonio was done directly from the model. Details of the pattern are incomplete, but the relaxed, flowing lines have a pleasing boldness. Shadows and folds have been indicated with a loose, slanted stroke. Shading of the upper half of the figure has been slightly smudged with the thumb. Overworked gray tones should be avoided. Too much smudging results in a muddy-looking drawing without character.

FREE-FLOWING LINES ■ The expressive line is developed through drawing the natural way. A relaxed, uninhibited line flows through this grease-pencil drawing by Barbara Pearlman. Tone was added with felt-tip pen in pale gray. Forgetting mechanical exactness, the artist used a continuous line following form of model and garment. "Effect" is the objective rather than a photographic likeness. Sureness of line and individual technique evolve from continual practice and working from the model. Drop your inhibitions. Mistakes are inevitable in learning. Observe and experiment. Only carelessness or indifference stand in the way of improvement.

DIRECT SKETCHING

Sketching directly from life is one of the best ways to improve your drawing and to get animation. It trains the eye to get an impression quickly and to record it with an individual style. The posed model is an invaluable aid to drawing the figure, but sketching from the scene at hand demands much more from the artist. To develop speed for on-the-scene drawing, try limiting the usual twenty-minute pose of the model to five minutes. In this way you learn to eliminate unimportant details and to simplify line and form. Next, let the model pose for a few minutes while you observe and make mental notes. Then sketch the pose from memory. If your observation and memory are good, you will have something; if not, try again. It is surprising how much repeated effort reveals. Some of your attempts may be nothing more than action lines, but these will probably be more alive than your more careful drawings and will really tell a story.

To find interesting subjects, take a sketchbook and set out for wherever there are people. The park, the zoo, the beach—all supply living models as well as the right background without faking. Perhaps you will find workmen digging or building nearby. The subject is up to you. The top fashion artists have always done on-the-scene sketching. Eric could be seen constantly making notes in the corner of a restaurant where the fashionable gathered or wherever there was action and interest. The result may be finished drawings or merely sketches of details and ideas for future use in small notebook form.

EXERCISES

The following exercises are suggested to stimulate new thinking patterns and to develop individuality in approach and technique. Trying various ways of drawing is invaluable in finding one's best method of working. It also relieves a tendency to be overly serious, a habit which can produce stereotyped and uninspired renditions.

GESTURE ■ Use scribbling lines to express gestures and movements quickly. The shape is suggested, not stated. Form in this exercise is not as important as conveying an action like thrust or pull, stiffen or relax, stretch or crouch. Lines may be spiral, suggesting roundness, or straight with a forward thrust—anything to loosen up those inhibitions. Draw large, with any type of pen or pencil that gives you freedom of line and a means of expression.

First premise: mass form. Forget outlines altogether. Look only at mass shapes. With a piece of charcoal, indicate what you see in gray tone as a mass form. Work for volume and solidity. Try unusual or crazy poses. The model might be seated with knees drawn up under her chin, arms hugging them close, the silhouette forming an egg shape. Draw it in that shape, later adding dark accents or lines to suggest a figure. Keep it simple. This method of working trains the eye to see simplified forms and mass shapes rather than lines and details. To see the subject this way more easily, squint your eyes until the whole picture becomes blurred, like a photograph that is out of focus. Then sketch that shape in one tone of gray. This trains you to see form as a part of design.

Give one whole session to this approach. If the shapes are out of drawing, this is unimportant. Perhaps you have created some interesting shapes or suggested a mood. Whatever you did, you made a statement in simplified form.

Second premise: three-dimensional form. Again, work on a large pad of inexpensive paper. With felt-tip pen, charcoal, or brush and ink, draw spirals as if the whole figure were made of wire. Or think of drawing lines around a figure made of glass so that you can see the lines going completely around through the glass. Keep a cylindrical feeling. The position of the arms and legs will dictate the ellipse of the cylinder. This not only gives a feeling of roundness to the figure, but automatically produces guidelines for drawing the garment.

Third premise: expression in line. Start drawing one unbroken line around the whole figure without lifting your pen or pencil off the paper. Do not cross or break the line, just let it continue around the hair, ears, neck, outline of garment, legs, and feet. If there is a chair within the outline, include it as part of the whole.

If your drawing does not please you, try again. Work slowly and deliberately to get your impression with a single line, concentrating on

Sketching mass forms

Charcoal quick sketching

MASS FORM ▪ Forget outline and think of shapes in mass form. Work for volume, exaggerating what you wish. To change your point of view, squint your eyes to eliminate sharp-focus detail and to see shapes as patterns of dark and light areas. Flat masses of color may be done with soft charcoal or with a very large brush and water color or ink. Work from live models, either in a class or wherever you find people to sketch.

QUICK SKETCHING ■ Spontaneity is the charm of quick sketching. The unstudied results of instantaneously recorded action and expression often have more life and excitement than those that are worked over too much. An exact outline of the image becomes less interesting than the exuberant gesture.

Southampton Horse Show
Junior Contestants

ON-THE-SCENE SKETCHING ■ Sports events provide both spectators and contestants as models, so make a point of carrying sketch pad and pen or pencil wherever you go. Constant practice develops keen observation and the ability to record action and gesture quickly. A good visual memory allows the artist to get people and animals in motion. You learn to eliminate unimportant detail and look for the few meaningful lines.

St. Croix, Virgin Islands
E. Sloane

ON VACATION ■ Take your sketch pad instead of a camera. Interpret what you see that seems interesting material from your point of view.

beauty of line itself. Relax, and let your line flow onto the paper. For fun, try drawing without looking at your drawing; just look at the model. The results may be hilariously funny, but you will lose the tenseness in your drawing.

Fourth premise: gesture. Forget contour, form, and line in your approach. Think only of action and gesture suggested, not stated. Work from a model, or sketch quickly from those around you. Let yourself go, using pen-and-ink lines that ramble unself-consciously over the paper. Express gesture, action, movement. Do not delineate outlines. The shape is suggested, not stated. The lines you put down will be scribbling, continuous lines devoid of detail. In some of the sketches, try suggesting the construction of the figure in action, indicating bone structure without being too exact. Continue this exercise until your line is relaxed and your scribbles tell the story of what the figure is doing.

NOTE: If working very large, you may find it difficult to see over-all proportions without getting a little distance between you and your drawing. For this reason, some artists prefer to sketch standing up at an easel or at a slanted table raised to the right height. This allows working at arm's length and backing up occasionally to see the sketch as a whole.

10.
FINISHED
ART

Along with proficiency in actual drawing of the fashion figure, the aspiring artist must learn the various methods of rendering finished art as the ultimate way of expressing his ability. If artwork is to be used for advertising in newspapers, magazines, or mailing brochures, a specific technique practical for reproduction is a necessity. Methods of engraving and printing demand clean-cut, professional artwork.

Eventually, you may develop a single technique and make it your own, but to learn only one is too limiting. In some cases you must adjust to the technique required for a specific job opening. It is only through learning various methods and continual experimenting that your potential develops and self-expression becomes evident.

Antonio, courtesy of *The New York Times*, 196

As in fashion, there are vogues in art techniques. One artist influences another or, his style being popular, other artists are asked to imitate it. One style, a deliberately streaked wash like a glaze, done on a slick surface, became so popular that it appeared on page after page of magazine advertising done by numerous different artists. Sometimes an artist may develop a style by accident or while experimenting; sometimes artists of the past are an influence on today's art.

TECHNIQUES OF RENDERING

LINE DRAWING

A line drawing is simply a black-and-white sketch without halftones (grays). It reproduces more easily and less expensively than the halftone. For this type of drawing, India ink used with pen or brush produces the most clean-cut line. The character of the line is influenced considerably by the surface of the paper or illustration board used. A slick surface gives an even, unbroken, clear line, while a kid-finish or rough-surfaced paper will produce more varied effects and texture. This is not to imply that one effect is preferable to the other. The choice is yours—whether to achieve a loose, sketchy type of drawing or a more meticulous, detailed, perhaps decorative, illustration.

A "dry-brush" technique is useful for many texture effects. The term is used to depict a stroke done with a partially dry brush giving the semblance of a soft, gray tone. This type of brush stroke can be controlled to taper into pointed ends, creating effects of long-haired furs or shaggy surfaces. For drawing hair, a soft, silky look can be developed equally well. Without tapering the line, fabrics such as tweeds and

BRUSH-AND-INK TECHNIQUE ■ These figures were rendered directly on charcoal paper with a large and a medium-sized tapered brush and India ink. The free style and loose technique were achieved by working very large from the model. Sometimes it is what is left out that gives a drawing character. The lines eliminated here, including details of the faces, give added strength to the bold patterns of the garments.

soft, thick woolens are produced effectively. To use this technique, simply work with water-color brushes in varied sizes and India ink. After dipping the brush in ink, blot it on a handy paint cloth and experiment. A little pressure on the brush fans out the hairs so that they make a wide stroke which can be tapered in again by lifting the brush gradually off the paper. (See examples on page 146.)

Charcoal, carbon pencils, or any of the other types of truly black pencils also produce interesting and varied textures and effects. Lead pencil must be excluded here as it will not reproduce as a black-and-white line drawing. For best results when working sufficiently large, use a regular charcoal paper. Other drawing papers with adequate texture and workable surface may be useful for the average job or smaller drawing. This requires individual experimenting. Pen and ink can be used in combination with charcoal for fine lines and black accents. With any of the pencil techniques it is possible to produce lovely, soft modeling of the figure through shading or weight of line. Control of the medium takes continual practice.

The felt-tip pen or marker has possibilities, though limited. Made in many types and sizes, they are fun to use for quick effect. The disposable kinds usually smear when used on a smooth surface and are therefore impractical for certain types of finished artwork. The most satisfactory one is a metal fountain-pen type that can be refilled with its own special ink. (Flo-Master is the trade name.) The disposable plastic pens dry out quickly but are handy to carry about and use for quick sketching, since the ink bottle is eliminated. Although these pens come in points of various sizes, it is impossible

BRUSH STROKE, JAPANESE STYLE ■ Again, economy of line creates a striking impression in these illustrations for cosmetic products. The original drawings were done very large. There is vitality in the swift, sure, tapered stroke, so like the Japanese technique.

Esther Larsen

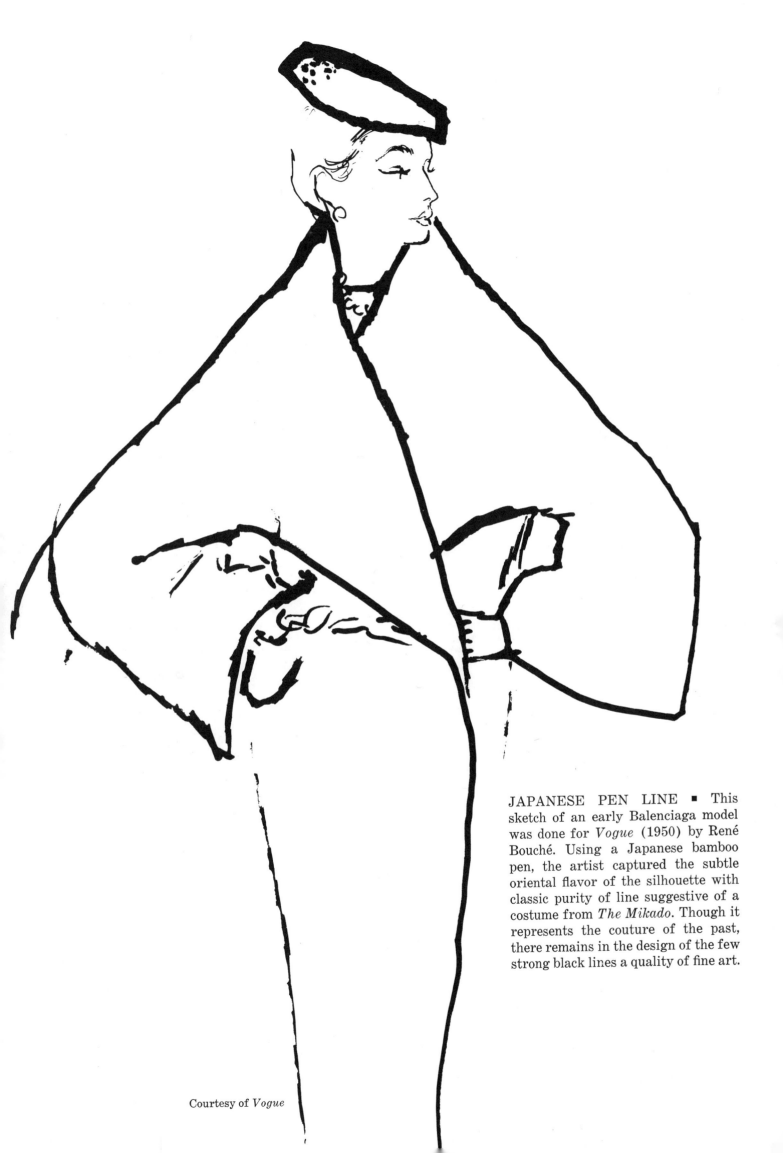

JAPANESE PEN LINE ■ This sketch of an early Balenciaga model was done for *Vogue* (1950) by René Bouché. Using a Japanese bamboo pen, the artist captured the subtle oriental flavor of the silhouette with classic purity of line suggestive of a costume from *The Mikado*. Though it represents the couture of the past, there remains in the design of the few strong black lines a quality of fine art.

Courtesy of *Vogue*

WHITE ON BLACK ▪ A decorative
style is achieved in this combination
of strong black areas and contrasting
light pencil lines. The jacket, cut out
of black paper, was pasted on the pencil drawing. The even stitching and
other details were added with opaque
white. The result is a clean, well-defined drawing of the merchandise plus
the charm of a stylized rendition.

Anne-Marie Barden,
courtesy of Bergdorf Goodman

Courtesy of *Vogue*

FELT-TIP PEN ▪ Another Bouché drawing, this one done with a felt-tip pen, appeared in a 1958 edition of *Vogue*. The lively pose and amused expression of the model help to lift this dull dress out of the dreary class. This was the era that produced the chemise style at its worst. The sketch, done directly from the model, maintains a clean-cut line without hesitation or correction.

DRY BRUSH ▪ The soft, fuzzy lines attained with a partially dry brush can be used to portray various textures. Use blotting paper or a soft cloth to wipe the brush on each time it is dipped in the ink. With practice, one can control the quality of line and the tones of gray. It is a quick method of depicting furs and thick, spongy, woolen fabrics for black-and-white line reproduction. It may also be used in combination with other techniques.

to get a flexible line with them. Their boldness of line, however, is suitable and effective for some types of illustration.

EXERCISES FOR LINE MEDIA

Pen-and-ink techniques require a fairly hard-surfaced paper, one that allows the pen to glide smoothly without catching or blurring. An inexpensive paper like newsprint may be used for practice and quick sketching; later switch to a good Strathmore or bond for finer lines and detail work. Using a variety of flexible drawing pens, from fine-pointed crow-quills to thick bowl points, see how many types of lines you can produce with ease. Try duplicating a delicate lace edging, working from an actual piece of lace. Practice doing areas of fine crosshatching, fine lines, and other surface textures. (See examples on page 146.) For interesting but unpredictable lines, try working with a Japanese bamboo or reed pen. Both of these may be sharpened with a razor blade if they become dull or scratchy.

Courtesy of *Women's Wear Daily*, 1966

Reed pen on
Smooth surface

Japanese reed pen
on rough surface

Dry-brush strokes

A brush can be more versatile than a pen once complete control has been developed. Good sable brushes are essential. Little can be accomplished with cheap, limp ones. A good brush has spring and flexibility when wet and maintains a point without separating. Practice long, tapered strokes with a medium-sized brush dipped in plenty of ink. Next, try blotting the brush with a paint cloth so that it has very little ink and experiment with a dry-brush technique. Try making both long sweeping lines and short feathery ones. Repeat, dipping and wiping your brush each time you use it. Rinse out the brush with clear water occasionally and wipe it dry. Experiment with both large and very fine brushes for contrast in weight of line. Do not expect perfection overnight. Facility comes only with practice.

For carbon-pencil, grease-pencil, or charcoal work, one must work on a paper with some texture. Newsprint is adequate for practicing, but a good drawing paper or charcoal paper is necessary for a finished drawing. To handle any of the *pencil techniques* properly, one must strive for delicacy of line and tone and have relaxed control. A tense hand and forced line are no good for charcoal. (See Chapter 9, "Getting Action and Swing into Your Drawing.") Be direct and definite. Remember that corrections are practically impossible in this technique.

WATER COLOR

The term "wash drawing" is used to designate a sketch done in water color in tones of gray. Such a drawing must be reproduced in halftone, a printing process more complicated and more costly than the line cut done from a line drawing. Reproductions of wash drawings in newspapers were somewhat unpredictable until the development of a solution called Kromolite, a so-called highlight solution that is used by the artist. It is

PEN-AND-BRUSH STROKES ■ Experiment with both pen and brush used with India ink. Use a soft cloth to wipe both clean and to control the amount of ink. Try various sizes and types of pens and brushes as well as papers with various textured surfaces.

Dorothy Hood, courtesy of Lord & Taylor

WATER COLOR (WASH DRAWING) ▪ This style of water-color rendering is referred to as wash drawing. Involving no outlines, the technique is
that of an academic water-colorist. The preliminary drawing is suggested
with a few light pencil lines on the water-color board (illustration board).
Important black accents are put in next, then the gray washes. Enough
white areas should be left to give the drawing light and sparkle. Too much
gray or overworking a wash can result in a muddy, dull effect. To get smooth
washes over larger areas, the paper can be first dampened with a wash of
clear water and allowed to dry partially.

Three-dimensional form and texture are expertly handled here by shading
defining planes of light and dark. Details are added with delicate pen lines.
The beautifully done backgrounds suggest glamorous surroundings for
glamorous "at home" fashions.

BLACK PENCIL WITH WASH ■
Flat, clear washes (Kromolite Highlight Solution is used instead of water for newspaper reproduction) are here added to these finely executed Conte crayon drawings done on charcoal paper. Note the carefree drawing of folds in the illustration of the long, backdraped crepe. The plaid pattern of the other gown is indicated with a precise gradation of gray tones, leaving out white areas for contrast. The hair styles are suitably chic and expertly defined. The over-all impression is one of good grooming and good taste.

Kenneth Paul Block, courtesy of Bonwit Teller

used in place of water and, since it is very much like water in appearance, it is quite simple to use. The engraver then applies a developer to the finished drawing which turns all areas washed with Kromolite a bright yellow, thus taking the guesswork out of indefinite gray areas and sharpening up white edges and highlights. Kromolite is now used for all newspaper halftone illustrations. While you are learning and making only samples, it is unnecessary to worry about solutions other than water. To master a good, clean, definite wash without streaks is your main goal.

There are many ways to use washes. Sometimes they are used in limited areas on a drawing that is mainly lines. Some techniques do not use an outline, just gray tones indicating form and color with accents of black and a minimum of line for detail. The artist using this technique draws lightly in pencil first as a guide for carefully worked out washes and white spaces. The famous Lord & Taylor ads are fine examples of this latter technique. They are not only well-drawn but beautifully handled water colors, rich in dark tones and sparkling highlights. The layouts are planned for adequate white spaces, and the whole forms a charming pattern or design focusing on the fashion story.

The line-and-wash combination, with very little use of gray tones, is used more often by specialty shops and advertisers whose ads are small. Because of limited newspaper space, artwork must be more open, with bold, simple lines and less complicated washes. Such drawings can be equally striking used large. Their simplicity and direct statement attract attention when done with assurance and flair.

WATER-COLOR MATERIALS AND METHODS

Since water color must be handled quickly, it is wise to get your working area and materials carefully set up before you start. It is best to work on a slanted surface, so have a drawing board or artist's drawing table that is adjustable to a slope. Obviously, one also needs a flat surface for water jars, palette, brushes, and other materials.

This drawing has only a minimum of wash added to suggest gleam of the fabric and emphasize the sparkles of opaque white paint.

Courtesy of Bonwit Teller

LINE AND WASH ■ Line drawings done with a fine felt-tip pen, these have accents and details added with assorted grays of felt-tip markers and wash tones. The technique is rendered with an airy, open style. The merchandise is portrayed with flair and accuracy of detail. Avoiding an overly serious approach, the style is particularly suitable for attracting the affluent young with sophisticated tastes. The lightness of line and tone are adaptable to the limited advertising space of a small shop.

Mona Mark, courtesy of Henri Bendel

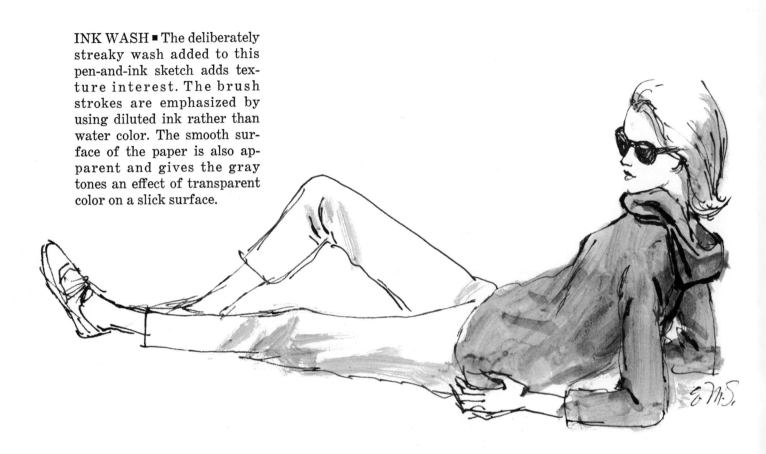

INK WASH ▪ The deliberately streaky wash added to this pen-and-ink sketch adds texture interest. The brush strokes are emphasized by using diluted ink rather than water color. The smooth surface of the paper is also apparent and gives the gray tones an effect of transparent color on a slick surface.

Clean paint cloths and a few blotters are a must. It is a good idea to have a blotter or sheet of paper to rest your hand on, since any moisture from the hand can spoil the surface of the paper. Have plenty of clean water and a clean water-color palette. These palettes come in metal, plastic, or china.

The best sable water-color brushes are the only type to buy. As a start, sizes #1, #3, #5, and #7 will do, later adding whatever you wish—perhaps a #10 and extras in the smaller sizes. For a delicate, flexible line there is a special fashion-artist's brush which is very long and tapered. It is only for lines, however, not for areas of wash.

Water-color papers vary in quality and price. The good ones are a delight, especially the imported handmade variety. They not only give richness to a wash, but the surface has a toughness that takes corrections and erasing. These are expensive and unfortunately are becoming very scarce, in some places nonexistent. The most practical buy is a good-quality illustration board. For practicing, an inexpensive grade is fine. Avoid a rough-surfaced paper unless you plan to work very large. Some water-color papers have an interesting surface or texture without being rough, having an appearance much like parchment. Avoid a one- or two-ply (thin) paper that will buckle when wet. Illustration board (mounted water-color paper) allows the unlimited dampening sometimes necessary for large areas of washes. A wet, or even slightly damp, surface eliminates streaks from overlapping brush strokes.

As an alternative to the heavy-weight papers and boards, it is possible to work on a lighter-weight paper and mount it later. Some artists use a light table for tracing their sketches onto water-color paper. This type of table is constructed with a large frosted glass mounted in a frame and boxed with a light inside. The idea is much the same as tracing something by holding it up to the window, which you may have done as a child. It is a simple method of tracing without pencil lines, resulting in a direct, simplified drawing eliminating fussy, unnecessary lines. Working with pen or brush, the effects can be spontaneous and authoritative. This way of working is best for line techniques with a minimum of wash.

A fine, handmade water-color paper, such as the English Whatman papers, can be stretched when wet. This method is used mainly by water colorists for fine art. For the average commercial job it is too time-consuming. To stretch the paper for this method, soak the paper first by holding it under running water (only a handmade paper with rag content can stand this treatment). Next, place the paper on a flat drawing board, blot up excess water with a cloth or paper towels, and while it is still wet, tape all edges to the board with gummed tape. When the paper dries it will be beautifully smooth. After repeated application of washes, the paper will continue to resume its flat surface. When the drawing is finished, it must be left to dry completely before removing it from the board. To remove, use a razor blade and cut out the drawing, leaving the tape sticking to the board. A true water colorist finds it worth the effort to have a resilient surface and a quality unlike any illustration board. These papers come in varied surfaces: cold press (slightly rough) and hot press (smooth-surfaced). A medium surface, #1, seems to have disappeared from the market. Materials change and new ones are developed continually, so it is difficult to name specific items. If there is an art-supply store nearby, it is always more fun to experiment and find your own favorites.

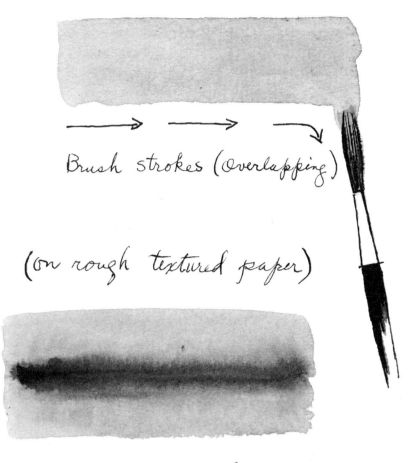

Brush strokes (overlapping)

(on rough textured paper)

Wet surface — dark brush stroke.

Pen strokes on wet surface

WATER-COLOR EXPERIMENTS ■ Practice laying an even wash with a brush, as demonstrated in the illustration. Experiment with various papers to develop the method most successful for your individual use.

EFFECTS WITH TONE[PAPER ▪ A medium-gra[charcoal paper provided th[background and all middl[tones for this drawing dor[with a bamboo pen. The pape[was slightly dampened, whic[accounts for the incidenta[dark accents. The darker gray[are in transparent water colo[probably "ivory black." Th[light areas were done las[washed on with broad, sweep[ing strokes of diluted opaqu[white and color (yellow). Th[escort in dinner jacket adds ir[terest and a nice contrast o[dark against the pale chiffo[dress.

René Bouché, courtesy of *Vogue*

There are various methods and various techniques that can be used for finishing. For a realistic rendition, I have found that dampening the paper first and allowing it to dry for a few minutes so that the wash will not run, then putting the shadows in is the most satisfactory method. Add the lighter-toned, over-all washes and the black lines and accents last. Some artists prefer to put in the blacks first, but they wash out or smear unless completely dry and waterproof. In using a wash technique such as the Lord & Taylor style, masses of tone and third-dimensional shading eliminate the necessity of outlines. The pencil guidelines are merely touched here and there with snappy black accents. Detail is indicated with pen-and-ink lines or, in dark areas, with opaque white or gray paint thinned out with water and applied with a pen.

For a wash-and-line combination, the approach is different. In this case the outline is done first. It can be done with pen and ink, brush and ink (diluted or full-strength black) or one of the many types of carbon pencils.

CHARCOAL AND WHITE CHALK ▪ The well-placed shadows in this soft charcoal drawing accentuate the action and form of the figure. The dark beige of the charcoal paper makes the white of the slacks snap out. The figure was sketched large (32 inches high), requiring two pieces of the charcoal paper pieced together. White pastel or ordinary chalk is used for this scale of work. For smaller drawings and fine white lines, pastel pencils with a finer point are more practical.

Antonio, courtesy of *The New York Times*

The paper may be illustration board or a lighter paper, whatever is best suited to the medium chosen. This might be a paper with a slick surface for brush or pen, or it might have a rougher surface suitable for charcoal or pencil. Even a heavy-quality vellum will take a limited wash without buckling. In fact, when speed is necessary, some artists turn in free-lance artwork done on vellum and mounted on heavier paper or board. Vellum has a good working surface and takes a beautiful, thin pen line that reproduces well. Washes may be added to any of these types of outline, but sparingly and with a light touch. Eliminate unnecessary lines and try for a clean-cut look.

A wash drawing must have a spontaneous quality with definite tones of gray and contrasting black and white accents. If it is worked over or done in a labored, uncertain way, it becomes muddy-looking and lacks sparkle and depth. Whatever you do, make a definite statement. If you can work directly on the board, fine. This takes sure drawing and lots of practice, but a loose technique can be charming if well done and not careless or sloppy.

Rough-surfaced papers or water-color boards may be used for working very large. In reducing for reproduction, the lines are refined as well as the texture of the washes. A rough paper sometimes gives an interesting tweedy look to a fabric rendition, especially in combination with a fine pen line. It is altogether impractical for working actual size, of course.

It is a great help to see original examples of the best artwork. Since this is not always possible, learn to observe and analyze work from magazine and newspaper reproductions.

EXERCISES FOR APPLYING WASH

1. Use an inexpensive sheet of illustration board for practice work. Mark off varied shapes (squares, triangles, circles) in light pencil outline. Have some forms large and some fairly small.

2. Have a tube of water color, matte or ivory black, or colors if you wish. Tubed colors are more practical than the colors in cake form. They can also be purchased singly rather than in sets. Put the color, or colors, onto a palette in small amounts and dilute with water what you need to cover the marked-off area. Be sure to mix enough paint to cover the intended space. Make tests on a separate piece of paper until you get the desired tone or depth of color. Be sure to have a cloth handy for wiping and blotting your brushes.

3. Before starting to paint, dampen the area to be painted with a large brush and clear water. The whole surface of the paper can be "painted" first with just water if you allow it to dry for a few minutes before beginning the washes. In either case, work from the top down in even, overlapping strokes. (See diagram on page 153.) Be sure to work on a slanted surface so that the excess water can be pulled down, thus eliminating puddles. Using plenty of water on the brush, start in

the upper left-hand corner. Quickly brush across the top of the paper and pull excess water, or wash, down on the right. Dip the brush again and apply the next stroke the same as the first, overlapping each time. Work evenly and quickly to the bottom of the board or paper, keeping the whole surface equally damp. As the surface dries out it is possible to repeat the process if you wish a deeper tone. This means working with very thin washes to avoid streaking. For soft, fuzzy effects, try moistening the wash area and adding dark tones to the wet surface. For sharp, clean-cut lines or detail, be sure the surface is thoroughly dry before adding brush or pen lines.

Keep practicing for proficiency, and experiment. As you work you will discover the degree of dampness which works best for you. Try gradations of one color in sets of joining blocks, say five gradations of gray from very pale to dark. It is wise to keep experimenting until you can control the medium before tackling your finished drawing.

THE FINISHED WASH DRAWING

It is important to work on clean illustration board with a minimum of pencil lines. For this reason many artists plan their drawings on tracing paper first, then trace them onto the water-color board. As a means of tracing, simply blacken the back of the tracing paper with a drawing pencil (2H or HB), rub off excess lead with a piece of cotton or tissue, and trace with a fine-pointed 2H pencil. If you wish, make a carbon this way to use for other tracing purposes.

Once your drawing is transferred to the illustration board, place another sheet of tracing paper over it and plan the arrangement of gray areas and dark accents so as to attain a pleasing over-all effect. First, try planning black accents alone to achieve balance and an interesting pattern; then fill in the gray tones, allowing enough white areas for lightness and contrast. Try several arrangements. It will soon become apparent which is the most striking and direct. This is a meticulous way of working and, although it seems slow, it avoids mistakes and disappointments in the finished art. As your eye and hand become quicker to grasp what you want to do beforehand, you may be able to e-liminate the tracing-paper and routine work directly on the water-color paper.

OPAQUE MEDIA

"Gouache" (pronounced gwash) is a term used to describe a type of water-color painting in which the colors are opaque and opaque white is used for attaining lightness rather than allowing the paper to show through as in transparent water colors or washes. Ready-made paints in this category include poster colors, which come in jars, and tubed colors, such as in a designer's series. There are also assorted grays and whites, such as Chinese white, or, a favorite of mine, Johnston's Snow White. A good illustration board is the most practical paper for this type of paint, as it is for all washes that buckle thin paper. Gouache is not used extensively for newspaper work as it is more difficult for the engraver than the transparent washes done with Kromolite. Tempera and gouache are used more often for magazine illustrating and sometimes are added to a water-color painting. The fashion illustrator may use these mediums to add fine lines or highlights of white or light grays on a darker-toned ground. Brass buttons on a dark coat, for instance, could be accentuated with white highlights.

Different and unusual effects can be achieved by using opaque colors on toned papers. For example, black and white on gray paper could be done in India ink and opaque white, or with charcoal and white chalk on a rougher-surfaced paper.

Effects are achieved through experimenting and practice. Opaque colors are useful in finishing detail on various types of artwork and for making necessary corrections. There is, however, no special rule or method for working in this medium. Methods used in all the other media apply here, except that this technique can be done in a slower way, unlike transparent washes, which must be handled quickly. Corrections are also much easier to make.

THE LINE CUT

Black-and-white line drawings which have no actual gray tones can be reproduced as line cuts by photoengraving with a zinc etching. A photographic negative of the drawing is copied onto a light-sensitized zinc plate, which is then etched so that all white spaces fall away, leaving only the black lines. Errors can be cleaned up by the engraver on the plate itself. Since all lines have a tendency to thicken slightly in the process of printing, especially on a rough or inferior grade of paper, it is important that the artist keep all lines clean and open. If lines are scratchy and too close together they become clogged with ink on the plate and form a messy blot. Fine lines should be kept to a hair's breadth.

Although it would seem that reducing a drawing would refine it, if your drawing is very large and is to be reduced to half its size or more, it should have even more space between lines since they automatically run together in the white spaces. Large drawings must therefore be very open and the lines bold and definite to retain the original effect. If overworked with fine detail, the whole drawing can become grayed down and the lines clogged together.

Pencil drawings (regular lead pencil) will not reproduce satisfactorily in black and white. The tones are gray and the delicacy of their values can only be reproduced in halftone. Charcoal and graphite pencils and the like can be used for line cuts, however, providing tones are achieved through the roughness of a textured paper and not through smudging, which is a gray tone. Some of these more complicated types of drawing require special engraving methods.

Isadore Seltzer, courtesy of Stern Brothers

CURRENT MOOD ■ Contemporary design is successfully handled in this strong black-and-white illustration. The artist combined two patterns, the bold stripe and the dark screen of the transfer sheets, with contrasting large black and white areas. The appliquéd patterns are particularly compatible with the geometric forms and stylized figures used. There is a sense of fun and adventure, of trying the new, in this type of illustrating. It has the attention value of being unique in concept and bold in technique and design.

THE HALFTONE

Halftone etching is used to reproduce all gray tones, photographs included. The gray tones are actually tiny black and white dots that can be seen with a magnifying glass. The drawing or photograph is photographed through a screen, and the negative with its pattern of dots is transferred to a metal plate (usually copper). In principle it is the same as a line cut. These plates can also be made with a combination of line and halftone.

THE TRANSFER SHEET

A popular vogue in line drawing is the use of the transfer sheet. The idea was originally devised as a substitute for halftone drawings, because it simulated the screen effect of black and white dots.

Now available in assorted patterns and even lettering, the transfer sheet is being used for all kinds of decorative effects—Op art, Pop art, and occasionally Art Nouveau. The transparent sheets are rubbed to transfer the pattern like a decalcomania to a black-and-white drawing.

Another type of sheet can be cut to shape and appliquéd directly on the drawing. Produced under several trade names (Instantype is one), the sheets are available at art-supply shops.

Picking up the mood of fashion following current vogues in art, the transfer sheet adds a touch of humor with a decorative flair. The many dots, stripes, checks are fun to use and the snappy black-and-white look can be strikingly effective.

Antonio, courtesy of the *New York Times*

PATTERN ON PATTERN ■ Appliquéd sheets in polka-dot patterns were cleverly used for background and theme in these illustrations. There is a strong influence of both Op and Pop art phases. Brilliantly conceived and executed, the compositions are also fashion art at its best. The spirited figures suggest the modern tempo of spy dramas and fast action.

11. DEPICTING TEXTUR

PORTRAYING FABRICS

Surface texture may be illustrated either in exact detail or by mere suggestion. Styles of rendering are up to the individual and the type of job required. The fashion artist needs to experiment with brush and pen to produce desired effects. (See Chapter 10, "Finished Art.") The handling of the outline can often more clearly indicate the physical characteristics of varied materials than the over-all rendering. Where the style of a garment is more important than the fabric used, the contour and fit may suggest the type of material. The line itself (hard pen line or soft brush line) can indicate the surface texture.

...ND PATTERN

Whatever technique you use—wash, pen and ink, charcoal, or other—remember that it is better to suggest and interpret than to copy literally. Prints and plaids, for example, must be simplified in order to keep them open and clear when reduced to scale. The main objective is to project an impression that attracts the viewer's eye and stimulates interest in the fashion pictured.

It is not always necessary to portray fabric detail in a fashion drawing. For some jobs the style of the garment is sufficient. Where a more literal, realistic rendition of the merchandise is required, a few pointers on approaching the problem will be helpful.

CHECKS AND VELVET ▪ Deftly handled with black line and shading, this crayon drawing convincingly portrays the contrasts of black velvet and checked wool. The black of the velvet hat and collar is dense at the center and light at the edges—a characteristic of velvet. The woven checks are accurately depicted with solid black squares where the horizontals and verticals cross.

TEXTURED PATTERN ▪ A minimum of detail outlining the paisley pattern here suggests the woven design of a heavy brocade. The pattern fades off nicely toward the hem, avoiding an overworked look, which can dull the effect. Some areas were left white to create a feeling of light and airiness. To know when to stop and what to leave out in a drawing can often save it from being drab.

Kenneth Paul Block,
courtesy of Bonwit Teller

Surface patterns like checks, plaids, and prints can be worked out individually. There is such a great range of patterns and sizes of patterns that the artist must work out each one separately. The only general rule is to simplify as much as possible, to keep a clean-cut pattern with open lines, and to have the pattern handled lightly enough to be secondary to the outline. There are various ways of interpreting surface patterns, depending on the general technique used in the drawing. A plaid, for instance, might follow the curving lines of the body if the drawing were done from a model in a very realistic way. It might also be done in a flat manner, using all straight lines and letting the outline carry the form. A third alternative is to indicate pattern on only part of the garment, letting it fade off into white space. If done well, the latter can be charming, sometimes giving the effect of sunlight on one side of the figure.

Lace should be done with a delicate pen line and kept light as a cobweb. Scalloped edging is usually incorporated into the design of the dress and should be carefully indicated. The lace pattern should be suggested rather than drawn in detail. Keep a transparent look by contrasting skin and undershift and by indicating the shoulderlines and arms if there are long sleeves. Lace does not cling to the body but follows its direction with airy, delicate lines. Heavy types of lace take a heavier pen line and may give the effect of a raised surface. A very light wash may be used over the pen lines where the flesh shows through and a darker wash over the underneath shift if it is a dark lace. This accentuates the transparent look.

Velvet, because of the depth of the pile, has a denseness of color that absorbs rather than reflects light. It appears almost wholly dark, with

LACE ■ An open, loosely-handled wash and felt-pen line give the impression of lace in the double flounced skirt of this evening dress. The body-fitting camisole in black satin damask has been held dark in tone to give contrast between the dense and the filmy, sheer characteristics of each fabric.

The hand-painted fern detail makes this halter-top dress with matching stole unique. The felt-pen sketch dramatizes the effect with a direct simplicity and style.

Kenneth Paul Block,
courtesy *Women's Wear Daily*

Courtesy *Women's Wear Dai*

PRINTS AND PLAIDS ■ Surface pattern should be simplified so as to retain the garment outline and details of styling. There are many ways to interpret pattern. Plaids and stripes may be done flat or with lines following contours of the figure. The latter is difficult to do without a model. One can develop a personal approach with experimenting. Avoid overworking detail, especially if your drawing is to be reduced for reproduction in advertising. A light touch helps to produce a clean-cut drawing.

light only around the edges of the garment and where there are folds or edges as the velvet rounds or turns in. To do a wash drawing of velvet, it is best to work on a rather wet surface, using the darkest tone in the center and letting it fade out near the edges. Fine lines and detail can be added with opaque water color in a lighter tone, using a pen or fine brush. If the drawing is to be done in black and white (ink only), most of the garment should be solid black with detail in fine white lines, again with opaque color.

Satin is the reverse of velvet, reflecting light rather than absorbing it and having many light, medium, and dark tones. The darker tones are apt to be found at the edges and in the folds. Satin is probably the most difficult fabric to fake without seeing it on the model to get placing of the many contrasts of dark and light.

Tweeds may be done in either wash or line, or a combination of both. A dry-brush technique is effective for expressing texture in outlines. (See Chapter 10, p. 145, for dry-brush technique.) Tweeds come in such a variety of patterns and surfaces that it is impossible to set up rules for rendering, except that a flat tone without contrasts should be maintained by minimizing strong lights and shadows. In other words, tweeds have a dull surface that should be done in a fairly flat tone.

Robert Young,
courtesy *Women's Wear Daily*

THE BOLD PRINT ■ The strapless tunic is actually a large rectangle of cotton print from Kenya. It can be wrapped and tied in a variety of ways to serve as a skirt or cover-up at the beach. The primitive motif of the silk-screen print, done here with a jumbo-sized felt pen, dominates the story and creates the silhouette.

Croquis of cap —
in black vinyl

CONTRASTS OF TEXTURE ■ In these sketches for a fashion-show booklet the clean-cut black-and-white drawings portray the fabrics in a direct way. The long black skirt has the outline characteristic of stiff, heavy satin or silk. The shading, done with a wide felt-tip pen in bold, angular strokes, also defines the sharp, stiff folds of this type of fabric. The dotted net is simply stated with emphasis on the full, gathered fabric flaring out from the high yoke of the dress. The heavy black accents indicate the dark color and sheerness of the dress.

Ben Morris, courtesy of Du Pont

LINE DRAWINGS ■ The strapless, bias-pleated crepe georgette (1) is given close-clinging lines in contrast to the full boa and hemline of matching organdy petals. St. Laurent's sheer cape over a black satin dress (2) is trimmed with black and white ostrich feathers, skillfully interpreted, here, with quick lines suggesting both depth and airiness.

Kenneth Paul Block,
courtesy *Women's Wear Daily*, 1973

Jerry Schofield, courtesy of Lord & Taylor

THE KNIT DRESS ▪ Knits of wool, cotton, linen, or acrylic yarns may look like woven fabric. This realistic wash-and-line drawing manages to illustrate both pattern of design and surface texture successfully. The black pattern and the edging are done with a strong pen line. Shadows and texture are rendered with sharply defined grays in transparent water color. Note that the main area of the garment is light, with simplified shadows kept to one side to delineate form and dimension. The modeling of face and figure are consistent in this respect. The sparkling wash technique projects the freshness of bright sunlight.

Shiny surfaces, on the other hand, must have plenty of white spaces with sharp contrasts of darks. Materials like black patent or vinyl may be done without middle tones. Also, accentuate reflected light by leaving light space, not shadows, at the outer edges. Sequins or metallic materials must also have lots of broken-up sharp darks and highlights.

FURS

Furs in earlier years used to be limited to types recognizable as mink, nutria, broadtail, and a few others. In the inexpensive furs, especially those that tried—and failed—to look like mink, styles could be described only as dowdy. Even in the expensive furs, styling was often secondary to the quality of the pelts. The fashion artist, in order to dramatize the best features, was expected to portray the fur in a very exact and literal way. A good drawing with beautiful washes had a rich quality and the furs were instantly recognizable. Badly handled, this approach could be stodgy and give an overworked, dull illustration.

With the swing to "with-it" fashions for the young and budget-minded, furs had to change. A new look with more excitement developed in small-priced furs. All kinds of pelts were styled differently, clipped or stenciled beyond identification with any known animal. Termed "fun furs," the inexpensive ones acquired a new chic. Long-haired furs like fox and lynx, formerly used for small wraps and trim, were now made into bulky, luxury-look coats. To appear dressed for a Moscow winter, complete with fur hat and boots, suddenly became fashionable. For cold weather anywhere it was practical, cozy, and chic.

CASUAL SWEATERS ■ Sharp-focus accents of gray and black, along with suntanned skin tones, make these white sweaters stand out on a newspaper page. The wash technique gives a realistic interpretation of surface pattern and texture with exactness of detail. Enough clear white spaces are left to maintain a feeling of light and color. With almost no outlines, the shading and gray areas create the shapes. The lively settings and casual mood stimulate interest in the merchandise.

Detail blow-up.

Dorothy Hood, courtesy of Lord & Taylor

AT-HOME ALLURE ■ Tunics of silk crepe de chine, a long one over pants, a shorter version over a long slit skirt. Gathered and tied at the shoulders, with armholes plunging to the sashed waist, the lines are soft and body-clinging. The pale wash, here, was used sparingly. Varying black-to-gray lines, done with a felt pen, suggest the soft silky texture.

Kenneth Paul Block,
courtesy *Women's Wear Daily*

The Enchanters

MORE FEATHERS ▪ Swansdown and short, curly ostrich with the old movie-star glamour still make the scene here and there. These bedroom fancies have a realistic appeal, begun with a light wash tone over the entire garment. Added shadows give depth. The fine gray brush strokes, used sparingly, suggest the texture of feathers. This type of drawing is impossible to fake and must be done from a model. Facility with the wash technique depends on a quick and sure brush stroke, which is developed only with practice.

Dorothy Hood,
courtesy of Lord & Taylor

Kenneth Paul Block,
courtesy of Bonwit Teller

THE FLAT FURS ■ Leopard, ocelot, and other pelts with a pattern should be kept mostly white with a minimum of shading. The contour lines of the coat are emphasized by the direction and irregularities of the sharply defined pattern of the dark spots.

MINK ■ Dark mink, finely pieced in evening style, is sketched here with strong blacks in a Conte crayon. Shining highlights are the white charcoal paper showing through. The fur gains richness and depth from the strategically placed dense blacks. The aspect of mink is indicated with a thin line between each pelt and a thick, smudgy line simulating the full stripe of the pelt. To maintain an impression of the lush softness of fur, avoid a mechanical rendering. The only way to achieve a realistic image of the fur and the styling is to work from a model posing in the garment.

DENSITY OF BLACK ■ Both the evening blouse of sable and the dark, velvety seal, made up in a casually belted coat, have very dense black areas. The seal coat gains richness and luster through the brightly lighted areas and the reflected light of the edges. The piles of velvet and seal reflect light in exactly the same manner. The heavy black of the seal coat is relieved by the leopard hat, which adds a note of chic and an interesting ornamental pattern to the illustration. In rendering furs or fabrics with pile, remember to keep the darks very dark. Halfhearted grays fail to express depth and richness.

Kenneth Paul Block,
courtesy of Bonwit Teller

175

THE FLAT LOOK OF BROADTAIL

■ The moiré pattern of broadtail is more evident in the sleek black coat. The lighter broadtail dress has an understated air of luxury, subtly illustrated with a flat wash. The dark accents and a minimum of moiré pattern retain the illusion of lighter color. Broadtail—a dressy, elegant fur—has been duplicated in appearance by so-called "processed lamb," which has less sheen. In a drawing, however, the rendering would be the same.

Fashion points of this well-planned illustration are worth noting: The black coat, for example, is shown to advantage over a white dress; the open V of white breaks up an otherwise heavy area of black. The pose also adds a casual look of assurance. The hair styles are suitably chic and restrained.

To illustrate fur fashions, then, let us think first of effect, without being tediously absorbed with the detail of hairs and overworked shading. One should have the actual furs to look at for sketching, preferably on a live model. The general characteristics of outline (bulkiness or slimness, fit, styling, etc.), are of first importance. Next should be indicated color—light or dark—and surface pattern, if any (leopard or stenciled giraffe, for example).

Soft, fluffy furs in a light color like lynx should be sketched with delicate lines. If done in pen and ink, use a fine-pointed pen and leave plenty of white, airy spaces. Dry-brush techniques should also merely suggest the fur. In wash or charcoal, only accents or shadows should have gray tones. Darker furs like sable or natural

Kenneth Paul Block,
courtesy of Bonwit Teller

THE OPULENT LOOK ▪ The bulky, fuller, rounded pelts can be indicated roughly as if they were enlarged mink. Sable, one of the most luxurious and expensive of all furs, has skins that are bigger and fuller than mink, and the look is softer, almost fluffy. But the same striping with wider spacing may be used. Other furs similar in silhouette and size of pelts and fashioned in stripes are fisher and marten. Opossum differs in color and texture, having a fuzzy surface and smoky-colored stripe, which is best portrayed with a smudged line.

Kenneth Paul Block,
courtesy of Bonwit Teller

mink need very deep darks to show depth, fading or blending gradually into light edges. If done in wash, considerable practice is needed to achieve the right effect.

To depict furs properly, it is necessary to learn to identify the various types, then practice rendering the fur in whatever medium is to be used: ink, wash, charcoal, or a combination of these.

BULKY LYNX ■ This long-haired fur with spotted pattern is best indicated with a mostly white background. Shading for depth should be kept fairly light in tone. The dark spots should not be flat-surfaced, as in leopard, but should be done with softened strokes to suggest the hairs. Sketches should be made from the actual garment. The overall pattern in this drawing is relieved by the flat gray tones of the hood and gloves. This fur is equally convincing done in just pen and ink if handled with a light touch.

Kenneth Paul Block, courtesy of Bonwit Teller

12.
FASHION
ACCESSORIES

ACCESSORIES

Always an important part of fashion, accessories include everything that cannot be termed a garment. The list is vast and the field open for good illustration in either realistic or decorative styles, depending on the type of job required. Whatever the approach, the drawing must sell the wares. There is always fashion news in jewelry (especially the costume variety), handbags, belts, shoes, boots, and hosiery. It is useless to make a long list of items in this category. With the exception of shoes, if you can draw one you can draw any of them.

Armed

DRAMATIC EFFECT ▪ Simplicity of design is the key. The mood and technique of Art Deco illustration again provide an eye-catching display, this time for jewelry trends of the mid-seventies. The strong black accents are emphasized by the contrast of finely drawn outlines of the figure on the large white background.

Pedro Barrios,
courtesy *Women's Wear Daily*, 1973

Shoes are a rather specialized area within this field. In addition to correct lines and construction, the artist must add a bit of style by emphasizing certain lines to achieve a look of chic and fashion news. The manufacturer or the shoe buyer in a store may have definite ideas about portraying shoe styles. It is necessary to follow fashion changes and to get the new look for buyer-appeal.

Along with handbags, gloves, and hosiery, which are volume items, the accessory artist may be given gift-shop items to do. So many objects come under this heading that the artist must have great facility in drawing and a knowledge of perspective. He should also be good at detail and have a clean-cut line and technique of rendering. If he also has a sense of good layout and feeling for design, he can attain a very high level in advertising or magazine work. A successful illustration of accessories should have a fresh, zingy look to attract the eye. Sharp accents of black and a pleasing over-all pattern can be accomplished through a well-planned layout.

Although headgear is a fashion accessory, it is usually done by the fashion artist because it involves drawing the head with the same style and flair as the figure in an ad. Gloves on the hand may or may not be done by the fashion artist. Any item sketched on the figure, or just the head, is usually assigned to the artist who specializes in the figure.

For the artist who enjoys fine detail, real jewelry is a specialty that demands careful drawing. Costume jewelry has a wider range and is found in volume in advertising. For inspiration in illustrating jewelry, start a file of clippings of ads you consider well-done or novel. Include magazine or newspaper examples of especially interesting techniques and layouts done by artists in the field. Observe and analyze what makes them clean-cut and outstanding.

The difference between a dull interpretation and one with flair makes the game exciting. Accessories can be a challenge to the competent and inventive artist.

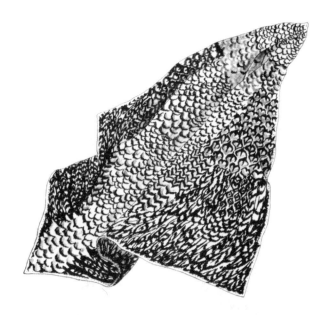

THE FLOATING ACCESSORY ▪ For this gift item to be ordered by mail or telephone from Henri Bendel, an accurate drawing was essential here. The seemingly careless arrangement shows the scarf to advantage without a figure. The folds are nicely drawn, and the fine detail of the print is indicated with professional exactness in clean pen-and-ink with gray wash tones. This type of drawing is best done large with a good separation between dark and light tones for clean reproduction in a smaller size.

Matt look of shag + capeskin (quilted at left.)

Striped cotton velveteen

Glen Tunstull,
courtesy *Women's Wear Daily*

SCARF NOTE ■ Curly lettuce edging adds frill to a breezy, six-foot long scarf of filmy georgette in an abstract print. It wraps the neck and is fastened with a matching flower pin. The mottled pattern of gray washtones suggests a play of evening lights and shadows across the rather sultry face.

Mock lizard portfolio

Courtesy of Henri Bendel

The Reptiles

Alligator — the finest from Madagascar.

Fine snakeskin in silver or gold for evening, a small scale envelope on a chain.

HANDBAGS ■ Meticulous detail here is beautifully handled in wash with pen-and-ink lines. Reduced in reproduction, these drawings maintained their sharp detail. Note the exactness of the reptile patterns and the textures of the velveteen and chenille. There are no tricks or short cuts to this type of art, just good draftsmanship developed from careful observation and accurate drawing. To retain clean, clear lines, some artists make preliminary pencil drawings, which are then transferred by tracing onto a clean illustration board. This eliminates erasures and messy corrections.

Knitted velvety chenille

Wave Lengths

Pedro Barrios and Steven Meisel,
courtesy *Women's Wear Daily*

SIMPLIFIED LINE AND FORM ▪ Figures and background spacing form a bold, well-designed composition of black and white and gray pattern. The cruise-wear figure suggests summer, and the soft belt bags look right with the knit dress in thin pen line.

Start by sketching whatever you have at home that would make an interesting drawing — a printed scarf, a compact, costume jewelry, handbag, hosiery, an umbrella, or anything that you find a challenge. Use a sharpened 2H or HB pencil and sketch in a careful, detailed way. Arrange the scarf so that it makes an interesting shape, and sketch the folds quite literally, putting in exact details of the pattern. Keep your lines clean and definite.

After you have made a number of pencil *croquis*, take a large pad of tracing paper and arrange the items in a pleasing layout. If your sketches do not fall into a satisfactory design, try doing a few thumbnail sketches of other arrangements for improved composition. Now sketch the items again to fit the new plan. Your drawing should have a swing and direction of line throughout, and the whole should be a related and harmonious composition of the various items.

Next, try working out your plan on a larger scale on the tracing paper. Plan your arrangement of dark and light areas to accomplish a definite pattern. Make those dark accents sing out, and let the white spaces give air and breathing room. *Remember contrast.* (See Chapter 13, "Design and Layout.")

Once you have achieved a composition that pleases you, trace the pencil sketch onto a good illustration board and make a finished drawing in pen and India ink, or add gray tones if you wish to make it a wash drawing. (See Chapter 10 on "Finished Art.") You may decide on either a realistic or decorative style. Whichever you choose, be definite and consistent throughout.

SHOES

Depending on the layout, shoes may or may not be illustrated on the foot. Either way, the same lines are right or wrong. A few basic rules can assist the artist to get an element of good drawing into a shoe illustration. To get style and flair,

OUTLINE DRAWINGS ▪ Jewelry in scale is designated here by suggesting a head or an ear for proportion. The few lines dramatize the jewelry and indicate the way each piece should be worn. The simplicity of line tells a fashion news story of design, disregarding realistic textures of the material used. The drawing stands out through economy of line, suggesting much without defining it.

FASHION NEWS ▪ A look that says "now," the contemporary presentation of seashell-clasped choker and earrings reveals a lively imagination. The artful arrangement within a circle, combining bold stripes and a small photograph, makes a strikingly handsome design. The strong black outlines complete the effective use of simple black and white.

Antonio, courtesy of *The New York Times*

Courtesy of *Women's Wear Daily*

COSTUME JEWELRY ■ These wash drawings, accurate renditions of spectacular fakes, combine pen-and-ink and opaque whites for fine detail and sparkle. Part of a full-page newspaper ad, they were done actual size on a medium-surfaced handmade water-color board. The head is in washes only and pen lines are used only to accent jewelry detail.

This is
Carnegie vermeil—
the precious new look
in jeweling

Yuskowski, courtesy of Lord & Taylor

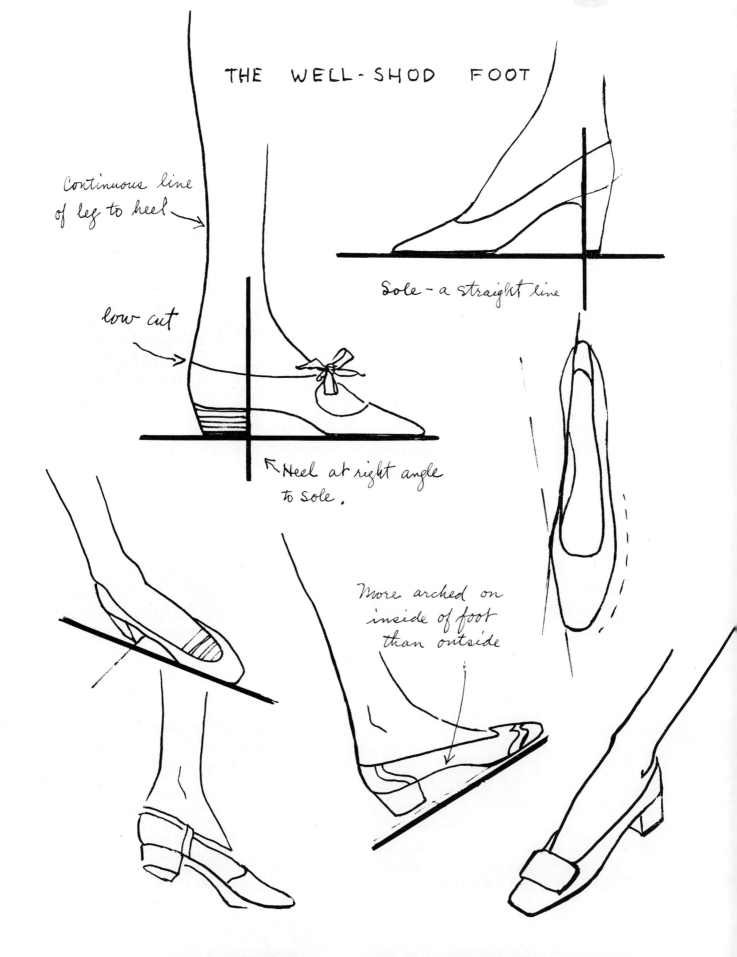

THE WELL-SHOD FOOT

Continuous line of leg to heel

low cut

Sole - a straight line

Heel at right angle to sole.

More arched on inside of foot than outside

SHOE GUIDELINES ■ Keep construction lines definite, such as the heel set at right angles to the sole, a decided curve to the arch, and the heel and sole lined up flat with the floor. All lines, curved or straight, must be clean and crisp (no turned up toes or soles that curl). Uppers should look pliable but not worn or shapeless. The heel, side view, is indicated with a continuous, unbroken line from the leg down to the lift touching the floor.

however, requires a knack and feeling for quality. To achieve a soft look without having the shoe appear worn and out of shape, to have it look new and trim but not stiff, these are accomplishments of value. Perfection must be faked for effect and flattery in a drawing. Listed are a few do's and dont's to use as guides in drawing shoes.

DO:

1. Line up the sole and heel with straight lines on the arched side of the shoe. These lines are merely a guide, done in pencil, to be eliminated in the finished sketch.

2. Indicate the outer line of the sole with a curved line in a down view, as illustrated on opposite page.

3. Have the heel properly balanced by sketching the inside line at right angles to the sole near the arch. (See side-view illustration on page 188.) In profile, the outside line varies with heel height and changing fashion.

4. Have a continuous line (also in profile) running up from the sole and curving into the back of the heel.

5. Give the shoe a well-defined arch.

6. Keep the top line of the shoe low-cut at the back of the heel. This feature is usually found in more expensive shoes. It gives a dainty look to the shoe and the ankle.

DON'T:

1. Have a sole that looks warped, with a turned-up toe. A well-made shoe has a sole flat to the ground all the way to the toe.

2. Draw a bulging curve at the back of the shoe, as if the wearer's heel jutted out beyond the ankle line. The line should be a gentle curve from the line of the leg to the heel of the shoe. See side-view illustration on opposite page.

Whatever the special features happen to be in a shoe, be sure to emphasize them. If it is a lightweight, delicate shoe, keep the sole thin and give the outline a look of slimness. Be accurate about

Susan Abbott, courtesy of Lord & Taylor

PALE SHOES FOCUSED ON BLACK ■ The black area of the head, centered in the large white background, acts as a target focusing attention on the shoes. All black and gray areas in this case are cut-outs. Dull-finish coated papers in black and light gray were used. The shoes, meticulously cut out in silhouette, were pasted on last. A minimum of detail was added in pen and ink. The decorative style gains a striking effect through simplicity of pattern and the large area of open white space surrounding the focal point.

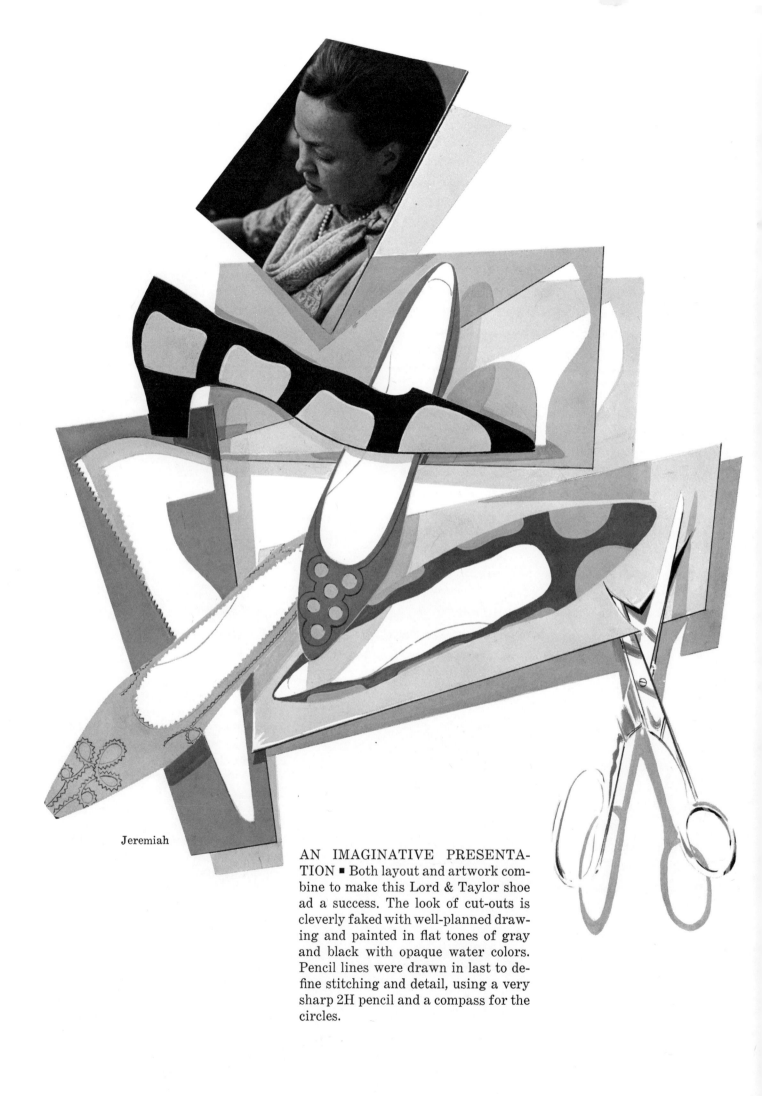

Jeremiah

AN IMAGINATIVE PRESENTA-
TION ▪ Both layout and artwork combine to make this Lord & Taylor shoe
ad a success. The look of cut-outs is
cleverly faked with well-planned drawing and painted in flat tones of gray
and black with opaque water colors.
Pencil lines were drawn in last to define stitching and detail, using a very
sharp 2H pencil and a compass for the
circles.

Worldly ways

Pedro Barrios,
courtesy *Women's Wear Daily*

HARMONY OF STYLE ▪ The flavoring of off-
beat accessories adds individuality to a basic dress.
The bicycle belt-bag, bold bangles of wicker and
sterling chain at the neckline complete the looks.
The purely decorative composition of the figures
and the geometric shapes outlined in fine, even pen-
line sustain the simplicity of the Art Deco period
at its purest.

How many ways to watch the world go by? *Come* to the Sand Bar and see!

Lord & Taylor

Our gala little shop
of beach accessories has
just opened for the season
with spectacular
collections of, say,
sun glasses, 5.00 to 20.00
—as well as beach hats and bags,
towel things, games, whims and so on—
**and the whole Sand Bar itself
is now part of our
brand new and
enormously exciting
Discovery Shop**
Street Floor,
Lord & Taylor
Fifth Avenue
at 39th Street
Sand Bar collections,
also at our
eight suburban stores

ESSENTIAL HEADGEAR FOR THE SUN ■ No longer merely protection, sun glasses have become a big fashion item. Worn up on the head to hold the hair in place or as a flattering mask for the eyes in or out of the sun, they are a decorative accessory. It is part of today's look of chic. Lord & Taylor artist Dorothy Hood has illustrated a wardrobe of "shades" with summery atmosphere sketches. The strong contrast of light and shadow done in clean, sharply defined wash adds realism and a look of strong sun and healthy tans.

THE FUR HAT ▪ The fur is obviously mink, and the style could be ordered by mail (a most attractive idea for the shopper who hates to shop). Dorothy Hood swings to a winter mood in these wash drawings from another Lord & Taylor ad. The deft handling of water color to get fur texture and pale tones takes much experimenting and practice. First drawn in pencil from a model, the faint outlines are filled in with wash tones, darks first. All grays and blacks are water color and brush strokes. Fine brush strokes indicating a few hairs of the fur are added in opaque white.

details such as type of heel (stacked, block, Louis) or shape of toe (square, round, oval).

Boots should follow the same rules for neat lines, except for a soft look at the ankleline, where they usually fall into easy folds to allow freedom of action. Fine leather has a supple quality that should be accentuated here.

Again, there is a choice of realistic drawing or a decorative style of illustrating. If your choice is a decorative interpretation, avoid emphasis on highlights and shadows, which give a third-dimensional effect, and indicate textures (leather or fabric) in flat tones.

EXERCISE:

Try making pencil sketches of a shoe from various angles: a down view, side view, and so on. If possible, have a new shoe; one that has been worn has usually lost its crispness of line. It is good practice to try the many textures available, such as patent leather, alligator, grained leathers, and the various fabrics used in shoe designs. Do a finished drawing in a combination of pen and ink and wash. (See Chapter 10, "Finished Art.")

HEADGEAR

The term "millinery" excludes so many items that are sketched on the fashion head that it is simpler to group them all under the one heading —"headgear." The casual look has promoted all types of substitutes for the hat.

In the past, no big-city daytime costume was complete without a hat. Sad as the fact may be for those in the millinery business, hatlessness today has become acceptable almost everywhere. The fashionable head can hardly be described as simple and unadorned, however. As hair styles became more complicated, they took over a large part of the job of adding to feminine beauty, and few women wished to lose a costly professional hair setting by flattening it out with a tight-fitting concoction of heavy straw or felt. To cope with this situation, millinery designers had to change their old ideas of a hat. They consequently came up with all kinds of clever ideas to protect the hair. Wind-defying fluffs of berets and turbans were made from lightweight silk prints or organza. Waterproof materials were used for fun hats to keep out the rougher elements of rain and fog. For winter warmth and flattery all kinds of fur hats and chic head coverings appeared. For summer sun, gay and colorful brimmed hats for city or beach wear appeared, some crushable for packing and travel.

To the new hair styles were added various kinds of hair pieces. Along with wigs and wiglets made of real hair, there were the obviously fake braids, chignons, and falls made of nylon. Hat bars in millinery departments added sections for selling these bits of flattery, with trained experts to style them and match individual hair color. "If you can't beat them, join them" seemed to be the idea. The fashion trend was younger, more casual, and much less serious than in the past.

For the fashion artist, flair is the first objective in illustrating headgear. As long as a drawing is a good "fashion head," the rest is a matter of portraying the merchandise in a way to stimulate interest. The head should be well-con-

THE CITY HAT ■ From *Vogue* pages, circa 1960, these casual drawings by René Bouché still have flair and style. Combined charcoal and felt-tip pen line were used to sketch directly from the model. The relaxed poses and the neat head, with little or no hair visible, project a chic type of well-groomed woman. The gesture of a hand directs the eye to the head and makes a pleasing line on the page. Drawn large, the heads have a look of authenticity and the faces an expression of unaffected assurance.

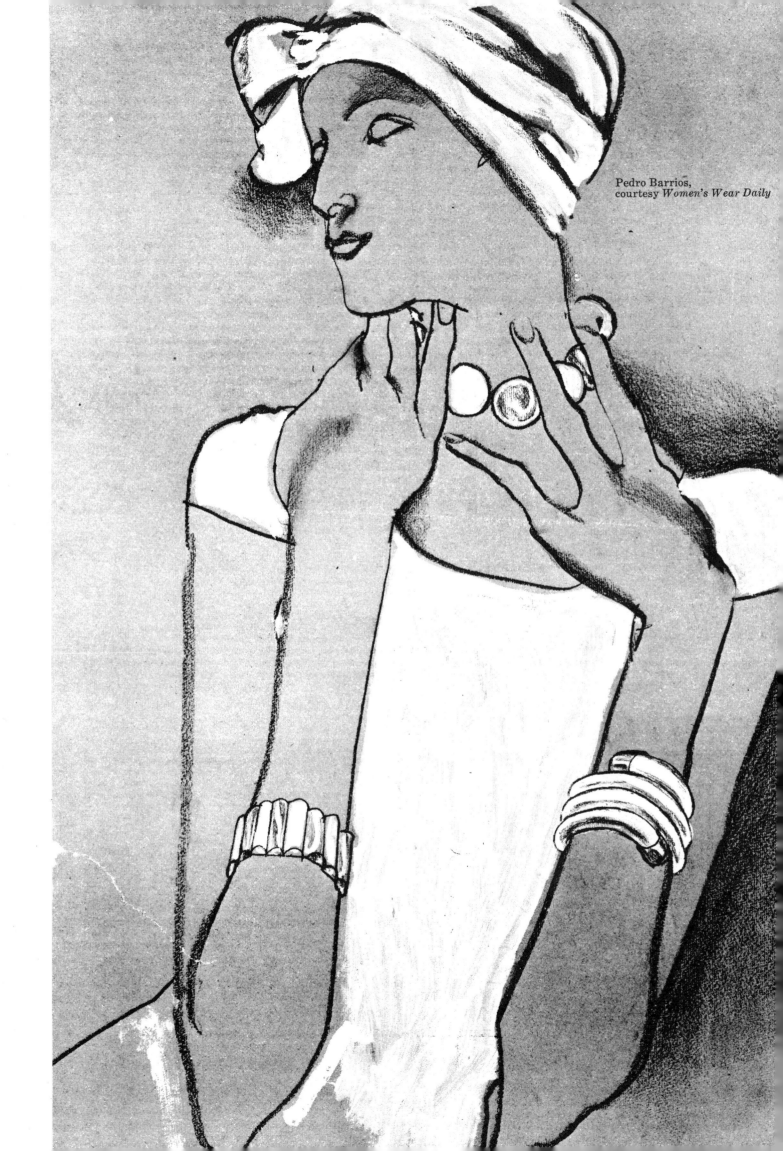

Pedro Barrios,
courtesy *Women's Wear Daily*

BRIMMED HATS ∎ As a guide to
drawing the hat in relation to the head,
think of the hatband first as a line cir-
cling the head. All other lines simply
determine style. Shapes have softened
and classic simplicity is the trend. For
summer shade or winter warmth,
functional design dominates the scene.
Most are pulled down on the head in a
casual, independent style.

structed, and the hat, scarf, beret, turban, or whatever, should fit the head and follow the lines of construction.

Headgear, whether functional or purely decorative, is an accessory which completes a particular image. Scarves or turbans may add to either a casual or an exotic effect. Brimmed hats are as varied in type as in shape and proportions. Some are compatible with the tailored classics; others team well with country tweeds. Simple rustic straws suggest dirndl skirts and many types of resort wear.

EXERCISE:

First, refer to Chapter 5, "Drawing the Fashion Figure," and review the rules for the construction and proportion of the head. Practice drawing heads and hair styles—from a live model, if possible. Draw large and put in as many guidelines as you wish at first to get a feeling of roundness.

Next, try a hat on the model. If no hats are available, use a scarf and try tying it different ways to show flair and style. Sketch the hat or scarf as if you could see through it and the head, the lines following the curve of the skull. Follow diagram illustrated on pages 196–197, using guidelines for drawing. The more sketching you do, the better. The head is the most difficult subject of all to draw well and with character.

Once construction becomes automatic in your drawing, start eliminating superfluous lines. Observe and simplify. Put down a direct line indicating the dominant characteristic of the hat style, the one that expresses the fashion silhouette. Try sketching the head from different angles (front, side, three-quarter view, and down views). Work directly on illustration board or Strathmore paper with pen or brush and India ink, or practice on tracing paper with ink instead of pencil.

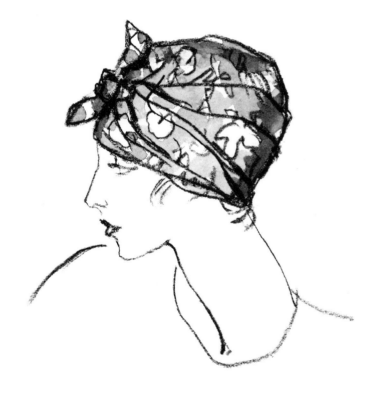

13. DESIGN ANI

To study art in any of its specialized fields without learning the fundamental principles of design is to ignore the true foundation of all good art. In fashion these rules are important not only to the designer who creates a style but to the illustrator who creates a picture. The picture should also be a part of the layout and planned on the same principles. It therefore seems essential to include here a few notes on design and its application to illustration and layout.

Do not confuse design with decoration. Design is the planned pattern of the whole subject. Decoration is a repetition of form for ornamentation and only a part of the total design. For example, polka dots of equal size repeated on a plain background form a surface pattern of decoration

LAYOUT

but do not create a design.

Design, in its broadest meaning, is a plan for order which is essential in all forms of creativity. It can also be interpreted as the cornerstone of all constructive and intelligent living. In visual design, as in every plan, the same elements of balance, unity, harmony, and contrast exist. Otherwise, there is only chaos or confusion. The principle of contrast is first in importance. Camouflage confuses the eye; contrast directs the eye through effects created by the artist. It is contrast that attracts the eye in advertising and stimulates interest in all the visual arts. It is the means of avoiding monotony by clever use of one or all of the other elements of design. These elements might be listed as:

This superb example of contemporary art by Antonio appeared in *The New York Times* (1966) illustrating fashion reportage. Reminiscent of a Fernand Léger painting, it is notably successful in composition. The repetition of circular forms and the poses of the figures carry the eye through a pleasingly rhythmic design. The original artwork, measuring 40″ x 24″, was done in pen line with appliquéd transfer sheets in varied tones of gray, each stripe and mass of tone carefully cut out and put together like a puzzle. Figures were first sketched realistically from actual merchandise on the model, then transposed into the carefully planned design.
Courtesy of *The New York Times*

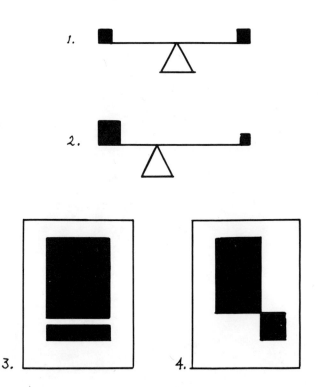

1. Balance: symmetrical (formal) and asymmetrical (informal).
2. Harmony (of): line, form (shape), proportion (of space or mass), and color.
3. Unity (unified whole): accent (emphasis on a single point of interest).
4. Rhythm (movement of line or form repeated).
5. Contrast (of): color (value or intensity), line (direction or weight), form (shape or mass), and proportion (scale).

FUNDAMENTALS OF DESIGN

BALANCE may be said to be a control over variety. Without a plan of dominant color or form, the result is confusion and monotony. Symmetrical or formal balance is the arrangement of identical parts on either side of an imaginary center dividing line. The parts are exactly equal in size, shape, and relative position. This formal or static balance suggests a quiet dignity, stateliness, or restfulness. In grouping furniture or decoration in a room, for example, a pair of lamps or a pair of chairs placed at either end of a sofa in identical positions would be a formal arrangement.

Asymmetrical balance is an informal arrangement that produces a dynamic rather than static composition. Through artful arrangement of unequal sizes and shapes, the forms or spaces have the optical illusion of equally distributed weight. The principle is the same as that of actual weights; i.e., equal weights balance at equal distances from a middle axis, unequal weights must be placed at different distances from the axis in order to balance. The imaginary axis in a picture or composition is at the center point of vision. There is a vertical axis and a horizontal axis. The vertical is visually dominant and unchangeable; the horizontal axis is secondary and therefore can be varied in position. The horizon line in a landscape, for instance, could be near the top of a drawing or well below center, thus

Visual balance is established on the same principle as balance of weight. Symmetrical balance (1) is the equal distribution of forms of equal size. Asymmetrical balance (2) is achieved through counterbalance of forms of unequal size.

Balance of forms in a planned design employs the same principle. A formal balance (symmetrical) is the arrangement of identical shapes repeated in the same position on either side of an imaginary center line (3). Asymmetrical, or informal, balance distributes forms of varied size (weight) to please the eye with an appearance of balance.

creating an unequal division of space more pleasing to the eye than if it divided the upper and lower halves equally. The center point of vision, however, would always be near the vertical axis. (See illustrations on symmetrical and asymmetrical balance on page 202.)

These principles should be used as a guide for checking your own work or that of other artists if a composition or drawing seems awkward or out of balance. They are not to be copied or followed slavishly. They should only give you a basis for viewing with a critical eye. To know how to criticize, not what, is one of the biggest steps towards self-improvement.

HARMONY in the visual arts pleases the eye as harmony in music pleases the ear. Lines and forms can complement each other or be discordant and disturbing. Identical forms have an affinity for each other in forming a pattern; i.e., a circle for another circle, a rectangle for a square, and so on. To be harmonious, an allover design should have a pleasing flow or continuity. This does not imply simple repetition; there must also be variety of proportion in color and form. One element should dominate to make a definite statement.

UNITY is the essential element of all good design. There must be a visual focal point, that necessary accent that attracts the eye. This is only possible if all other parts of a composition complement or become secondary to the main point, thus creating a unified whole. If there is more than one point of equal interest, the eye is distracted and confused and the picture or layout is a disjointed collection of parts adding up to nothing. It has no climax, so we are left in midair. To tie any design together, then, it becomes necessary to have a definite plan. Limit yourself to a dominant form or color and make all other parts secondary to it to create a unified whole.

RHYTHM in nature is evident in the cycles of the tides and changes of season. In music and in art it has two elements: repetition (suspense)

SYMMETRICAL DESIGN ▪ In the approach to fine art, the principles of good design are a basis for the best, and much can be learned from observing and analyzing the ingredients. This rough copy of a Matisse drawing, though symmetrical in plan, avoids a mechanical exactness of line.

ASYMMETRICAL BALANCE ▪ This rough copy of a Matisse still life might be described as "out of drawing," since the artist ignored accuracy and employed distortion for the sake of design. The flowing, off-center lines of the vase and the S curves of the flower stems express a style of lyric gaiety. The one straight line with dark blossomed top adds a staccato note (emphasis) to the composition, and the continuity of line achieves harmony in the design.

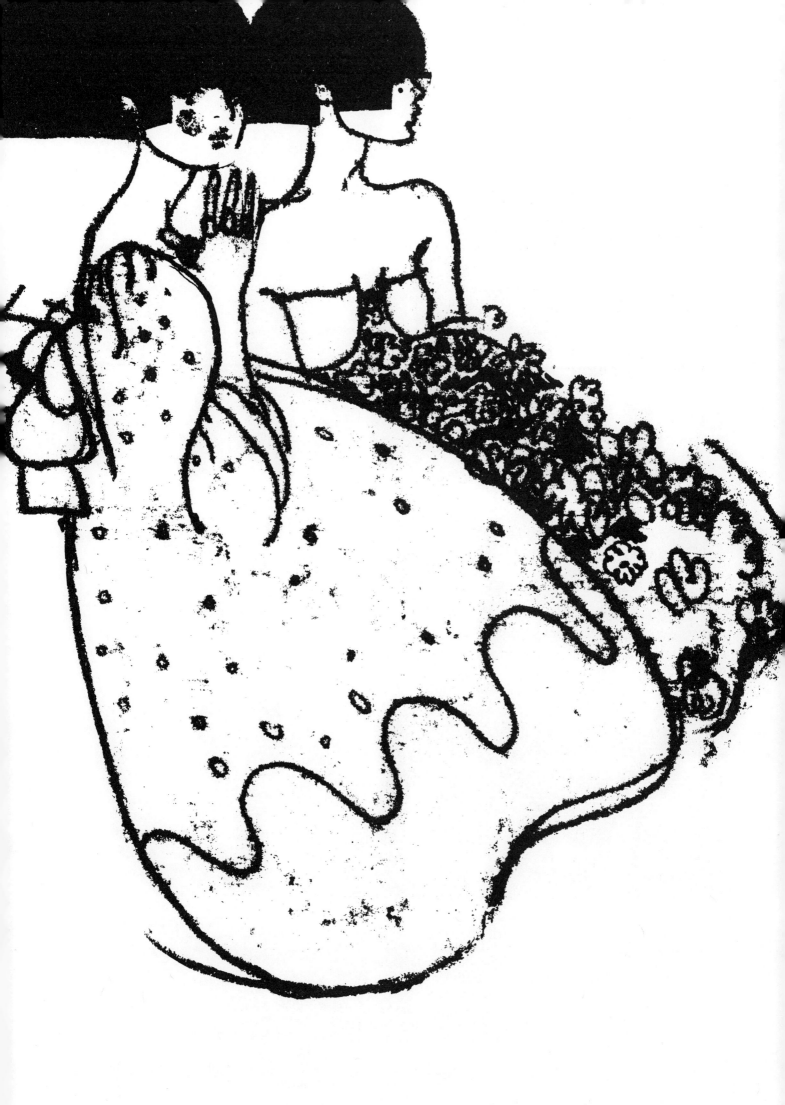

From *Young Flair*

HARMONY OF LINE AND FORM ▪ The predominant curving
lines and rounded forms have an affinity that produces harmony
of design in these two stylized illustrations by Anne-Marie
Barden. A fine sense of over-all pattern and consistency of style
give the compositions authority. The artist's personal technique
and the whimsical doll faces have an individuality that commands attention.

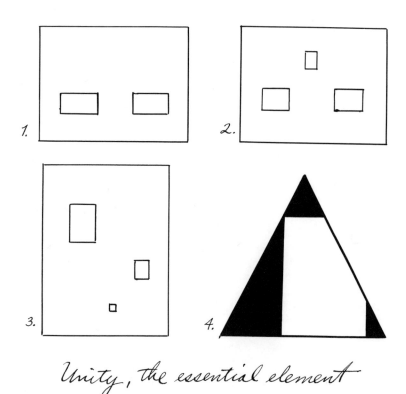

Unity, the essential element

(1) LACK OF UNITY ■ Forms of equal size brought together lack unity, having no point of interest.
(2) UNITY ACHIEVED ■ Forms varied in size gain unity through dominance of the largest form.

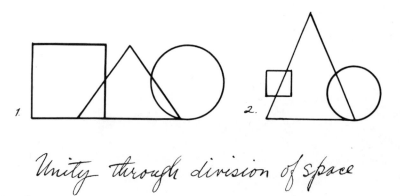

Unity through division of space

(1) Two units of equal size placed side by side are static and uninteresting. The composition is visually divided in the middle.
(2) A triangle is formed by the addition of a third unit, which groups the pieces and brings the eye to a point of interest.
(3) A progression of forms, varied in size, produces unity through a visual line of transition.
(4) Unity is gained through unequal division of space and contrast of size by producing one dominant form or focal point.

and climax (emphasis). In picture form, rhythm creates continuity and movement by an easy flow of form and line that carries the eye to the point of interest (emphasis). In ornamental pattern, repetition of form is also more interesting with the addition of the second element than with repetition alone. Climax is the accent of a drumbeat. Without that accent there is no rhythm, only monotonous repetition of sound.

CONTRAST is necessary to bring out all the other aspects of design. Color, line, form, and proportion all need contrast for expression. Color needs contrasts in value or intensity. Equal amounts of black and white, for example, do not register anything other than a divided whole. A small square of black against stark white stands out like a beacon light when the whole is surrounded by grays, as does a bright color surrounded by neutrals. It is by means of contrast that attention is riveted to the point of interest.

Lines may also direct the eye, flowing or moving dynamically towards a climax. Lines of varied weight and character may express contrasts of texture, even concepts of mood. (See illustrations on page 208.) A horizontal line expresses restfulness and tranquility; the vertical line is climbing, reaching, inspirational, as in the architectural lines of a Gothic cathedral. Curving lines are more lyric, suggesting beauty found in nature. Oblique or diagonal lines are chaotic, create excitement, suggest action. All can be used for contrasts.

Forms should vary in size as masses of color or of dark and light. As shapes alone there is contrast in a circle against a square shape, but one should dominate through size or repetition. Any form on a contrasting background creates a new background, which should become an interesting shape itself. (See illustration on page 208.) A background shape therefore is of equal importance in good design to the object illustrated.

Proportion and scale, the bases of classical Greek architecture, are also elements of contrast. Spaces and forms divided into unequal proportions are easier for the eye to accept than equal division of space and form.

THE IMPORTANCE OF LAYOUT

Most fashion illustrating for advertising follows a planned arrangement in the form of a layout. This is usually a rough sketch of the page as it will appear as an ad, with headings and copy space indicated along with suggested illustrations. It should be a well-balanced arrangement of pictures and words following the principles of good design. Its objective is to attract attention and to stimulate desire for the item being sold.

Since layout concerns the artist who does any form of advertising illustration, he should have some knowledge of its relation to his work and of the aesthetic principles of design involved. A poor layout with ill-chosen type detracts from a good drawing, but a good layout can enhance even a mediocre piece of artwork. It is up to the artist to do the best with whatever layout he must follow. At times he may be required to do his own layout, in which case a knowledge of visual presentation in advertising is an asset. As an alternative to illustration, the artist may even decide to switch to layout work as his specialized line.

The basic principles of design are evident in all concepts of good layout. Each should be a well-balanced unit of areas of illustration and copy. It should have a single point of interest, either headline or picture, which tells the story with clarity and impact. If a drawing or layout is divided in equal halves, the result is confusing and lacks unity. Equal amounts of space allotted to copy and illustration have the same lack of contrast as equal amounts of light and dark areas in an illustration. Whether the arrangement is symmetrical or asymmetrical, unequal spacing and areas of dark and light are more pleasing to the eye. In a layout, the areas of light, being white spaces or background areas, are of great importance to the over-all appearance of

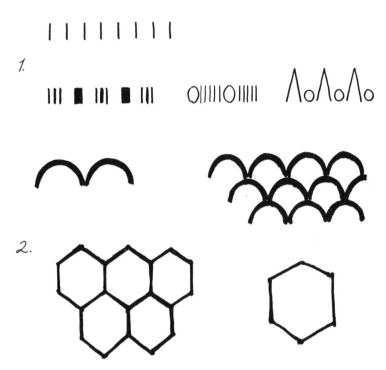

1.

2.

(1) REPETITION AND RHYTHM ▪ Identical forms and equal spacing produce a static repetition and monotony in design. Repetition with an accent produces rhythm with a beat that adds interest.

(2) PATTERN FROM REPEATED FORMS ▪ The repetition of simple line or form produces the design for all ornamental pattern.

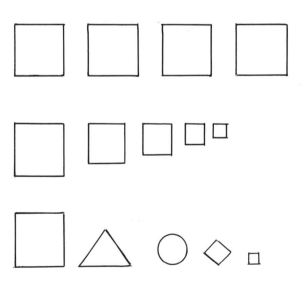

PROGRESSION ▪ Repetition of form expresses an orderly progression. Gradation (forms of graduated size) expresses a more dynamic progression.

RHYTHMIC LINE AND PATTERN

■ The curving, fluid line and uneven spacing of nature produce a pleasing pattern. The continuity and flow of line in this abstract design suggest the movement of the ocean wave. There is good variety in spacing of both black and white areas. The zebra pattern is, by the same principles of good design, more interesting than mechanically even stripes.

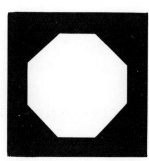

COLOR AND FORM ■ The sharp contrast of white against black or bright against dark emphasizes a point of interest. Any form on a contrasting field creates another shape—that of the field itself. Figure 1 appears flat as form and background focus on an equal plane. Neither one surrounds the other. In Figure 2 the background (black) completely surrounds the object (white) so that the object stands out from the field and creates a center focal point.

an ad. The shape and size of the field (background) in a design is as important as the form placed on it (object illustrated). As an example, in a newspaper a small ad might be surrounded by gray areas of type or by other ads with heavy black areas. If the small ad carries a light, airy sketch, surrounded with plenty of white space, it would probably attract attention simply because of contrast of light against dark or of calm against confusion. There is no set formula or rule which can be applied at all times. However, the idea of large drawings and heavy blacks as attention-getters may be defeated through lack of white spaces to rest the eye and serve as contrast.

The eye must be guided or allowed to follow with ease to the point of interest. A heading may rivet attention by being placed in the middle of a page (the visual axis) with illustrations grouped around it. Through habit, our eyes read a page of printed matter from left to right. They see a layout or illustration the same way. Correct placing of objects (or figures) directs the eye toward the focal point. A figure walking from the left side and facing right seems to be entering the page, but reversed (coming from the right) does not create quite the same impression.

Contrasts of mood are also indicated by basic principles of design. Lines may be dynamic and attract attention through action or even discord. Restful lines create dignity. Developing fresh ideas and making the best use of these principles is the recipe for good layout. There is no one rule for all problems. Repetition of any formula or idea soon becomes boring and creates indifferent

PROPORTION ■ The impact of contrasts is demonstrated in this design of abstract forms. First, there exists a contrast of shapes (a circle and a line within a rectangle). These contain the contrasts of unequal proportions and color (small white forms on large dark ground). All are arranged to direct the eye to the small form within the circle, a simplified principle of good design and a forceful pattern for selling a product.

MEANINGFUL LINES ■ To understand lines as a means of expression is as important as facility in drawing them. Lines of varied character direct the eye, create contrast, express mood, portray texture, and delineate form. Lines of transition, opposition, and radiation are all directional lines. One of these dominates in a good design or composition. Illustrated are examples of expressive lines listed singly.

(1) HORIZONTAL – The line of tranquility, repose, quiet cool.

(2) VERTICAL – The architectural line of ascendancy, growth, loftiness, warmth, or inspiration.

(3) DIAGONAL – The line of motion, progression, or unrest.

(4) OBLIQUE *(alternating)* – The dynamic lines, suggesting speed or flight.

(5) CONVERGING – Lines pointing upward, also dynamic, may suggest loftiness.

(6) SEMICIRCLE – The arc is joyous, graceful, the line found in nature.

(7) CURVING, WAVY LINE – The lyric line, or S line of beauty, is liquid, suggesting continuity or flowing motion.

(8) OPPOSING *(straight)* – Severe lines that attract attention, may be disturbing or constructive.

(9) ZIGZAG – The lightning lines that suggest chaos or conflict.

(10) OPPOSING CURVES – Branching lines of nature, they suggest growth, progression, and harmony of movement.

(11) SPIRAL LINE – The continuous line, one of nature's shell designs.

THE STRUCTURAL LINE *(Contour)* ■ Line enclosing space creates a mass, delineates the contour of a circle, a square, etc. Abstract forms are distortions of the basic shapes. They should not, however, be a circle or a square that is slightly off or uneven. As a design, this would be merely disturbing or negative.

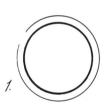
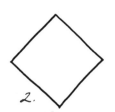

layout and illustration. The basic premise of all fashion is to stimulate interest with the new and different.

FOLLOWING THE LAYOUT

Let us suppose you have a real job to do for department-store advertising. The art director has given you a layout to follow. In some cases a dummy layout might be smaller than the actual size to be reproduced, but more than likely it will be exactly the size of the ad as it will appear in the newspaper. The headline and copy space will be indicated and the space for artwork shown with rough sketches. It is important that

Antonio

The decorative packaging of assorted cosmetic articles is artfully displayed in this design for a magazine page. A preliminary drawing to be used as a working plan, it is executed with precision in pencil lines. The flat, two-dimensional style and the aesthetically balanced arrangement of items complete a well-ordered and exciting pattern.

Anne-Marie Barden, courtesy of *Mademoiselle*

The geometric pattern of action figures and copy in this magazine illustration is a successful combination of good layout, good art work, and well-chosen type. The design and size of the numbers are harmonious in scale, character, and placing. The type becomes part of the design, radiating from the figure 5 and creating another shape as part of the figure 4.

As a graphic designer of the first rank, George Tscherny deserves applause for this cover for an art school booklet. The contemporary use of typography and lettering as a dominant part of the design is handled with imagination and finesse. The sophisticated color scheme is orange and purple on a white background with black lettering.

the artist follow the plan carefully to keep within that allotted space.

The easiest and quickest way to follow exactly is to trace off the space, but this means working actual size, which may be quite small. Many artists prefer to work for reduction in order to have more freedom in sketching and finer detail in the final reproduction. Working large, too, often gives a look of importance to a drawing. This choice is usually up to the artist. If you do work large, it is imperative to make sure that your drawing will still fit the space when reduced. A single figure produces no problems, but a group of figures or a staggered arrangement must be checked carefully for size and placing. The figures must also offer uniform reduction.

It is usually easier for the artist if the figures in a layout are suggested rather than sketched in definite poses, which is restricting. This allows the artist freedom of expression and his choice of poses. An arrangement of accessories, however, is easier to follow and a definite layout helpful. Occasionally an artist may make his own layout or turn in separate figure drawings to be arranged in a layout later.

ENLARGING YOUR GIVEN LAYOUT SPACE

The point here is to get the same proportion of height to width as the layout, but with increased size so you can work larger. First fasten a large sheet of tracing paper on your drawing board. With T square or triangle, make a right angle as the left-hand lower corner of your working space. (This could be the corner of the tracing paper.) Place the layout under the tracing paper, fitting its lower left corner under the one you have drawn, matching horizontal and vertical lines exactly. Draw a diagonal line from the lower left corner of the layout and extend it beyond the layout. Any point on this diagonal line will indicate the upper right-hand corner of your enlarged working space, depending on how big you want it to be. Then simply draw the top and the right-hand edge, meeting at the point on the diagonal line, and you have the right proportion for your working space.

The elements of good design combined in layout and artwork here produce a striking balance of well-placed darks against a larger proportion of white. There is contrast in the variety of shapes and sizes of the blacks (thin curved lines, thick straight ones, small circles, and larger triangles). Partially accidental, they are all used to produce an effect of continuity with clarity and impact.

Ben Morris, courtesy of Du Pont Company

Fashion is the Costumed look! Carsons is fashion! If it's with-it...it's with its own jacket or coat! Sizes 8 to 16. Left, Jerry Silverman basket-weave wool in red-pink or green-blue, $125; Center, Joan Leslie by Kasper double-knit wool jacket, vest, pleated skirt in brick-gold-charcoal, $100; Right, Rembrandt double-knit wool dress and coat, charcoal-caramel, $125; North Room dresses, fourth floor, State; Edens, Evergreen, Hillside, Randhurst.

Carson Pirie Scott & Co

The artist devised his own layout, which became the design for this series of half-page newspaper ads. They are calculated to sell a "fashion look" in each case, and the story is conveyed with imagination and clarity. Placing and grouping of the figures in the horizontal shape is nicely balanced. Cropping at the top brings them forward to an important size. The airy space, simply framed with a bold black line, and the unusual use of script contrive to spotlight an ad anticipating the surrounding gray of newsprint. The model types are suitably chosen for the style of costume in each ad. Flair and good drawing combined with careful attention to garment detail make these illustrations a stand-out. The direct pen-and-ink technique skillfully emphasizes important fashion details with economy of line.

Fashion is paisley! Carsons is fashion! Pure pow... here and now... paisley prints propelled by dirndl skirts. Sizes 8 to 14. Left, jacket, tank top and dirndl skirt, $60. Center, cowl-neckline overblouse and dirndl skirt, $60; Right, jacket with its own float of scarf and dirndl skirt, $60; Better sportswear, fourth floor, state; also Edens, Evergreen, Hillside, Randhurst.

Fashion is the costumed look! Carsons is fashion! Of all the ways the fall '65 Costume can look, your way is here. In sizes 10 to 16. Left, Camel-Color wool Coat, white wool knit dress, $150; Center, grape wool tunic, cowl-neck plaid overblouse, $140; right, grape and gray checked wool, grape wool shell, $110; Miss Carson shop, North Room, fourth floor; represented at Edens, Evergreen, Hillside, Randhurst.

Antonio, courtesy of Carson, Pirie, Scott & Co., Chicago

What is your sport?

Sailing! Just off-shore or deep-water breed—
there's nothing like the lure of the sea and the clothes
designed for it, that are sweeping the sporting world.
The Sports Floor, Fifth, has everything—
long and short pants, culottes, all kinds of tops,
a marvelous slicker. 7.95 to 17.95. Lord & Taylor
—and at Manhasset, Westchester, Millburn,
West Hartford, Bala-Cynwyd, Garden City and
Washington-Chevy Chase

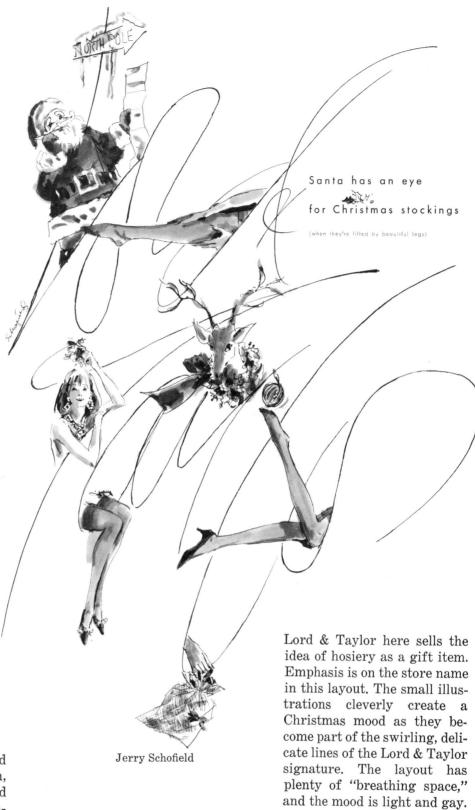

Santa has an eye
for Christmas stockings
(when they're filled by beautiful legs)

Jerry Schofield

Lord & Taylor here sells the idea of hosiery as a gift item. Emphasis is on the store name in this layout. The small illustrations cleverly create a Christmas mood as they become part of the swirling, delicate lines of the Lord & Taylor signature. The layout has plenty of "breathing space," and the mood is light and gay.

full-page newspaper ad designed ith a good balance of illustration, py, and white space. The staggered rrangement of figures has visual connuity. The nautical scene adds emhasis of color and creates a mood for ne clothing advertised. The illustraons, done actual size, carefully follow ne planned layout. They are handled ere with skill and verve by the late arl Wilson, whose versatility and nagination contributed much to the ord & Taylor style for many years. hough the fashions are dated, the ght touch of humor and gaiety comes rrough in good drawing and a crisp endering of wash and expressive pen ne.

COUTURE '65
A REPORT FROM
DU PONT

Scale is the means of contrast here. The small object (the figure and type grouped as a unit) on a large area of white space has dramatic effect. The division of space is pleasing, the approach disarmingly simple. The figure is suggested, not overstated.

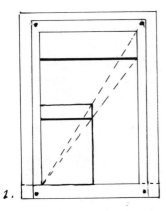 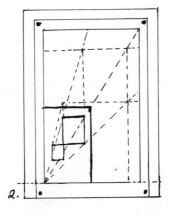

To enlarge a given layout space, follow diagrams 1 and 2 using a T square and triangle for accuracy.

GROUPING FIGURES

To do a single figure is relatively simple if one does not have to consider its placement on a page in relation to type or other drawings. There exists in this case a complete choice of pose and direction of line. If, however, there are three or more figures to group or arrange pleasingly, careful planning before sketching is helpful. To arrive at the best possible composition, try doing a few thumbnail sketches to get a quick over-all effect and placing of dark accents.

Two or more figures in a single illustration must have a plan of arrangement to unite them as a group. The plan may be purely decorative with a pattern of line and form that makes a solid design, as illustrated in the horizontal panel in the beginning of this chapter. Here repetition of form and harmony of line carry out a plan for design.

Figures drawn singly and scattered over a page with areas of copy should have an easy flow of line designed to guide the eye. The arrangement should be an over-all design, pleasing in pattern of dark and light and white spaces. A general theme that sells an idea at a glance is essential for unity of the layout.

In grouping figures for a realistic illustration with a single background (a group or gathering of persons), the perspective of the figure should relate to the background. A dominant point of interest (a centered main figure or group) creates unity of composition and tells a straightforward story; otherwise the eye wanders over a monotonous line-up of figures and registers nothing. Poses suggesting related activity or interest (conversation or focus of attention) help tie up an illustration.

With a little imagination, artists often use one model for all poses in a group, altering the general aspect of each. Unfortunately, the disguise is sometimes thinly veiled, especially if a camera has been used instead of the live model. This is where your quick sketches, done on the scene and kept for future use, are helpful.

14.
MEN'S
FASHIONS

The advantages of specializing in this field are noteworthy. There are always openings for the artist who succeeds in producing quality work that sells the merchandise, and a style, once achieved, can be continued for years. Men's fashions do not change as rapidly or as drastically as women's, and the figures are less stylized. Since the figure proportions remain more realistic, the artist can work to a greater extent from photographs than is possible for women's fashions.

The chief requisite for good illustrations in this branch of merchandising is the ability to portray, on the right type of man, correct fit and tailoring detail, with an accurate rendering of fabric. Whatever type is

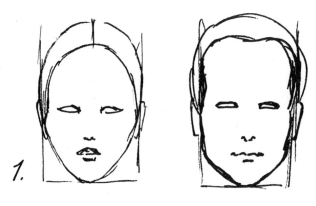

The Male Head

COMPARATIVE PROPORTIONS ■ Placement of the features follows the same rules as those for the female head. It is in the general proportions that they differ. The angular jaw and forehead of the male head appear as wide, in the front view, as the cheekbones. The muscles around the mouth are more pronounced, and the mouth is wider.

PLANES, ¾ VIEW ■ In this view the angular construction of the head is shown in three dimensions. The main plane of the face, the forehead, projects beyond the cheekbones but is narrowed in width as it turns back at the temples. The second plane runs from the width of the cheekbones down to the upper lip. A third block-shaped plane, around the mouth, reaches from the nose to the chin. The chin projects beyond the cheekbones in line with the brow. The jaw is longer and more pronounced in the male head. To observe the head with a knowledge of its planes and general construction is essential to drawing it with conviction.

represented—sportsman, business executive, college student—he must, above all, look masculine. It is important to project an impression of masculinity with a certain refinement, rugged features without coarseness, character without toughness. Briefly, the man should appear to have discriminating taste in dress and grooming as well as casual good manners.

BASIC MALE FIGURE PROPORTIONS

As with the female figure, the ideal male is about eight heads tall. The same horizontal lines are followed for placing the rib cage, pelvis, kneecap, etc. The chief differences in proportion are that the shoulder and chest are wider and the pelvis smaller than the same female measurements. The bone structure is heavier but otherwise the same. The outline of the figure is altered mainly by the flesh. Muscles, bones, and tendons are more obvious in the male and therefore easier to delineate. The female figure is not only more delicately boned but muscles are usually well covered by flesh, which makes them more difficult to study in learning anatomy. For this reason it is helpful to sketch the male figure as much as possible in learning how to draw the female figure.

ANATOMY

Anatomical diagrams are, after all, only guides for training your eye to observe. It is important to know something of the bone structure and the way it works when the body is in motion. Without this knowledge, no amount of guesswork will give your drawings a look of authority. To spend a great amount of time copying anatomical diagrams of the body standing straight and rigid is of limited help, since the body in motion changes completely. To study and sketch from life will do more for your drawing. Acquire a visual comprehension of body structure, and refresh your memory from time to time by referring to good anatomical drawings. You can continue to

R. & B. HERRMANN SET A HIGH STANDARD
■ As illustrators of the well-dressed man, this husband-wife team does an outstanding job in the Lord & Taylor style. The good drawing reveals a solid foundation of figure construction and a freshness of expression. Nothing is faked. Superbly rendered in water color, these small drawings on illustration board are done with minute details clearly and simply defined.

R. and B. Herrmann, courtesy of Lord & Taylor

CLASSIC TAILORING ■ The unself-conscious ease of conservative good tailoring and good fabric is exemplified in this illustration of a well-groomed young executive. His rugged good looks are emphasized with the three-dimensional shading of chiseled features. The subtly defined facial expression and naturalness of the pose are convincingly masculine and clean cut. Garment details are indicated with a few hairline brush strokes deftly placed. The dark and light threads running through the fabric in a fine check pattern have been suggested with crosshatching in dark gray using a dry-brush stroke.

TWEED CLASSIC ■ The country gentleman's classic tweed jacket is never out of fashion. Wearing this one with the proper "old school" tie and white shirt with buttoned-down collar is a type who might be a distinguished professor or busy advertising man who commutes from his country home. The natural shoulderline and conservative cut of the jacket are effectively shown in the informal pose. The dark tweed pattern is represented with two tones of gray stripes and broken, nubby lines over a flat wash. Folds and shadows are kept simple and sharply defined. A few black accents suggest the lapels and pockets.

R. and B. Herrmann, courtesy of Lord & Taylor

THE CITY TOPCOAT ▪ The easy style of this classic topcoat looks right as worn here with an air of self-assurance. The rolled umbrella and soft fedora complete the picture. Note particularly the casual lines of the suitably chosen hat, which is pulled down on the brow and slightly tilted. The hatband, following the lines of the skull, is the basis for drawing the hat to fit the head properly. The wash technique is handled with professional skill. Shadows are definite and simply stated. The herringbone pattern, done with minute brush lines, is confined to the lighted areas of the gray wash. A swift, sure black line defines some of the outline and details of tailoring. The original drawing, only 6 inches high, was done for actual-size reproduction, which demands clean-cut drawing and rendering.

CLASSIC RAINWEAR ▪ The raglan-sleeved town-or-country poplin raincoat is handled here with casual style and flair. The collar flipped up slightly and the firm grip on the umbrella add a note of ease. The pale-gray tone of the coat is relieved by the darker shadow and sharp black accents. The flat wash carries the outline, and the only lines used are those of stitching and seaming details. The head and hat here also have correct contour lines and good modeling of planes emphasized with well-placed shading.

R. and B. Herrmann,
courtesy of Lord & Taylor

COUNTRY CASUALS ■ The warm, bulky look of this pile-lined and hooded winter cover-up is portrayed with a bold contrast of dark washes against the woolly white lining. The three definite tones of gray wash help to spotlight the detail lines and white-accented clasps.

do this for years whenever your thinking gets static and your work lacks freedom and ease of line.

There are a number of books which concentrate on the male figure, many available from the public library. Some are more inspiring than others. For a visual presentation of the figure in motion, I highly recommend *Anatomy for Artists*, by Reginald Marsh. Eliminating written explanations, it is a compilation of examples of the best anatomical drawings of past centuries, including those of Albinus, Vesalius, da Vinci, and Michelangelo. These are not to be copied slavishly but used as a comprehensive study. George Bridgman's *Constructive Anatomy* is another excellent book for the anatomy of the figure as well as the head. It is now available in an inexpensive paperback edition. Good books on this subject are worth the investment, since they are used for years as reference.

Remember that the fashion figure must be slimmed down. Muscles should not be overemphasized as in anatomy studies.

THE MALE HEAD

Although general proportions of the head and placing of the features follow the same rules as for the female head, the planes differ and are more pronounced. The skull is heavier, and the brow projects out above the eyes and slopes back toward the cranium. Proportions vary with each individual but should follow a standard based on a more-or-less ideal masculine type.

The forehead, the main plane of the face, turns sharply at the temples, narrowing down to the cheekbone, which is wider than the forehead. The second plane, divided by the nose, runs from the width of the cheekbone to the center of the upper lip. (See diagram on page 220.) Another block-shaped plane runs from the nose to the chin. From the chin the plane of the jaw widens out and is divided into two secondary planes, one running toward the cheekbone and the other to the ear.

R. and B. Herrmann, courtesy of Lord & Taylor

DARK PLAID ▪ The clearly defined plaid of this warm, casual shirt is done with two darker tones of transparent gray over a flat, pale wash that shows through between the wide and narrow stripes that cross each other. Garment details are drawn with crisp black lines. Shadows on the head and neck define the structural muscles and tendons.

THE TURTLENECK SWEATER ▪ This increasingly popular fashion is shown here in a suitably relaxed pose. The back-lighted head and partially lost profile in shadow add an interesting effect. Note the drawing of the head and features in this view. The hair is rendered with simplicity and an assured style.

R. and B. Herrmann, courtesy of Lord & Taylor

IN A LIGHTER VEIN ■ Sleepwear is illustrated here in an amusingly informal mood. A few quick camera shots can catch the spontaneity of gesture
and facial expression in this type of pose.

The Man's Shop

Lord & Taylor

THE BLACK-TIE EVE-
NING ■ This casually posed
figure has an air of non-
chalance. The sketchy background creates the right atmosphere with a few unob-
trusive lines that add glamour to the well-cut dinner
suit.

R. and B. Herrmann,
courtesy of Lord & Taylor

SWEATER LOOKS ■ The merchandise is depicted with accuracy and shown to advantage on suitable types in both drawings. The tennis player in cable knit looks ready for whatever his opponent may serve, and his sweater has eye-catching contrasts of white and dark.

The college man looks so right with a touch of white collar showing at the neck of his brushed wool pull-over. Light areas of the sweater have been barely touched with a dry-brush stippling of a darker gray to suggest the heather-textured surface. The book adds a sharp black accent, and the hand is naturally posed and drawn well with few lines.

R. and B. Herrmann, courtesy of Lord & Taylor

To achieve a rugged quality in a man's face, character lines, such as those from the sides of the mouth up to the nose, can be emphasized in more mature types. Subtleties of facial expression and proportion are matters of individual taste and the artist's way of expressing them. A comparatively low hairline is usually indicative of youth. Although the receding hairline does not always follow maturity, a lofty brow can add a look of distinction to an interesting face.

Further study of the construction of the head and features can help the artist to portray character and facial expression without a model.

The Young Man's Shop's

view on summer sportsmen —

They can't have too many comfortable
knit shirts and well-tailored walk shorts!
Here are a few from our collections —
each shirt is made in England of fine cotton.
Above, striped shirt in red or navy
with white, or navy with burgundy, 5.00
Dacron® polyester-and-cotton poplin
walk shorts, natural, black, blue, olive, 7.00
Top left, shirt in dark green with white trim,
navy with white, or white with navy, 4.00
Indian cotton madras walk shorts, 10.00
Below left, shirt in navy or white, 4.00
Dacron polyester-and-cotton seersucker
walk shorts, blue with white, 10.00
Shirts, S, M, L. Walk shorts, sizes 28 to 40.
Lord & Taylor, Bala-Cynwyd and Jenkir
Open Monday through Saturday 9:30
and Wednesday nights until 9:00

R. and B. Herrmann,
courtesy of Lord & Taylor

R. and B. Herrmann,
courtesy of Lord & Taylor

THE YOUNG SURFER TYPE ▪ The sun-bleached
hair and healthy tan of this youth in his Henley
shirt are the natural good looks of one dedicated
to sailing or surfing. The few pen-and-ink lines
that define the eyes squinted against the sun and
suggest the convolutions of the ear are masterfully
done, as are the rest of the features.

KNIT SHIRTS AND TAILORED
SHORTS ▪ A good layout is followed
successfully here to sell summer resort classics. Ample white space and
snappy dark tones add zing to the
carefully indicated stripes and plaid
patterns.

THE WALKING POSE ▪ The neat-fitting slacks
of this fresh summer outfit are captured here in a
good, striding action pose. The few wrinkles and
definite shadows are placed accurately. The black
sweater tossed over the shoulder adds a necessary
color contrast to the pale striped shirt and wash-
and-wear slacks.

Lou Beres for a *New York Times* men's supplement

THE LOOSE WASH ▪ The sketchy quality of these shirt drawings was achieved through a complicated means of working with transparent overlays. The black outlines were done on sheets of clear vinyl, which can now be purchased in pad form. The loose wash, colored in this instance, is on the illustration board underneath. One advantage to this approach is the opportunity to experiment with various colors and wash effects and still keep your original drawing separate and intact.

THE PAINTING STYLE OF LOU BERES ▪ The effect of brush strokes in this illustration follows the trend among artists to free their work from duplication of what the camera can do. The realistic drawing and the loose technique of modern painting here produce a quality of strength. The drawing was done large, in outline first, with brush and waterproof ink on a slick-surfaced paper mounted on illustration board. The background tone was next brushed on with transparent color (burnt sienna) over the entire surface using a large brush and allowing the strokes to streak with a freehand effect. Opaques were added last on the shirt and background area around the head. The cardigan sweater is in an opaque vermilion.

THE MOD LOOK ■ The forceful character of the fashion independent is here typified by artist Barbara Pearlman in this somewhat modified "mod" look for men. The antithesis of everything traditional, the idea was to appear fashionably bohemian with flair. The use of the two figures here, wearing the same outfit shown in different views, makes an interesting illustration.

Once you have the general structure of the figure in mind, sketch from life around you. Draw from scenes in everyday life. If you are surrounded by students, sketch them as you see them, in natural poses. Put down their gestures, no matter how quickly or roughly. Try to express the natural, human quality in their attitudes. For the time being forget detail and exactness of line and concentrate solely on action. If your drawing lacks conviction, go back to the anatomy lessons from time to time for review. (See Chapter 9, "Getting Action and Swing into Your Drawing.")

For more detailed and finished drawings, get someone to pose for you. Try seated as well as standing poses. Have your model hold a pose for twenty minutes, if necessary. Take time to draw the clothes as you see them, putting in folds and meaningful wrinkles. Emphasize a straight crease in the pants and details of tailoring such as the fit of the collar, shoulderline, and width of lapels. A gentle slope to the shoulderline is more graceful than a too-square appearance. Try sketching a casual sweater-and-slacks outfit, giving a feeling of bulk and softness to the sweater in contrast to the smooth fabric of the slacks.

THE FASHIONABLE MALE

Though men's fashions retain a certain stability, there are some drastic changes every decade or so, with minor changes or new ideas added for interest each year. As Paris has always been the trend-setter for feminine fashions, so London has led the field in men's wear, from hats of every type to shoes and boots. The classic styles of the leading English tailors, though slightly altered for American tastes, still have the most universally accepted look for the well-dressed male. Their styles continue to set the trend for formal city wear and country tweeds as well as establishing the best cut in officer's uniforms for army and navy standards. From the American prep-school boy to the successful executive, conservative good taste has been inspired by British

The Man's Shop

Leslie Saalburg, courtesy of *Esquire* magazine

LESLIE SAALBURG, ILLUSTRATOR OF ELEGANCE ■ Though not an illustrator of men's fashions, Leslie Saalburg is known for his authentic portrayals of a diminishing world of elegance and the well-dressed men of that small world. His handsome, full-color illustrations have appeared in *Esquire* magazine regularly for many years. (That magazine, in the sixties, named him "the best-dressed artist on either side of the Atlantic.") He has traveled from London to Paris to Singapore, sketching and making notes on the scene to depict famous British and European hotels and bars, men's clubs, the races at Ascot, and other gathering places of the "beau monde," which he knows well.

The Leslie Saalburg illustrations here were done for an article written by him about a few exclusive London shops that still cater to the individual tastes of a select clientele. Of the Englishman, Mr. Saalburg says, "He knows what he is doing, and he is wary of violent new changes in style. . . . There is the effect of great assurances—elegance even in their attitude." It is interesting to note here that the Englishman's traditional habit of correct dress for an occasion did not stem from an exaggerated interest in clothing per se but to create an effect which would give the wearer distinction. Today's youth combs London's antique and secondhand shops for clothing and uniforms of a more romantic past. They may not revere their finds or wear them with dignity, but they do sense the style and flair and quality of workmanship.

SADDLERY AND HARNESS SHOP ■ Traditional London still maintains a few long-established shops for the individualist who has everything made to order. This illustration was done in color from sketches made in the shop of Champion & Wilton Ltd., London. The tweed suit worn by the gentleman shopping is obviously cut on classic English lines—nipped waistline, high armholes, and trousers that hang straight and neatly cover the tops of the shoes.

Leslie Saalburg, courtesy of *Esquire* magazine

LONDON BOOTMAKER ■ The Paris establishment of John Lobb, where some of the world's finest leather goods may be purchased. The pencil sketches with written notes were made on the scene for use in developing the finished water-color drawing. The composition in detail was done on handmade water-color board in light pencil lines. Outlines were emphasized with pen and gray ink for the light areas, black for the darker outlines. Pencil guidelines were then eliminated with a kneaded eraser before filling in exact colors with transparent water color.

Leslie Saalburg, courtesy of *Esquire* magazine

JAMES LOCKE & CO. LTD., LONDON ▪ A hatter for generations of well-dressed men, this shop is famous for its range of styles and standard of excellence. The bowler hat, worn straight and low on the brow, is an accepted style for distinguished Londoners.

ACCESSORIES FOR MEN ▪ To sell this assortment of costly items to the likely buyer, an atmosphere of luxury and a "snob approach" were created in the illustration. The artist, Carl Wilson, carried out the theme extremely well in this Lord & Taylor ad.

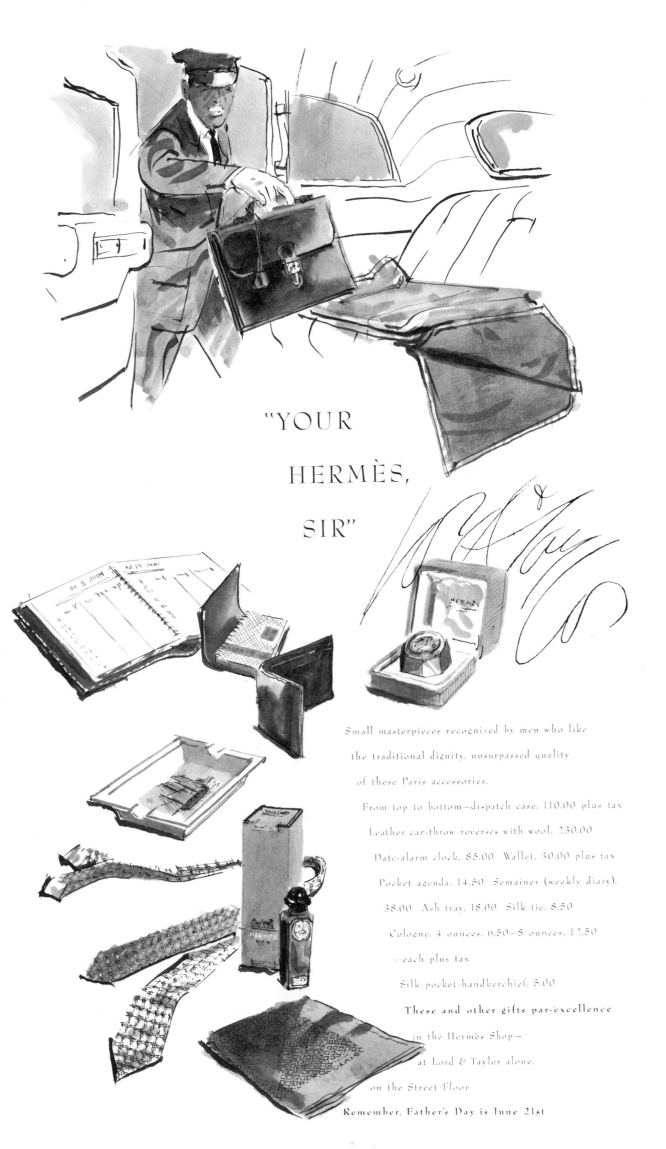

"YOUR

HERMÈS,

SIR"

Small masterpieces recognized by men who like

the traditional dignity, unsurpassed quality

of these Paris accessories.

From top to bottom—dispatch case, 110.00 plus tax

Leather car-throw reverses with wool, 230.00

Date-alarm clock, 85.00 Wallet, 30.00 plus tax

Pocket agenda, 14.50 Semainer (weekly diary),

38.00 Ash tray, 18.00 Silk tie, 8.50

Cologne, 4 ounces, 9.50—8 ounces, 12.50

—each plus tax

Silk pocket-handkerchief, 5.00

These and other gifts par-excellence

in the Hermès Shop—

at Lord & Taylor alone,

on the Street Floor

Remember, Father's Day is June 21st

SUMMER CAMP ▪ A lively imagination and a sense of fun are valuable assets in this area of fashion illustrating. These exuberant young figures are masterfully done with a clean-cut wash rendering and realistically perfect drawing, expressing character and gesture with professional skill. Figure proportions of this in-between age group are exactly right at about six heads tall. The head still has a childish quality, with small features and large size in proportion to the body. The legs are long and the hands and feet are a bit large at that age. The scene is set with a mere suggestion of background, allowing the action to tell the story.

R. and B. Herrmann,
courtesy of Lord & Taylor

standards. The fit is fairly close, jackets cut high under the arm and with flattering, clean lines done in the best worsteds and tweeds.

The London mod fashions of the nineteen-sixties are something else, chiefly an influence of the antiestablishment feeling of rebellious youth. A bohemian, nonconformist trend, it has a touch of the dandy from a past era and has become part of the young international look.

Learning the current look of fashions for men is possible by studying examples of the best artwork, much of which appears in newspaper advertising and direct-mail advertising for department stores and men's shops. Magazines for men carry news of men's fashions, and others, such as *Town and Country*, give regular, limited space to their story. Occasionally even *Vogue* devotes a few pages to men. For action pictures showing golfwear and other sports attire, you might find exceptionally good examples in publications such as *Sports Illustrated*. A collection of clippings of this sort can be invaluable for action poses and suitable background atmosphere. With a little initiative, you may find material for a comprehensive and useful file from many sources.

In working from photographs, be sure to elongate the figure for fashions so that the effect is that of a tall, slim man. If you are taking your own pictures or Polaroid shots, you might hire a suitable model and get enough basic poses to use for a number of jobs. Details of style and tailoring can be changed to follow the merchandise to be illustrated since basic types of suits or sportswear have similar lines.

FINISHED DRAWINGS

Techniques of working and rendering vary. (See Chapter 10 on "Finished Art.") One of the most popular and practical procedures is that of working first in rough pencil outlines either directly on illustration board or first on tracing paper and then transferring to illustration board. Washes are used extensively for fabric textures and tweeds. Lines should be strong and clean-cut. Clothes should appear well cut and fit without wrinkles except where the elbow bends or the action of the body forces folds in the material. The general effect should be that of casual good grooming.

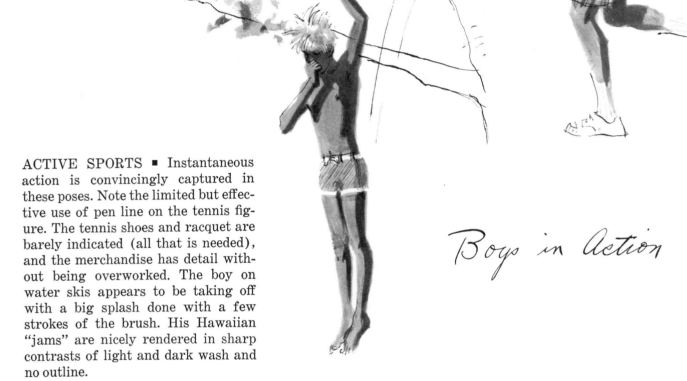

ACTIVE SPORTS ■ Instantaneous action is convincingly captured in these poses. Note the limited but effective use of pen line on the tennis figure. The tennis shoes and racquet are barely indicated (all that is needed), and the merchandise has detail without being overworked. The boy on water skis appears to be taking off with a big splash done with a few strokes of the brush. His Hawaiian "jams" are nicely rendered in sharp contrasts of light and dark wash and no outline.

Boys in Action

15. CHILDREN I

A growing interest in children's fashions has created a demand for original and imaginative illustrations in this field. Designers have produced charming ideas for fashionable small fry, dressing the young in everything from way-out modern to costume-inspired modes of the past. Some of these styles are whimsical, others have a charm reminiscent of more romantic eras. The field is broad, with a wide range of types and age groups, as well as a price range from budget to expensive.

Artwork may vary from simple, quick sketches to beautiful and imaginative illustrations in full color. Work may be used in all kinds of newspaper and magazine advertising. There is also a demand for engaging portrayals of children in such places as magazine editorials and book illustration. If you have the knack and a genuine interest, the subject can be a delight.

ASHION

PROPORTION AND EXPRESSIVE GESTURE

Proportion and expressive gesture are the most important ingredients involved in portraying children. Constructive anatomy is of little value in learning to sketch the infant whose bone structure is well-hidden by baby fat and whose muscles have hardly begun to develop. As the child grows, the structure is still secondary to action, gesture, and stance. These are qualities of expression different for each age. Proportions can be achieved mechanically, but they are insufficient without the keen observation and study necessary for depicting the ingenuous charm of children. Unself-conscious gestures, sprightly imagination, and whimsical antics are the keynotes of a true and revealing portrayal.

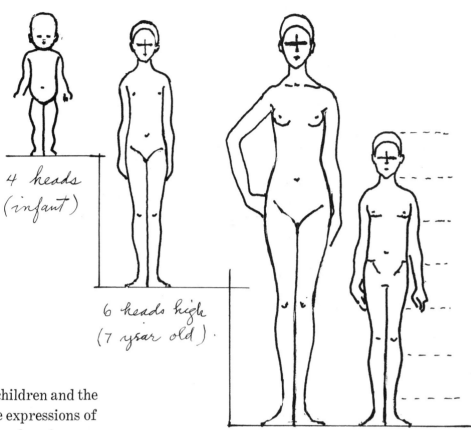

Children's Proportions ···· Comparative heights.

4 heads (infant)

6 heads high (7 year old)

8 heads high - adult, 6½ heads (9 year old)

The engaging innocence of some children and the guile and artfulness of others are expressions of character that can be revealed in a drawing.

PROPORTIONS

In infancy the head is extremely large in proportion to the body, about one-quarter of the over-all height as compared to one-eighth of the adult height. In the first year the child's head is already two-thirds the size it will be at maturity. The body continues to grow more than the size of the head so that, at five or six years of age, the head equals one-sixth of the total height. The head retains a slightly round, baby look for some time, but the neck gradually lengthens, the body slims down, and the legs and arms stretch out longer and longer.

ROMANTIC REALISM ▪ A quality of portraiture was captured in this charming pose of mother and child by Antonio. The sensitive little face is ideal for the romantic style of the ruffled frock. The mood is enhanced by the soft charcoal rendering with the white chalk lighting up the infant's dress.

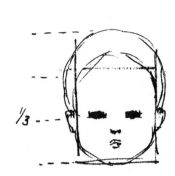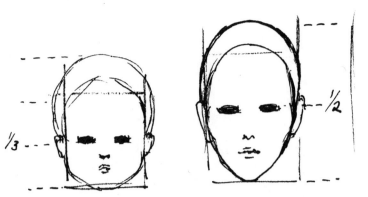

Comparative Proportions of the Infant Head:

1. Eyes rounder, same width between as in adult.
2. Very small mouth.
3. Nose a mere button, with no bridge yet developed
4. Wide cheek bones, small chin.
5. Skull large, face small. As the child grows, the face grows larger and longer.

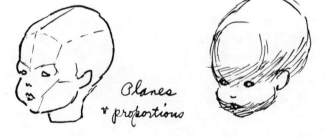

Planes + proportions

Side + ¾ Views

1. Skull elongated, more oval than the adult.
2. Forehead projects, somewhat pointed.
3. Chin set back, jaw small.
4. Neck small + short.

MORE REALISM ■ These gay eight-year-olds show a natural exuberance in both attitude and facial expression. The charcoal line on vellum tracing paper has a free style that contributes to the lighthearted charm of the illustration. The two figures are grouped in a pleasing composition. To sketch children such as these in motion one must get very quick impressions on paper while the action is going on, being sure to capture gesture and expression. Details can be worked out later.

Barbara Pearlman

PLAIN & FANCY

PROPORTION AND GESTURE ▪ These sketchy line drawings for fashion reporting emphasize new style trends for children. Proportions must be correct for each age group, the head proportionately larger in the 3-to-6 size range, etc. Note the narrow width of the shoulderline in relation to the head and the small neck. The body becomes larger in proportion to the head as the child reaches the age of seven or eight.

Courtesy of *Women's Wear Daily*

The in-between "subteen."

Courtesy of *Women's Wear Daily*

A MODERN CONCEPT ■ Children are charmingly illustrated in a stylized way in these drawings by Anne-Marie Barden. The off-beat grouping of the three little beach figures is from a *New York Times* report on children's fashions. The vertical arrangement is pleasing in design. The expressionless faces and geometric haircuts are amusingly sophisticated and contemporary. The simple pen outline of the figures clearly displays their patterned surfing gear.

This drawing, using the same style in a horizontal grouping, avoids a too-serious approach to showing pantyhose for juveniles. The poses and individual hair styles are both decorative and amusing.

Anne-Marie Barden

The neck of the infant, up to a year old, is almost nonexistent it is so short. From the small, narrow shoulders the rest of the body can be divided into two halves, the upper half being the rather large body, and the lower half, the legs. The short arms hardly reach above the head.

The baby head is quite round with a large proportion of skull and a very small face that is about as wide as it is long. In the front view, the face would fit into a square rather than a rectangular shape. The eyes, nose, and mouth are all bunched together, the eyes being the largest of the features. The tiny mouth should be less than the width of the eyes, except in a smile. The little button nose is barely suggested with a curved line or a wisp of shadow underneath. At that age the bridge of the nose is undeveloped and should not be indicated at all. A faint shadow across the line of the eyes sometimes accentuates the rounding forehead above the fat cheeks. (See illustration on page 246.)

Keep all lines and shadows light and delicate. Roundness and softness are the qualities to emphasize in doing heads of children. The baby head has no hard, definite hairline. The hair around the face is usually fine and wispy with a tendency to grow toward the face, not away from it. As the child grows, the hair becomes thicker and acquires weight and body, but it still falls forward. For this reason, bangs of one type or another are the most practical and charming hair style for both boys and girls. The roundness of the head and shallowness of features are evident for quite a few years, although the face gradually elongates and the cheeks slim down as well.

CHILDREN AS MODELS

The small child cannot be expected to pose at all. It is up to the artist to sketch what he sees quickly or from memory. If the child has something of interest to hold his attention while you work, so much the better. To sit and observe and make sketchy notes is the most you can expect. An older child will often gladly pose for you if

Anne-Marie Barden, courtesy of *Bergdorf Goodman*

Spacing of light areas and dark accents of balloons and figure give this layout an over-all design that is eye-catching.

Antonio, courtesy of *The New York Times*

TODAY'S CHILDREN ▪ The new look as viewed
in a fashion report on children's fashions. The bold
felt-tip pen outlines and appliquéd gray areas suggest an influence of the Pop art phase.

These action figures also form a strikingly simple
design of diagonally opposed lines. The dark sky
balances the composition and emphasizes the white
snow.

Antonio, courtesy of *The New York Times*

The grown-up sweater-and-skirt fashion looks convincingly juvenile on this subteen figure. The background is contemporary in character and completes the composition in an interesting design.

Antonio, courtesy of *The New York Times*

NURSERY NEWS ■ Convertible furniture for children is given an interesting play in these illustrations for a Home Furnishings page of *The New York Times* (Dec. 25, 1966). A Christmas morning scene is suggested by the pajama-clad young demonstrators, who seem to be very much at home with the contemporary styling.

Anne-Marie Barden,
courtesy of *The New York Times*

he is going to be paid for the effort, but do not expect lengthy poses. The patience of children is short, and when they tire it is time to quit.

Try quick sketching in the park, at the beach, or wherever you find a variety of ages and types. In sketching, concentrate on action lines of stance and posture. Try to capture children in the act of doing something, playing a game or intent on watching. All action is fleeting, so observation and memory are needed to depict the natural exuberance of children. Photographs can be helpful for action poses and for the fit of clothing, but one should avoid copying too literally. No matter how realistic your rendition may be, a spark of imagination adds much to the spirit and charm of illustrations of children. Create a situation or story in your drawing, with a touch of humor, perhaps.

Quick Sketches - in the Park

EXERCISE

Take a pencil and small drawing pad with you to a playground or a place where you will find a gathering of children. Do not draw details of the figure at first, simply sketch it as a series of circles to get proportion and action. See how fast you can get the impression of contour, stance, and proportion that are typical of a particular age. Make as many quick notes as possible of heads, for example, or of the way the clothes fit and hang. Sketches need not be complete. They are mainly for use in making your finished drawings later.

Quick sketching for proportion & gesture

(at the beach)

16. GREAT NAMES I[

Of all sources of inspiration, the most obvious is the work of other artists. Even the greatest painters have influenced one another over the centuries. As a method of learning, keen observation and analysis of the best in art is of immeasurable value. Many young artists understandably copy an idol's technique, eventually developing a style of their own. But to be content with an exact imitation of another's work reveals a lack of imagination or effort. Little can be said for outright plagiarism.

Most of the notable artists represented in this chapter were, or could have been, great names in fine art. Some of their work reveals the influence of the Impressionist and Post-Impressionist era, reflecting the taste trends in art on fashion and illustrating. Examples of the best of their fashion work may be found in old editions of *Vogue* and *Harper's Bazaar*,

ASHION ILLUSTRATION

which may turn up in secondhand bookshops and some libraries and museums. The costume department of the Metropolitan Museum of Art in New York has most back editions of these two magazines from the early nineteen-twenties through to recent years.

All the artists presented in this chapter added much to the image of the fashionable magazines of their day. The most recent contributor of the group is the late René Bouché. His vitally brilliant illustrating followed that of Eric, who set and kept the high standard of art in fashion for well over a quarter of a century.

These few set the pace and represent a sophisticated art form at its best. Collectors are still avidly buying originals from the widows of both Eric and Bouché.

RENÉ BOUCHÉ (1906-1963)

Fascinated by the human image, René Bouché was painting portraits in Europe as early as 1933. In Paris, a few years later, an offer from *Vogue* proved to be a turning point in his career. Aware of the know-how behind fashion at the higher levels, he took immediate steps to learn its subtler ingredients. Prevailing upon a chic and knowledgeable model to devote two uninterrupted weeks to posing, he did endless and detailed sketches to get the character of an elegant hand, a well-shod foot, the studied look of assured style. An analytical eye and the ability to record with accuracy and flair came through in superb style.

Following the fall of France in 1941, Bouché went to New York. His work was to appear in *Vogue* from then on. With great versatility and energetic drive, he experimented successfully with various media and covered many subjects. *Vogue* reproduced page after page of his spirited on-the-scene sketches from around the world, from fashion showings in Paris to the Dublin Horse Show to backstage views of geisha girls in Tokyo.

He continued to paint, going through many phases. The influence of an abstract period was reflected in his later work. Returning to portraiture, he achieved momentous success. There was a sense of today in the large and thinly painted canvases and the sure, linear style that brilliantly depicted character and physiognomy. Among his more significant portraits were those of Braque and Stravinsky and a painting of Jacques Lipchitz now owned by the Whitney Museum. A long list includes famous names from all worlds of endeavor. Revealing a sharp wit, the Bouché portraits were candid, sometimes biting portrayals that delighted New York sophisticates. Even his grotesque image of Elsa Maxwell was no doubt accepted with good humor.

Early in the sixties, Bouché's work showed the beginnings of another phase. His last drawings were powerful, semiabstract heads expressed in heavy black lines. Prolific in output and with a sustained enthusiasm and devotion to art, he left a heritage of work recognized by museum and private collector.

PORTRAIT OF SOPHIA LOREN ▪ In this life-size drawing in Conte crayon on charcoal paper, the figure is merely suggested, emphasizing the magnificent eyes with detailed rendering.

tesy of *Vogue*

DUBLIN'S HORSE SHOW WEEK
■ These on-the-scene sketches were done with felt-tip pen on a large drawing pad. The panel required three sheets of paper pieced together. The genius to see accurately and record quickly is apparent in these brilliant drawings.

Courtesy of *Vogue*

Courtesy of *Vogue*

SOMERSET MAUGHAM ▪ Here is a quickly sketched portrait of the famous author and some friends, done by Bouché on a Riviera visit. Felt-tip pen, ballpoint pen, and pencil on charcoal paper were employed to gain these results, but methods and tools are unimportant for this type of sketching. Observation is what really counts.

GIRL WITH DALMATIAN ▪ Softly textured line is here rendered with Japanese bamboo pen and felt-tip pen on dampened pastel paper. Opaque white and water color were added later.

Courtesy of *Vogue*

1955 FASHIONS SKETCHED IN ITALY ■ Using the sumptuous interiors available, Bouché cleverly indicated them with few lines so as to supply an atmospheric background which would not overpower the gowns. The result is a glamorous scene in tune with the clothes.

rtesy of *Vogue*

Courtesy of *Vogue*

Courtesy of *Vogue*

SUMMER WHITE ▪ is rendered on toned paper, dampened again for soft effects. Pen-and-ink and opaque white succeed in creating the luxury image of this appliquéd fabric.

TINTED CHARCOAL PAPER ▪ is used as a toned background for the combination of felt-tip pen, charcoal, and pastel drawing. The original was done directly from the model. Corrections are not possible with this medium. Such freshness of expression and sureness of line are developed only through constant practice.

1959 GIVENCHY SUIT ▪ Here is a great example of the fashion silhouette accurately revealed in its purest lines with texture and contour beautifully depicted in varied pen lines.

Courtesy of *Vogue*

Courtesy of *Vogue*

Courtesy of *Vogue*

A BOX AT THE RACES ▪ The atmosphere is suggested by pose rather than by sketched-in background. With a minimum of garment detail, this illustration sells a fashion through chic accessories and the type of persons portrayed.

Courtesy of *Vogue*

BOLD BRUSH LINE ▪ a Japanese-style stroke, attained with a large, tapered brush, illustrates a Paris fashion of the past.

Courtesy of *Vogue*

ERIC (CARL ERICKSON) (1891-1958)

The brief signature "Eric" appeared on distinguished illustrations for *Vogue* magazine for more than thirty-five years. Eric's brilliant draftsmanship was not confined to superb drawings of fashions and elegant people. With great sensitivity, he recorded scenes and people wherever he went. His genre subjects included the French circus, nightclub entertainers, the chic Riviera, or any scene he considered colorful or

WORLD WAR II SCENE ■ sketched in Grand Central Station shows the timelessness of good taste and good drawing. The original water color, eventually purchased by a private collector, first appeared as a coat story illustration for *Vogue*.

dramatic. He was often referred to as the American Toulouse-Lautrec, and there was, between the two, a similarity in artistic genius and in their sympathetic impressions of humanity. He could not bear anything faked or drawn from memory. Preferring to sketch from life, he consistently made on-the-scene notations in a sketchbook. Working later from the sketches, he might redraw a subject many times before reaching the standard of perfection he demanded of himself.

His perceptive eye and sensitive line produced superlative portraits, completely honest but charmingly sophisticated. Among the more famous of hundreds of sitters were Franklin D. Roosevelt, Queen Elizabeth, and Gertrude Stein. He often worked in charcoal, and his economy of line was deliberate and accomplished only after lengthy consideration. A close friend, once posing for a portrait sketch, said that Eric observed him endlessly without putting a single stroke on paper. Finally he drew one eye which took an hour and a half. (This was his favorite starting point.) The three-quarter seated figure, with few lines and no indication of shading, took four hours of intensive concentration.

In a story of his life, *Vogue* recorded a youthful interest in boxing and gaming cocks and mentioned his marriage to a *Vogue* artist. Their daughter also grew to be a sensitive and talented artist. American born, he spent much time in Paris and was, in appearance, more European than American. His round face had an innocent expression of detachment that concealed a sharp eye. He was always well-groomed and correctly tailored, and his attire usually included boutonniere, walking stick, and bowler hat. He is said to have worn the hat while working.

CLASSIC GREEK DRAPING ■ handled with classic simplicity and statuesque poses. Not unlike Picasso's pen drawings in the same vein, it has a casual quality only achieved through the confidence of a great draftsman.

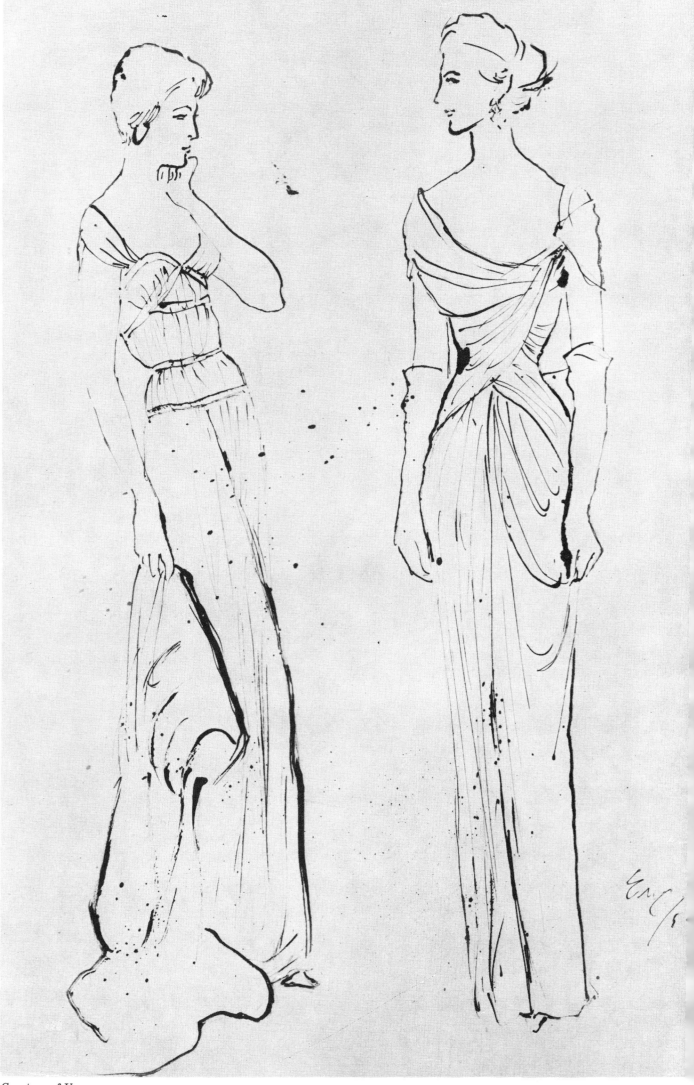

Courtesy of *Vogue*

Courtesy of *Vogue*

THE FAMOUS "ERIC" LINE ▪ expressive, fluid, elegant. Each stroke was carefully thought out before putting charcoal to paper. Rather than correct a drawing, he discarded it for another try. Alternately firm and delicate, his line always revealed a keen observation of human character and form as well as the subtle contour of a fashion.

A HAT SUGGESTED ▪ by one knowing brush stroke. The fashion story (1956) here was focused on the cabbage roses; all else was merely indicated without detail.

Courtesy of *Vogue*

Deauville

Courtesy of *Vogue*

PORTRAIT ▪ from a one-man exhibition at the Philadelphia Art Alliance (1949). A candid study of Benjamin Sonnenberg, public relations expert.

DEAUVILLE, 1954 ▪ At the Bar du Soleil, the painter Van Dongen (at right in beret) appears among the gathered celebrities. The finished water color was probably done from many sketches made on the scene. The flavor of an unhurried, uncrowded, chic world of the past is captured here by Eric with a great sensitivity found only in one of his artistic genius.

tesy of *Vogue*

Courtesy of *Vogue*

tesy of *Vogue*

Although he was basically shy and often inarticulate, his occasional comments could be salty. Eric once brushed aside the sharp-focus style of a famous surrealist with, "That's not painting, that's knitting." Invited to lecture one evening at the Society of Illustrators, he made up for a skimpy talk by quietly doing a magnificent drawing onstage before a fascinated audience of other artists.

His one-man show in 1949 at the Philadelphia Art Alliance was reviewed by art critic Aline Saarinen, who commented, "He has never exhibited at a museum, but more of his work has been seen by more people than even the prolific and immodest Picasso."

Artists, still imitating his fluid lines in brush and charcoal, fail to capture the same human qualities and uncontrived look of elegance. As an artist, Eric ranks among the historically great. His drawings of peasants and clowns and his portraits of the famous will successfully survive many current art trends.

WASH OVER CHARCOAL LINES ■ The original 20-inch figure, sketched directly from the model, has the mature elegance of the fifties. The portrait-like drawing was meticulously done with charcoal on illustration board and sprayed with fixatif to prevent smearing. Water color was then washed on for gray tones over the lines.

MARCEL VERTÈS (1895-1961)

Vertès is here represented by a delightful *Bazaar* cover, which appeared in an exhibition at the Hallmark Gallery in New York commemorating "100 Years of *Harper's Bazaar*." Always poetically lighthearted and gay, his illustrations were charmingly decorative. Many of his paintings, including trompe l'oeil murals, decorate the walls of private homes, clubs, and a theatre or two. His people and animals, always whimsical, often naughty or suggestive, are pure fantasy displayed with delicacy and subtle taste in drawing, composition, and color.

In 1956 his designs for Ringling Bros., Barnum & Bailey's "The Flowered Circus" were exhibited at the Carstairs Gallery in New York. The motifs were enchanting costume versions of flowers, frogs, bugs, and imaginative ideas for a fairy-story décor.

HOSIERY AD ■ with a lighthearted approach. Attention value is achieved by a touch of humor in a delicate line drawing with sharp black accents.

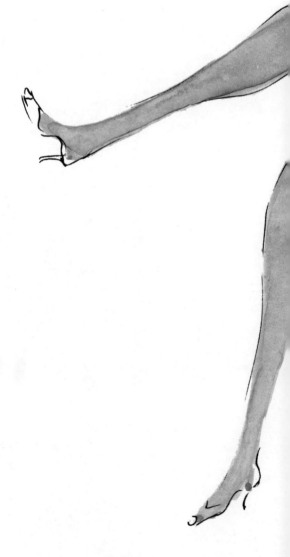

Courtesy of Saks Fifth Avenue

Harper's BAZAAR

April 15

His kind of creativity hardly seemed to fit the background of the Hungarian-born Vertès, who served in that country's army from 1914 to 1918 and later worked on posters for the underground fight for independence.

He moved from Vienna to Paris to do book illustration and stage design. In 1939 and 1940 he was in the French army, before coming to the United States, where his talents were much in demand. He received two Academy awards for his artistic contributions to the film *Moulin Rouge*, the story of Toulouse-Lautrec. Since his death, silk-screen prints of his work as well as originals are valued items.

POSTER-STYLE ART ▪ in gay colors made this magazine cover a decorative eye-catcher. The loose, sketchy technique was Vertès' trademark. His paintings were often a combination of opaque and transparent washes with features and details added with quick, short brush strokes.

rtesy of *Harper's Bazaar*

CHRISTIAN (Bebe) BÉRARD (1902-1949)

A favorite pupil of Vuillard in the nineteen-twenties, Bérard was a serious painter, choosing acrobats, peasants, and urchins for subjects. Though modern, his canvases had both an intellectual and an enchantingly romantic quality. His taste for color was subtle and sophisticated but dramatic. The modern baroque of the theater of the thirties drew him to designing costumes and stage décor for the ballet.

Success in the theater, the product of long hours of dedicated work, usurped time which could have been devoted to painting, but he found the world of fashion too beguiling. His genius was put to illustrating books, designing dress fabrics, or whatever was offered at the moment. His instinct for the excitement of unusual color combinations, such as mauve and orange, the drama of a touch of one of the poisonous greens or golds added to a conventional arrangement, created shock at the time. He would cleverly spark pastels with a rich plum or deep green, giving the scheme character and impact.

Editors of fashion magazines, who were in Paris for the collections, were quick to appreciate the Bérard flair. His fashion illustrations soon appeared in *Harper's Bazaar* and, later, in *Vogue*. Bérard's drawings often left out details, such as a face, suggesting rather than delineating and setting the trend of freer drawing in fashion. Art students, imitating his Japanese-style brushline, missed the knowledge of the connoisseur behind the simple technique.

Bérard's great taste developed through extensive reading and study and a background of training in architecture as well as painting and appreciation of all the creative arts. His influence with the creators of fashion is said to have helped launch Dior when the designer set out on his own.

A complex man, admired and cherished by aristocrat and bohemian alike, bearded and sloppy in appearance but with a zest for life, he left all creative Paris mourning his early death.

THE ROCOCO INFLUENCE OF THE THEATER ▪ The rich coloring of this sketchily painted, decorative illustration from *Vogue* contributed much to this work by Bérard. The loose technique and imaginative approach is limited to a magazine editorial type of illustrating rather than the more exact drawing demanded for department store advertising.

Courtesy of *Vogue*

289

Courtesy of *Vogue*

R.B.W. (Count René Bouët-Willaumez) (Contemporary)

These initials appeared as signature to many of *Vogue's* illustrations on both editorial and advertising pages, projecting the haute couture and the elegant world of the thirties and forties. His was an individual style, devoid of tricks. The expressive pen line and technique of rendering a careless-looking wash that sparkled with a sure stroke and exciting contrast had the sensitivity of fine art. Like the best of that era, he was also a connoisseur of color.

Technique, as always, was only a means of expressing a fine instinct for elegance in all he did. His talented and chic wife was sometimes his model, and he, a continental type, looked much like the distinguished men-of-the-world portrayed in his drawings. None of the top fashion artists of the period relied on photographs as a substitute for models. Time and money was spent for the best models available to produce a look of authenticity. Sometimes the fashion magazine provided their highly paid photographic models.

Occasionally, an R.B.W. drawing (or reasonable facsimile) appears on an advertising page today and still stands out as a classic style of transparent water-color and ink drawing handled with clarity and dash.

A LUSH WATER-COLOR RENDERING ■ The spontaneous effect is gained here through elimination of outlines and quick handling of washes. Such a convincing portrayal of satin must be done from a model wearing the garment with her own personal flair. Although of a past era, the great style of the figure, the freshness of technique, and the fine composition make it still an exciting illustration.

SUNLIGHT ■ indicated through a mere suggestion of shadow in wash adds much to these brush and pen line drawings. The original, in color, contained outlines in burnt sienna, grays, and greens rather than all black.

GATHERS AND DRAPING ■ shown in these soft, clinging gowns of the thirties are depicted in pen line and white pastel. A heavy quality of paper with a medium surface or "tooth" (roughness) was first prepared with a wash of water color (burnt umber in this case). Outlines, done with a flexible drawing pen probably over a light pencil tracing, were added and highlights picked up with the white pastel pencil.

Courtesy of Vogue

Courtesy of

ELIMINATION OF DETAIL ■ gives these ink and wash sketches a freshness. The airiness of uncluttered white areas and the sharp accents of almost black shadows suggest brilliant sunshine and clear desert air.

Courtesy of *Vogue*

Courtesy of *Vogue*

AN EXHIBITION ■ is always part of the fashion scene. This illustration from the thirties creates a casual mood of reality. The poses of the figures are natural, probably sketched at the gallery.

Courtesy of *Vogue*

RUTH SIGRID GRAFSTROM
(Contemporary)

The signature "Grafstrom" identified another gifted *Vogue* artist of the thirties and forties. Sound art training and knowledge, as well as a lively imagination, showed through her many impressive illustrations. *Vogue's* pages proved a good showcase for her work, and many advertisers sought her out to illustrate their products. Her beautifully planned groups of figures in story-telling situations and suitable backgrounds also appeared in newspaper ads for Saks Fifth Avenue. Atmosphere might be suggested by a uniformed doorman or a scene at the opera, attracting the buyer with stage settings in tune with the times. Masterfully drawn and correct in detail, Grafstrom's illustrations were always charming compositions that enhanced the fashions displayed.

Technique, again, was merely a means of expression. Defining an accurately constructed body, form was often indicated with fine pen line and soft pencil shading. A classic sculptural quality was evident, not only through three-dimensional drawing, but also in the serene types of individuals portrayed. Her fine painting and superb drawing came into play for fashion, and clothes had the same look of quality and elegance, depicting fine fabric, fine tailoring, and chic lines.

The Matisse-like freshness and deliberate simplicity of her work were lost to fashion when she turned to serious painting.

BLACK ORGANZA ■ is conveyed in obvious brushstrokes with the hand of a fine painter. The diluted inks and water color used here project the delicate character of the fabric. The sculptural quality of the figure, well defined by planes of light and shadow, reveals a thorough knowledge of anatomy, especially notable in the arms.

Courtesy of *Vogue*

Courtesy of *Vo*

SKI CLOTHES, CIRCA 1938 ■ Diluted inks are used on smooth illustration board, with fine lines deftly indicated with a fine brush. Outlines have been eliminated and the larger areas have been washed in with a very large brush. The composition contains a well-planned arrangement of figures with a pleasing pattern of gray and white with sharp black accents.

SIMPLICITY OF LINE ■ here achieves the decorative style of a pen sketch by Matisse. On Bristol board with a medium-smooth finish, outlines were done with a flexible crowquill pen over a carefully planned drawing in light pencil (later removed with a kneaded eraser). Note the economy of line used to indicate the stripes and folds of the draperies.

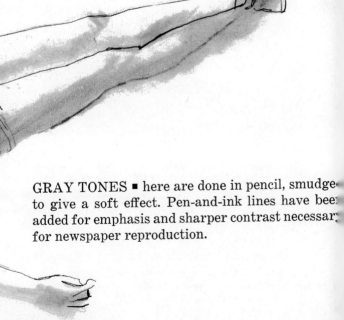

GRAY TONES ■ here are done in pencil, smudged to give a soft effect. Pen-and-ink lines have been added for emphasis and sharper contrast necessary for newspaper reproduction.

Courtesy of Saks Fifth Avenue

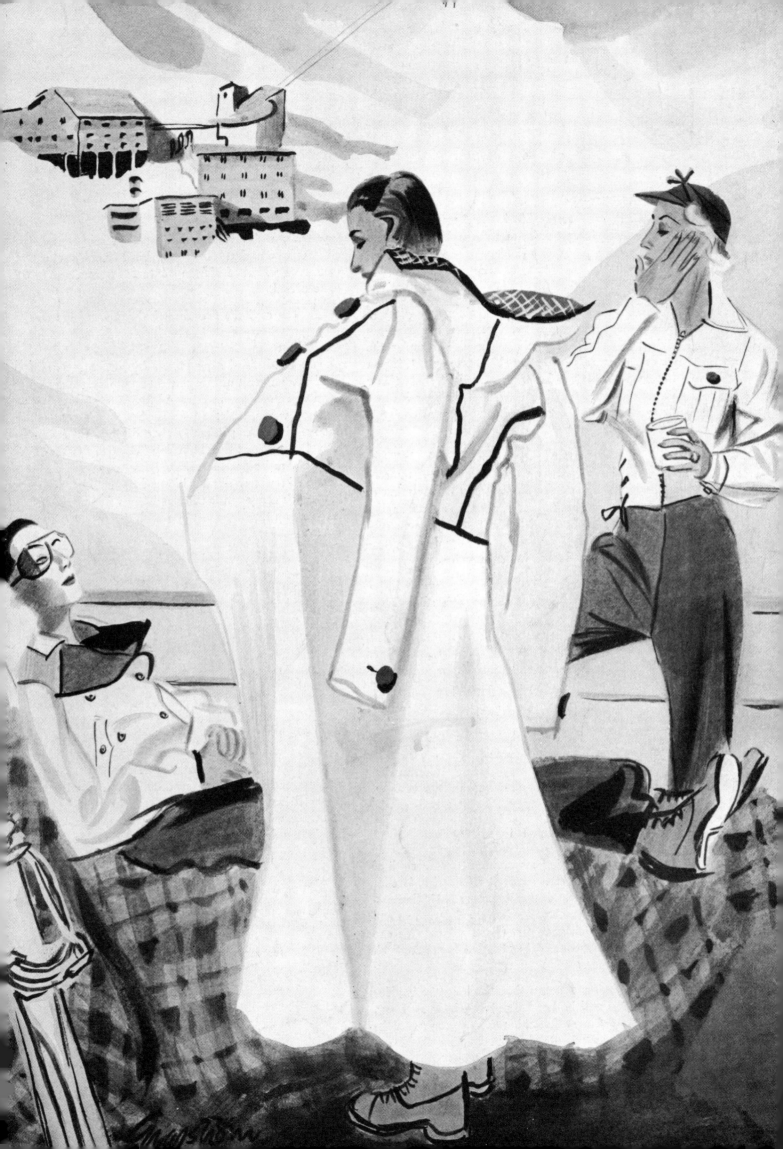

PENCIL DRAWINGS ■ This style, consisting of lines ruler-drawn with an architect's precision, had a strong influence on fashion art in the late twenties and early thirties. The types are also characteristic of the sophisticates of the era.

BERNARD BOUTET DE MONVEL (1884-1949)

The artistic talents of French-born Boutet de Monvel included architecture and portrait painting. His first exhibition in New York was in 1927. Others followed, with portraits representing the internationally chic and socially important from New York to Palm Beach. He often chose profile views and painted them thinly in soft color. They were accurate, decorative, and meticulous in detail, carrying a suggestion of the Italian Renaissance in their two-dimensional drawing and classic simplicity of design and composition.

In the field of fashion illustration, Boutet de Monvel's style and technique set a trend in the twenties and thirties. His elegant people and interiors were delicately drawn with an architect's precision and an eye for purity of line and geometric form. The two-dimensional effect in his magazine work was created with flat washes over fine pencil lines.

Unique and restrained, his drawings exemplified the sophisticate of that period of short, sleek hair, short skirts, and angular body lines. Imitators, following tricks of technique, failed to achieve the look of savoir-vivre that distinguished his figures. The technique used is, nevertheless, interesting as a classic style.

THE PANTS SUIT OF THE THIRTIES ▪ Interpreted with classic good taste, this sophisticated drawing still holds its own today. The natural pose of the figure shows the fashion in a relaxed way. The backgammon game on the beach suggests a leisurely atmosphere. The precise but delicate pencil lines and flat washes are consistent with the decorative style of composition.

TROPICAL BEACH SCENE ■ Sophisticates of a past era are charmingly grouped against the background of this impeccable beach scene. The graceful, geometric design of the palm trees was uniquely de Monvel's style. Again, the main figure in V-necked T shirt and long shorts still has the timeless quality of simplicity. Good drawing is especially noticeable in this starkly exact technique. Nothing is faked or suggested. Each form is definitely stated in the purest of lines.

17. A CAREER IN

OPPORTUNITIES IN THE FIELD

Opportunities for artists in the field of fashion are many and varied. One job can lead to another, and to have your work seen is your best form of publicity. Clippings of your work that has appeared in print also add much to a portfolio. Job openings, in a general way, come under the six main categories of advertising, editorial, pattern drawing, general sketching, display, and teaching. Of these, advertising offers the largest scope, taking in department-store, specialty-store, mail-order, and general advertising agency work.

SPECIALIZATION: Apart from straight fashion-figure drawing there are also, within the realm of advertising, specialized fields in fashion

'ASHION ART

art. You may find yourself more proficient at one than another, or a job opening may decide your course. The specialist, if outstanding, sometimes commands more money than the Jack-of-all-trades. As you work and learn you may find that you have a flair or particular interest in one of these branches. To feel that you do something particularly well is good enough reason to develop and follow that course. Some of these specialized lines, such as shoes, are large fields and have a continual demand for artists with flair and a talent for detail. Hair-styling illustrations, though usually done by the fashion illustrator, could become a specialty if enough work were available.

If drawing children fascinates you, perhaps you should encourage the leaning. This is a specialized line that calls for imagination, an appreciation of the light and gay, and a touch of humor. Illustrators of men's fashions are always in demand. Although male artists predominate here, a few women have successfully made a career in this field. For further discussion on these subjects, see chapters under the various headings.

DEPARTMENT-STORE ADVERTISING: Pick up the Sunday paper and you will probably see page after page of department-store ads to lure the potential customer. These ads are the result of the combined efforts of many artists, including layout artists. Some may be part of the regular staff of the store's advertising department, some may work on a free-lance basis, depending on store policy. A large department store often has openings not only for fashion artists but for those who can sketch merchandise from the various other departments, such as home furnishings, sporting goods, giftwares, or whatever the collection may be. Staff jobs are often open to the beginner who can fill in by being able to sketch whatever comes along or handle odd jobs. Along with newspaper advertising, department stores send brochures and booklets by direct mail to their charge customers. Sometimes these are done by the manufacturer with the artwork handled by an advertising agency, but often it is done by the store artists.

ADVERTISING AGENCIES: Depending on their size, agencies handle anything from local accounts to national advertising that appears in magazines with circulations running into the millions. Larger agencies have full-time art directors with assistants in various capacities from layout men to artists who do paste-ups and mechanicals. Illustrators, though uually free-lance, may be hired on a full-time basis to do "roughs" or even finished art. So-called roughs are often far from roughly done. Although not finished, they are exact drawings in black and white or color and, as part of the planned layout, are called "comprehensives." Comprehensives are presented to the advertiser and advertising heads who select the one they consider best. A copy of their choice is then given the artist or photographer to use as a guide in doing the finished illustration, either fashion or whatever other subject is wanted.

Occasionally a fashion artist fills an agency staff job, though generally they are used on a free-lance basis. Before seeking interviews with agency art directors, be sure that the agency you have in mind handles fashion accounts. Information about advertisers and agencies may be found in the *Standard Advertising Register*, usually available in the public library.

ADVERTISING BY MAIL: This branch takes in all types of material sent directly to the consumer, including the mail-order catalogue and small brochures sent out by stores and manufacturers. Some of this work is handled by the advertiser and some through agencies. Photographs are being used more and more in this field, but there are still numerous openings for artists in this vast business.

MAGAZINES: Editorial sketches and illustrations are handled through the art department of a magazine, the artist usually working with one of the fashion editors. The editorial staff has nothing to do with the advertising section of a magazine. The fashion artist is usually allowed more freedom of expression in magazine work than in other fields. The fact that they are selling ideas and information about fashion rather than the merchandise illustrated allows the artist more freedom of expression.

It is a limited field, with most of the well-known magazines published in New York. Here, photography dominates the field, the most creative photographers and top fashion models working together to turn out a magnificent job. Fashion editors, or their assistants, work with the photographers and, as a result, may have endless shots of a subject from which to make a choice. In spite of this, there are still many openings for artists' work.

PATTERN ILLUSTRATING: If you have ever tried to make a dress yourself, you have doubtless looked through pattern magazines and catalogues for the type of design you had in mind. Perhaps you decided on a *Vogue* pattern, *McCall's*, *Simplicity*, or one of the others. These companies, mostly located in New York, all have large staffs of artists to produce their catalogues, magazines, and pattern envelopes. From the designer who plans the style and does a color sketch of her idea to the artist who does the finished drawing for reproduction in printed form, it takes many hands. Finished art is often done by free-lance artists, who work from the designer's sketch or a muslin made from it. The muslin (a garment of unbleached muslin) is more or less unfinished, and it takes a good deal of imagination to produce the effect of various fabrics such as tweed or velvet from a muslin. The work is fairly exacting since all seaming and details must be indicated as the designer planned. When photography is used, the finished garment must be made up in exactly the right fabric. Obviously, using artwork has a time-saving advantage here, and most of the illustrations are apt to be artwork rather than photography.

POSTER AND DISPLAY WORK: This is still another outlet for fashion art. Display advertising includes posters and large background paintings for window or floor display. As a rule these are one-shot sketches to be used as originals and not for reproduction in printed form. For this reason, although the drawings may be large and impressive and often in color, the artist is seldom paid proportionately more. Also, they are sometimes very sketchy and quickly done, which may add to their charm but not always to their value. It can be in some ways a very satisfying field because it allows a freer technique and the opportunity to draw large and enjoy working with color. This type of work is found in display firms or in department stores having a display department.

FASHION REPORTING: Reporting current fashion news and forecasts is a field with limited openings for artists. A few newspapers with full-time fashion editors use artists to sketch highlights of fashion showings; some editors go abroad for the couture openings, taking the artist along. Magazine editors and members of the press are usually given a preview showing at the various couture houses before the buyers and manufacturers are invited. Some of the sketches are done in New York for publications such as *Women's Wear Daily*. Reporting for notices to buyers and merchandising personnel is also done locally. Most of this type of work is quick and sketchy but not every artist is capable of getting the essence of a fashion trend or working at the necessary speed.

DESIGNERS AND MANUFACTURERS: Occasionally there are staff jobs to be had in this business. Usually, however, the designers do their own sketching and other drawings are handled by those doing the advertising or reporting.

TEACHING: There are always openings for qualified teachers in the various branches of art training. Schools affiliated with a college or the public-school system usually require a degree. In the average art school it is not essential; ability or success in your particular field is enough to make you desirable as an instructor. Many free-lance artists enjoy part-time teaching and find it stimulating to get away from the drawing board and work with receptive students. If you decide to make a full-time career of teaching, degrees may be acquired through college evening courses. If you can afford the time and money for college while you are young, the time spent can be worth while not only for a degree but as a personal asset.

RELATED FIELDS

It is possible for an artist starting out with the idea of being a fashion illustrator to end up in some different but related field. Either some other line is more to his liking or a job possibility opens a different door. Some artists work at fashions for a while, then decide to switch or progress to another type of work. It might be designing, another kind of illustrating, layout, anything that is a part of fashion or art. Case histories include artists who have progressed from fashion art to layout, to art director, to advertising manager. The latter takes executive ability not always found in a person of creative or artistic temperament. It is not to be considered a goal, just one of a list of possibilities.

Fashion photography has also attracted many an artist who finds this medium his best means of self-expression and livelihood. Portraiture, too, has attracted many artists whose knowledge of fashion and the chic world has given them a sophisticated approach to portraying women. To do portraiture well one must have a thorough knowledge of bone structure and basic drawing as well as a talent for achieving likenesses. In most of these other lines specialized training is worth while and can always be sought through extracurricular courses, or recent books on the various subjects.

THE IMPORTANCE OF A GOOD PORTFOLIO

Once you have an objective in mind, spend time making your portfolio of samples as interesting and impressive as you possibly can before making appointments for interviews. Your portfolio of artwork will open doors if it appears to have something to offer.

First of all, pick out your best work and lay it out so that you see the over-all effect. There should be a consistency in the collection that gives an art director assurance of your ability. In other words, it should look as if one artist had done all the drawings. Even though you may have used more than one medium or technique, the feeling of style and types portrayed should have a personal or individual quality. If not, discard what appears to detract from the collection. If necessary, add something more of the same type as the best examples, even if you must redo a few drawings.

Avoid an overabundance of samples. It is better to have six or eight consistently good drawings than a portfolio bulging with odds and ends. Suitability is also a wise consideration. Be sure exactly what type of work is used by the art director you plan to see. If he handles newspaper advertising, it is pointless to show him poster-type color work.

To make your artwork attractive and presentable, mats add immeasurably to a clean, finished look. Mats may be ordered from a framer, but it is comparatively easy to make them yourself with careful measuring. A metal T square and a good mat knife (or one that holds razor-type blades) are essential. Buy a lightweight mat board, usually white, although grays in some cases make a nice contrast in framing. Plan the size of frame opening that best suits each sample of artwork. The inside measurements will vary, but the outside measurements appear better if they are of uniform size. It is also simpler for an art director to handle one size.

To mat an illustration the neatest way, it should have a backing of smooth cardboard exactly the same size as the outside measurements of the mat. Attach them together at the top with masking or Scotch tape on the inside so that the two are hinged together. The easiest way to tape them is to place them together opened flat, put the tape over the two, and then fold. Next, place the artwork between the two and adjust to best position. Secure drawing to back cardboard (not the mat) with rubber cement or tape.

In some instances, drawings may be left unmounted or be mounted directly on a light cardboard without a mat. These decisions are up to the individual. Mainly, the effect should be orderly, uniform, and harmonious. Samples should also look clean. Be sure to eliminate any smudges or unwanted pencil lines with an art-gum eraser.

To protect a charcoal or pencil drawing and keep it from smudging while handling, spray it with fixatif and then cover it with a sheet of clear, heavy cellophane or vinyl.

To protect and transport your artwork, some type of portfolio or carrying case is practical. Choose one large enough to take your largest matted drawing. Art-supply dealers have a type with carrying handles especially for this purpose. The newest and most expensive portfolio is a ring-binder type with clear vinyl protector sheets into which mounted drawings may be placed. This type of portfolio is a great timesaver, eliminating mats and allowing quick changes in your collection.

WHERE AND HOW TO GET A JOB

In any of the various branches of the art field, what you have produced in picture form is your real selling point. Samples of your artwork in a neat, well-planned portfolio will do the talking for either free-lance work or a full-time job. Not all buyers of artwork are connoisseurs of art, nor do they all look for the same qualities, so it is a matter of doing, showing, and hoping to be accepted by the right one.

GEOGRAPHIC LOCATION has much to do with job possibilities. Naturally, outlets for all types of work in this field are more numerous in large cities. New York has always been the leader here, not only as an art center but as the center of fashion design, garment manufacturing, advertising, and publishing. Los Angeles, on a smaller scale, also produces fashions and is an art center, as is San Francisco. Many large cities, like Chicago, have raised their standards for artwork in department-store advertising. Department stores like Neiman Marcus in Texas have put many topnotch artists to work and, in some cases, started them off in other directions.

It is needless to go through a list of the many fine cities here and in other countries offering attractive futures for artists. It is up to the individual to find out the possibilities in the city of his choice or the one available to him. It is possible to find opportunity in a small city if you have the ingenuity to seek it or even create it. Once you have an objective in mind (and feel that you have something to offer), the next thing to do is to start looking up the right contacts and seeking interviews.

NEWS OF JOB OPENINGS: One source of information concerning jobs for artists is the newspaper want-ad section. Some cities also have employment agencies specializing in advertising jobs of all kinds. The names of these agencies appear in the want-ad sections of newspapers, or might be found in the yellow pages of the telephone directory. If you are interested in a full-time job, agencies can find out-of-town openings for the artist meeting the necessary qualifications.

If the job that turns up is not exactly what you had in mind, it may be worth considering as a start. The chance to observe experienced artists' working methods and to learn something about reproduction and printing is of definite value. There is also the likelihood that the job you take will open the door to something better. If you are determined in your aims, it is a matter of planned and persistent effort to see art directors and wait for the right opening.

GETTING INTERVIEWS: In nearly all cases it is necessary to telephone ahead for appointments with art directors. Some set aside special days for interviews or looking at portfolios. Never expect an interview without your portfolio of samples. You may be asked to leave your work and never win an interview. If an art director sees you personally but shows no interest in your work, he might give you helpful criticism if you ask for it. He might even suggest other job possibilities. Be sure to show the director the type of work he uses, not just a hodgepodge of unsuitable artwork.

If you find your samples continually rejected, try to review your portfolio objectively to find its weaknesses. Is it bad drawing, poor rendering, uninteresting approach, or sloppy presentation? Are the drawings of an even standard of quality, or are some good and some bad? If suggestions have been made, try to make use of them to produce some new samples and throw out the bad ones. Once you have produced something better, try calling again on the same art director after a reasonable lapse of time.

If you are seeking a staff job, personality and appearance may influence your chances of being hired. Although this may have little to do with your ability as an artist, it can indicate good or bad character traits. Remember that good grooming and an agreeable attitude are always appreciated by those with whom you hope to work.

GETTING STARTED: Remember that it pays to get your work "in print" even if you have to take small pay at first. Do not insist on top prices if you are a beginner. Nothing quite takes the place of experience. Showing a reproduction of one of your works that has been used can make more of an impression on an art director than reams of impressive originals. First of all, it proves that you can equal your samples in doing a specific job. Secondly, it gives the art buyer an idea of how well your work reproduces—to see if it is clearly stated, has clean lines, and makes the right impression when reduced to a small size. Psychologically, too, there is nothing like letting a prospect know that someone else wanted your work and had confidence in your ability. If your work appears in an outstanding ad, it is the best possible publicity for you. The goal you set is up to you. It is also up to you to recognize your qualifications and limitations and realistically estimate your potential.

THE FULL-TIME JOB

For the average artist a full-time staff job is the answer to many problems. Security of income, a major requisite for most of us, is at least assured by a steady job. Insurance and other benefits are a consideration, and responsibilities of bookkeeping and budgeting can be forgotten. For the beginner it is a chance to watch experts at work and to clarify methods of technique difficult to learn without demonstration. It is also an opportunity to see original artwork of other artists and to pick up a knowledge of reproduction possibilities and limitations. The chance to get your work in print is another advantage.

The guidance of a good art director can be stimulating, if you are lucky. Unfortunately, many art directors are given so little say in making decisions that inspiration, if any, soon evaporates. It becomes easier just to please those in charge of advertising policy. Needless to say, they cannot battle in behalf of the artist whose work fails to please a buyer or whose sketches fail to attract the business sought in costly advertising. The fact that one artist's fashion drawing brings in thirty responses to a small ad and another's brings in only one does not escape a buyer's notice. In business, results are calculated in dollars usually not in artistic achievement. Since advertisers keep close accounts and calculations of results, the artist's work is valued, justly or unjustly, for attention value and pulling power.

If a first job holds no prospects for an attractive future, it is wise to try for a change while you are young. If you hang onto a dull, unsatisfying job through lack of courage, you must accept the idea of settling for security. Security being somewhat uncertain anyway, the challenge of trying for a better job seems worth while, providing your objectives are valid.

It is not always possible in the beginning to find exactly the right opening. As a student just out of art school and supposedly ready for fashion work, I was offered a staff job doing furniture advertising (with a few figures thrown in now and then). In the middle of the depression there was little choice, so I took it. Not content to make a career of anything but fashion, I finally headed for New York and a bigger field. I have never regretted that move.

THE FREE-LANCE ARTIST

If free-lance work is available in your location, it is possible to set up your own business in a small way. With comparatively little expense, one can start working at home or in a studio apartment. The bare necessities, apart from basic supplies and equipment, are good light and a telephone-answering service. Once you start getting jobs, models' fees and messenger services, if you use them, are the major expenses.

In a town where art jobs are scarce there may be no market at all for free-lance artwork. To depend on one account is risky. One is independent only with two or more sources of work, in case of possible changes. Then, too, accepted prices may be too low to make it worth while.

Some artists rely on agents to get them work and cope with the problems of delivering, and so on. In New York the average artist's agent collects 25 percent on all jobs obtained by him; some demand even more. Unless the agent has good contacts and gets better-than-average prices, it is hardly worth while if you are capable of getting work yourself. This is a personal problem to be decided by the individual. Some artists do better with personal contacts, others need a good agent to do the ground-work. It is wise to have an agreement in writing that binds the agent as well as you, prior to giving the agent any work. Such questions as who should do the billing, how long the artist should pay the agreed percent-age on a contact that the agent does not service, and so on should be set-tled. With a reliable agent these problems may not arise, but when they do, it is often too late to straighten out such matters.

There are many advantages in being a free-lance artist if you are capable of coping with the disadvantages. The self-employed do have certain problems. If your work is in demand, you can accept the jobs you wish and refuse those which offer little or are uninteresting. If you can budget your time and money, do the necessary bookkeeping, and main-tain a reputation for reliability, you may make a success of free-lancing. There is also the problem of getting work and the pressure of keeping an account once you get it. The first takes initiative and groundwork, the second takes self-discipline and the ability to produce what is wanted.

There are pitfalls for those without self-discipline or the ability to keep a time schedule. If you have a tendency to sleep late or put off work-ing, this is not for you. Failure to meet deadlines is unforgivable, and if you fail to maintain a reasonable standard of quality in your work, you may lose an account to another artist.

Another pitfall, since you are getting paid by the job, is the temptation to take more work than you can handle well. It is possible to gather speed and produce under pressure. It can even be stimulating at times, but as a continual practice, the habit may lead to inferior work or nervous exhaustion. A rest period or vacation takes care of exhaustion, but in-ferior work means resignation to the routine and boring.

Rush jobs are often given the free-lance artist at the last minute to be done overnight or over the weekend. Some artists prefer working at odd times when they are not disturbed by telephone calls and other inter-ruptions. Others simply take last-minute jobs through desperation and fear of refusing work. Personally, I have always liked to relax and enjoy friends in the evenings and on weekends. I found that by maintaining a definite stand on this question jobs could often be organized to give the artist needed time. There are, of course, times when emergencies arise unavoidably and a rush job is really necessary. It is then up to the artist to help out with grace and understanding. To make a habit of taking emergency jobs is not only detrimental to your own standing but to the standing of artists as a group. If you believe in yourself, have the courage to show it, but without resentment.

Offsetting all the above disadvantages is the attractive side of having your time to use as you see fit, working at home or in a studio, and, if success is your lot, your work bringing increasingly higher prices. In spite of the problems and lack of security, free-lancing in New York suited my personal habits and temperament for many years. I loved to travel and enjoyed having the time and money that allowed me not only several trips to Europe but one to South America, with short vacations in the Caribbean. I always managed to do sketching and painting along the way, and even did some fashion jobs on a trip to London and Paris. The occasional change of scene made up for the pressures and hard work. The forties and fifties were perhaps particularly good years, but there is always a market for work that fills a demand or in some way excels.

FINANCIAL REWARDS

With present-day income taxes taking their bite, it is unlikely that a fashion artist will become a millionaire. An artist should, however, expect to be well paid for work that excels. It is a highly specialized field and few are gifted enough to make even a try in this direction. The old saying that a picture is worth ten thousand words applies perceptibly in advertising. Without the artist and photographer, where would the ad man be? The picture is the most direct means of communicating ideas. Words written or spoken in a foreign language express nothing to one unfamiliar with the tongue, but a picture can explain and delight. Europeans now use picture signs on their highways to warn motorists from other countries of traffic rules and danger signals.

As in everything, supply and demand are big factors in pricing. If there are many artists who can equal your standards, then you can easily be replaced, or there may be an oversupply of artists for a particular job. In either case one must at times accept the "going rate." Opportunity, ability, and reliability all contribute to success, but having something special to offer puts you above the crowd. Some mediocre artists, for example, make up for lack of greatness in speed, turning out perhaps ten times the number of figures per day that another does. This should not be a prime goal unless a job requires it. Some artists can only work rapidly while others must take a reasonable amount of time for everything they do. Each must find the right opening and try to adjust to individual demands. Given time and a good price for a free-lance job, it is sometimes a personal satisfaction to use that time and expend the extra effort to produce something outstanding. Speed does count in the advertising world, and it is essential that the artist devise short cuts and budget his time.

Artists have never been bound by unions or set wages, nor are they likely to start conforming to such dictates. They enjoy a freedom unlike that offered by careers in other fields and, though money is a prime concern, most artists would not change their chosen work for any other. Some are more creative than others, some more practical about business, and some combine the two extremely well.

To be realistic about prices for artwork is to consider the budget for your kind of work. For example, artwork that reaches a small audience cannot earn as much as artwork that appears in a magazine or newspaper with a large circulation. To be sure, a well-planned ad with attention-getting artwork can have ten times the pull of a dull one with poor work if it reaches the right audience. The advertiser, therefore, needs to get a return on his investment in order to make the allowance for advertising worth while. In turn, the artist is in a bargaining position if his work brings results. It takes many talents to make a good ad, but the picture part is up to an artist or photographer or both.

It is important to stress the position of the beginner and his prices. He may not meet the standards of his samples at first, and art directors realize this fact. This by no means suggests starting off as a cut-rate artist. One should ask fair prices for free-lance work and a reasonable salary for a staff job. If in doubt as to what to ask, let the employer make an offer. Once you have made a start, let your work earn its own reward by constant improvement.

To have a showcase for your work may make it worth while to do a job for very little money at first. If it is good, it will be noticed. If you are allowed to add your signature to a good job, it amounts to personal publicity. I know of one publication in the fashion field that had so many calls for the names of their artists that they were asked to sign their work to eliminate answering the question via telephone. To do a job well may lead to other and bigger opportunities.

If your work is seen it sells itself. My first example of this point came to me while still in art school. Some of my work had been bought at the end-of-term exhibit, examples of pure design and color done in design class. Through this exhibition I later had a call from a large store for something similar. They wanted a series of newspaper ads done in a modern vein for their chic gift shop, which carried a wide variety of imports. To illustrate them as ordinary merchandise would not have projected the idea. They wanted a small, imaginative, eye-catching bit of modern art as a promotional idea for the shop. I came up with a grease-pencil technique that looked different from anything else in the paper. It apparently made a hit because I was given the series to do and later offered a job on their staff. As a beginner I would almost have paid someone to publish my work, so when they asked my price I said "Five dollars." In those days that was worth at least three times what it is today, but it was still ridiculously cheap. Later, I heard that someone had criticized the ads as being amateurish. Frankly, I think this might have been their charm. At any rate, I was off to a start.

To make a list of prices for free-lance artwork or a standard scale of artists' salaries would be to state the uncertain and changeable. There is a certain air of secrecy attached to prices paid individual artists, and it is also a matter of bargaining. A general scale of prices for certain types of artwork varies from city to city. It also changes according to the existing market for each type. Fashion illustration for newspaper advertising can be as high as $100 per figure or as low as $10 for free-lance work, even in New York City. It depends on the job and on the merit of the artist's work. Rates for magazine advertising, especially if done through an advertising agency, are usually higher, but again there is no set rule. It is pointless to tell the beginner what to ask. This he will have to find out for himself. As there is a demand for your work, your prices can be increased. It is vital to believe in yourself and your capability, but be realistic about your limitations.

Financial rewards are seldom automatic for "length of service," as in some types of work. Even on a staff job they must come from a need for your work because of its superior quality or usefulness in some way. It is the artist's problem to sustain quality or, better yet, improve his work.

As to billing for free-lance work, if your completed artwork has been accepted, it is up to you to send a bill to the attention of the art director or whoever ordered the work. The price should have been settled before you accepted the job. If possible, get an art order beforehand. If this is not standard procedure with the company, it is pointless to insist.

INDEX

ABOUT THE AUTHOR

The Pacific Northwest, where the author lived as a small child, left with her an undying love of the out-of-doors. It also offered a comparatively good opportunity to acquire an appreciation of art. At the age of seven Eunice was taken to a fashion show and was captivated. The gayer aspects of the fashion world seemed infinitely more appealing than exhibits of serious painting. An early interest in drawing veered toward fashion and consequently produced crude water-color copies of magazine illustrations.

From the start, much encouragement came from her mother, who enrolled her in a Saturday morning art class as a substitute for the longed-for ballet school, which apparently met parental objections. The art lessons were dreary sessions based on the old academic theory of learning to draw from casts of sculpture and odd bits of uninteresting crockery. Later art instruction from notable schools in San Francisco and Los Angeles provided more inspiration and a broader scope.

Serious art training began at seventeen with a full-time course at the Chouinard Art Institute in Los Angeles. The curriculum included study of the basics of fine art along with all phases of commercial training, which led to advertising illustration. The young artist's work attracted the attention of an advertising executive, who called her in to try a series of small promotional ads. Having her first work reproduced in the newspaper seemed so exciting that she charged only five dollars each for the drawings. The ads apparently attracted attention and brought a subsequent offer of a full-time position on their art staff. The job required more furniture illustrating than figure drawing, so the fashion training temporarily had no outlet.

Several unrewarding job changes led to the decision to try New York, where the field was greater. Before long her fashion drawings were appearing in New York papers. She became established as a free-lance illustrator for some of the better stores, including Saks Fifth Avenue.

Eventually, her work also appeared in the editorial pages of such magazines as the *Ladies' Home Journal* and the advertising sections of *Vogue* and *Harper's Bazaar*.

Missing California and a more relaxed pace, she returned to Los Angeles for a three-year stay before deciding that New York was the only place to work the way she pleased, as a free lance. The security of being on an advertising staff seemed unimportant compared with the freedom of movement allowed the artist who can put on the pressure when necessary in order to enjoy periodic long vacations.

World War II had, by then, changed everyone's life, and those artists who were not in the battle were trying to do their bit. Eunice Sloane joined other members of the Society of Illustrators who devoted many evenings and weekends, sometimes flying out of town, to do volunteer portrait sketching of men in the armed forces. The portraits were sent to the families of the servicemen, and the personal interest shown by the artists provided a great morale booster. The experience kindled a continuing interest in portraiture and motivated study with John Carroll, the late portrait painter, who was then teaching at the Art Students League.

As travel opened up at the war's end, beguiling invitations to visit friends in foreign countries took the author to South America and the Caribbean. Sketching along the way produced material for later work as well as minor bits of finished art. Europe provided the most stimulating atmosphere for fashion, as might be expected. One assignment to sketch for B. Altman & Company brought the opportunity to accompany their merchandise manager to the formal couture openings in Paris and London. To see the original models of the great designers dramatically shown was impressive and inspiring. Drawings of the Altman purchases were sent via air mail to New York for the store's magazine and newspaper advertising.

About this time, mid-career, a brief and tempestuous marriage changed the set routine of work and travel. The marriage was legally dissolved after three years.

In the early sixties fashion entered a transitional period, starting with the sack dress. It was an uninspiring era of mainly unbecoming styles which eventually broke outmoded ideas of fashionable dress. At this point portraiture appeared to be an alternative interest. The experience was enlightening but costly in time, energy, and money.

Teaching fashion illustrating on a part-time basis has added dimension to Miss Sloane's career. Starting in California with the Chouinard Art Institute, she afterward joined the faculty of the Fashion Institute of Technology and, later, the School of Visual Arts, both in New York.

Recently sketching fashions again, this time for reporting, she claims that fashion has never been more inspiring and less restricting. Today's fashion, with its sense of fun and extravagant choice of individual style, offers a broad field in fashion art.

ST. LOUIS COMM. COL.
AT FLORISSANT VALLEY

ST. LOUIS COMM. COL.
AT FLORISSANT VALLEY